# William Ellis

1. Frontispiece of *The Country Housewife's Family Companion*. This is a modified version of a seventeenth-century Dutch engraving, not a representation of Ellis's farm.

# William Ellis
Eighteenth-century farmer,
journalist and entrepreneur

Malcolm Thick

HERTFORDSHIRE PUBLICATIONS
an imprint of
University of Hertfordshire Press

First published in Great Britain in 2022 by
Hertfordshire Publications
an imprint of
University of Hertfordshire Press
College Lane
Hatfield
Hertfordshire
AL10 9AB

© Malcolm Thick 2022

The right of Malcolm Thick to be identified as the author of this work has been asserted by him in accordance with the Copyright, Designs and Patents Act 1988.

All rights reserved. No part of this book may be reproduced or utilised in any form or by any means, electronic or mechanical, including photocopying, recording or by any information storage and retrieval system, without permission in writing from the publisher.

British Library Cataloguing in Publication Data
A catalogue record for this book is available from the British Library

ISBN 978-1-912260-49-2

Design by Arthouse Publishing Solutions
Printed in Great Britain by Henry Ling Ltd.

# Contents

| | | |
|---|---|---|
| List of illustrations | | vii |
| Preface and acknowledgements | | ix |
| 1 | Introduction | 1 |
| 2 | Life before Little Gaddesden and at Church Farm | 5 |
| 3 | Agriculture | 23 |
| 4 | Advertising and trading | 75 |
| 5 | Food, drink and medicine | 101 |
| 6 | Ellis the man | 129 |
| 7 | Other matters | 143 |
| 8 | Conclusion | 165 |
| Appendix | | 168 |
| An annotated bibliography of the works of William Ellis | | 172 |
| Bibliography | | 188 |
| Index | | 193 |

# Illustrations

1. Frontispiece of *The Country Housewife's Family Companion*. ii
2. Dedication by Ellis of the 4th edition of *The London and Country Brewer* to William Murray, the Solicitor General. 10
3. Upnor Castle, Kent, 1781. 12
4. Hertfordshire parish map showing the location of Little Gaddesden parish. 14
5. Methods of plashing hedges in Hertfordshire, recorded by Arthur Young in 1804. 27
6. *Husbandry Methodized* (1772), vol. 1, engraving of the Hertfordshire double-wheeled plough. 31
7. Digging chalk, Hertfordshire. 33
8. Engraved frontispiece of *The Farmers Instructor*, showing Ellis's four-wheeled drill plough in operation. 43
9. Frontispiece of *The Timber-Tree Improved*, 4th edition, 1745. 52
10. *The Modern Husbandman*, for May. 80
11. Frontispiece of *Dictionarium Domesticum*, 1736. 106
12. Brewing on a small scale using eighteenth-century techniques. 126
13. Little Gaddesden church. 133
14. William Ellis's entry in the Little Gaddesden Churchwardens' Account Book, December 1721. 138

# Preface and acknowledgements

My interest in William Ellis was greatly stimulated by a commission to write an introduction for a new edition of *The Country Housewife's Family Companion*, published in 2000. Other more pressing tasks intervened to prevent more research on Ellis but I had him in the back of my mind and steadily accumulated copies of his books. Then came Covid. This book is one of the few positive results of the pandemic – I was, for many months, virtually housebound and I read Ellis's books, either in my own library or courtesy of Google Books. I came to appreciate fully the amount of agricultural, food and general social history they contained. I had not realised until I started to acquire his books how his publications dominated the market for agricultural (and brewing) textbooks in the second quarter of the eighteenth century. I am surprised that mine is only the second book on Ellis. The first, a relatively short work, was written over sixty years ago. I hope that, with all its faults, my book will stir up further interest in William Ellis and his writings.

Many people have helped me in the writing of this book. Foremost is my spouse, Jane Card, who helped in many ways: reading, rereading and correcting the drafts; genealogical research; scanning illustrations; chasing up references; and suggesting new sources of evidence. She also kept me going when my enthusiasm flagged, producing many cups of afternoon tea. I thank the staff at the University of Hertfordshire Press, particularly Sarah Elvins and Jane Housham; Cathy Soughton for research in Little Gaddesden parish records and Barbara Sheard for supervising access to these records; Dr David Drummond for genealogical research; Professor Christiana Payne for information on the engraved frontispiece of *The Country Housewife*; Victoria West, archivist at The Worshipful Company of Barbers, for information about Ellis's son William; and the staff of The Museum of Rural Life at Reading University. Thanks to Tony Shahan of the Newlin Grist Mill, Glen Mills, Pennsylvania, for the picture of eighteenth-century brewing and to Marc Meltonville for advice on brewing techniques. Dr Graham Sumner and Phillip Owens helped me to interpret Ellis's observations on four-wheeled vehicles. The parish map of Hertfordshire and photographs of 'chalking' in Hertfordshire are taken from H.W. Gardner, *A Survey of the Agriculture of Hertfordshire*, Royal Agricultural Society of England (London, 1967).

# Chapter 1
# Introduction

William Ellis, a farmer who, for many years, lived and farmed at Little Gaddesden in Hertfordshire, is an important figure in the history of English agriculture. He wrote many books and periodicals in the 1730s, 1740s and 1750s (he claimed nineteen books in all) and was, at this time, the most prolific writer on agriculture in England. He was read not only in the British Isles but also in the American colonies and in continental Europe; some of his works were translated into German. Most were on general farming, but he also wrote on timber trees and published the first book in English devoted entirely to sheep. His book to instruct rural housewives on their duties contains much on the food and medicine of the ordinary farming community of his day. In addition, he penned what was considered at the time to be the best book on brewing.

Ellis was essentially an agricultural journalist, a relatively new occupation in his time. The agricultural journalism of Ellis's day was characterised by both articles drawn from personal observations or communications from readers and publication in the form of weekly or monthly periodicals. Ellis's *Modern Husbandman* appeared in twelve monthly parts, later being collected as a multi-volume work; two other books, *Agriculture Improv'd* and *New Experiments in Husbandry*, began life as monthly periodicals but both ran for only two months. There were other writers in Ellis's time producing agricultural periodicals, most notably Richard Bradley and Stephen Switzer. Ellis stands out from his rivals by the immediacy of his writing and the content of his works. He wrote about his own farm, that of his neighbours, those in his county of Hertfordshire and the way agriculture was carried on in many other parts of England. He brought into his books his subsidiary business as a supplier of agricultural instruments, seeds, plants, trees and fowls, peppering the text with subtle advertisements for his wares. Ellis got most of his copy directly from farmers, their wives and others living in the countryside, by interviewing them. Ellis's contemporary and rival Richard Bradley also produced periodicals in monthly parts and reported on current agricultural topics, but his works relied more on correspondence than farm visits. Switzer – seedsman, nurseryman and garden designer – did travel extensively on business and met with many farmers, but his and Bradley's works were aimed squarely at the gentry and aristocracy.

The content of a late work by Ellis – the *Country Housewife's Family Companion* of 1750, a new edition of which was produced in 2000 – exemplifies his discursive style of writing.[1] Ostensibly a manual of country living for farmers' wives, the book is full of material for the social historian: accounts of the doings of labourers and farmers, beggars and travellers, wives and maids, as well as the gentry and aristocracy. Ellis found it hard to stick to the topic about which he was supposed to be writing, going off at tangents to relay a piece of gossip, to tell of a notable success or disaster of a neighbour in farming, household management, cookery or medicine. In this and his other books he was opinionated and moralistic, condemning rural vice, theft and the sharp practices of shopkeepers. Ellis, in all his publications, was clearly writing about his own life as well as that of the ordinary people of his village of Little Gaddesden and his county of Hertfordshire. Moreover, he travelled extensively on business in southern England, the West Country, the Midlands and East Anglia half a century before that other great agricultural commentator and traveller Arthur Young. His books contain the fruits of these travels. In short, he absorbed information from whoever he encountered who could provide it and he poured it out in his books: both information relevant to his subject and 'all those random ridiculous details which have so much disgraced his page', which were the despair of the editor who produced a two-volume synopsis of his agricultural writings some years after his death.[2]

In contrast to other agricultural writers of his time, journalists included, he broke free of the need to allude to, or begin a topic with, reference to classical authors. A book written by a contemporary, Edward Lisle, has a long quotation from Columella on its title page and the first line of the text on arable land begins: 'Palladius has laid down the following rule'.[3] Richard Bradley invokes Xenophon on the second page of his dedication of the *Country Housewife and Lady's Director* to 'The Ladies of Great Britain', and by page nine he summarises the opinions of a number of classical authors on the lifespan of pigeons![4] The only mentions of such authors in Ellis's books are reproduced from John Evelyn's *Sylva*, the text of which he plunders for the second part of his *Timber Tree Improved*. Indeed, Ellis specifically condemns 'meer Scholars, who, because Virgil does not mention it, by no Means will

---

1  William Ellis, *The Country Housewife's Family Companion, 1750* (Totnes, 2000); references in this work refer to page numbers in the 2000 edition of this book.
2  [William Ellis], *Ellis's Husbandry, Abridged and Methodized* (London, 1772), vol. I, pp. iv–v.
3  Edward Lisle, *Observations on Husbandry* (London, 1757), pp. i, 23.
4  Richard Bradley, *The Country Housewife and Lady's Director* (London, 1736), pp. A4v, 9.

allow a Thing to be valuable, tho' there be a Thousand Improvements at this Day in Practice, that he never had the Knowledge of'.[5]

The wealth of information, especially his own, that can be extracted from Ellis's books on farming is augmented by the report of a visit to Ellis in Little Gaddesden by the Swedish botanist Pehr Kalm. Kalm, who was born in 1716, was a graduate who studied under the botanist Carl Linnaeus and joined the estate of a wealthy Swede, Baron Sten Carl Bielke, under whose patronage he continued his academic research. Kalm obtained funds to go to America and he came to England en route, arriving in the winter of 1748 and spending some months here. Living in London, he made excursions to the countryside and recorded both the native flora and what he saw of farming practices. Crucially for us, between 25 March and 15 April 1748 he stayed at Little Gaddesden.[6]

Kalm kept a voluminous diary and on 25 March records:

> This morning, I set out on a journey at the request and expense of Vice President Baron Bielke to Mr. Ellis who lives at Little Gaddesden in Hertfordshire. Mr. Ellis is a man who for his practical understanding of rural economy and even more for his writings in the same science merits attention.

The main reason for the journey was to see the various farm implements Ellis advertised in his books and to obtain 'models of the most useful of them'.[7] In this objective Kalm was largely disappointed, seeing very few of the new implements in action and finding that Ellis had them made on demand rather than ready and waiting. Kalm did, however, have several long conversations with Ellis and also talked at length with other farmers at Little Gaddesden. These farmers told him that, despite the emphasis in Ellis's books on new farming methods, he did not, on the whole, farm differently from his neighbours and they did not consider him to be a particularly good farmer. It is clear from Kalm's diary that he did not warm to Ellis and that Ellis was in turn irritated by Kalm. This must be borne in mind when reading Kalm's account of his visit. Nonetheless, this independent observation of Ellis and his farming activities is an extremely valuable addition to the information we have about Ellis at Little Gaddesden, which otherwise comes solely from the pen of Ellis himself.[8]

---

5   See below, p. 141; William Ellis, *New Experiments in Husbandry, for the Month of April* (London, 1736), Preface. Vigil's *Georgics* was still regarded as a valuable agricultural textbook by many in the eighteenth century.
6   W.R. Mead, *Pehr Kalm in The Chilterns* (Aston Clinton, 2003), pp. 7–15.
7   Mead, *Pehr Kalm*, p. 34.
8   Vicars Bell, *To Meet Mr. Ellis* (London, 1956), pp. 147–53.

Ellis has been dismissed by many writers as a minor figure both in English agricultural literature and as a commentator on rural life in mid-eighteenth-century England, but on both counts he has much to offer historians. This book begins with a review of his life, or as much of it as can be discovered, for we have virtually no details of his boyhood and adolescence, and only sketchy information on his adult life before he arrived in Little Gaddesden and started farming. Some false assumptions, however, about these early years have been corrected. The farming section will concentrate on his own farming and that of his neighbours, based on what he tells us in his books, augmented by the diary entries of Pehr Kalm. It will also cover some of the agriculture he found on his travels around England. Some may ask – why devote so much of the book to obsolete farming practices? As well as answering that history is inherently interesting, we may observe that farming is at present undergoing major changes as it comes to terms with such challenges as global warming and carbon capture, food security, biodiversity and soil exhaustion. We may smile at Ellis's attempts to build a reliable seed drill and his advocacy of other horse-drawn machines, but he was thinking along the right lines: where would English farming be today without row cultivation and mechanised weed control, fertiliser spreading and harvesting? And what of his numerous comments on such farming activities as maintaining soil quality by crop rotations, marling, fertilising and the like? At the time this book was written, the British government was preparing to announce a complete overhaul of government subsidies to farmers to replace those removed following Britain's withdrawal from the EU. The old emphasis on maximising output will be swept away and new support for farmers will be conditional on improving the environment. We could well find that some of the farming improvements observed, implemented or recommended by Ellis will again be applicable to British farming.

As well as agriculture he was involved in various non-farming enterprises, which will be reviewed along with his writings on country food, medicine and veterinary matters. An attempt will be made to discern his character and religious opinions and to assess his contribution to the local government of his parish. We will consider how he viewed the changes in English agriculture and economy during his years as a farmer and writer. His fluctuating posthumous reputation will be discussed. Finally, a bibliography of his books is appended, providing a brief synopsis of each.[9]

---

9    Mead, *Pehr Kalm*, pp. 34–139; Bell, *Mr. Ellis*, pp. 14–33, 55–64, 88–98, 138–56. In discussing his own farming, I have tried to use instances in Ellis's books where he specifically states that *he* has carried out a farming operation, or Kalm has observed him doing it.

## Chapter 2
# Life before Little Gaddesden and at Church Farm

This chapter will try to tease out, from official records and stray remarks made by Ellis in his books, evidence of his life before he moved to Little Gaddesden, and his family life after he commenced farming there. The landscape in which he farmed will be explained, and an attempt made to describe his farm.

*Before Little Gaddesden*
Matilda Dodson, spinster, married William Ellis, widower, in March 1717/18 at St James's church, Duke's Place, a small parish in the City of London.[1] Of Ellis's first wife nothing is known, apart from the fact that she must have died young, after only a few years of marriage, and that she was alive in 1715, for in the preface to *New Experiments in Husbandry for the Month of April*, published in 1736, Ellis says his eldest son by her was 21. The baptism of a Philip Ellis, son to a Mary and William Ellis, is recorded in 1713/1714 in the register of St Clement Danes, a parish with which Ellis is known to have had connections. Added to this is a daughter named Mary, born to his first wife. The only Hertfordshire marriage involving a William Ellis that fits the timing of the birth of his children by his first wife took place in Bishop's Stortford in 1705, the spouse being Elizabeth Hemmings. On balance, it is more likely that his first wife was Mary.[2] This second marriage, if local gossip in Little Gaddesden was true, gave him the capital to set up as a fairly well-off yeoman in that village. Matilda died aged 67 in 1750 and thus she

---

1   The date is written thus because, between 1582 and 1752, two different dates for the start of the year were used in England. The official and 'legal' year started on 25 March, whereas most people started their years on 1 January. So, dates between these two dates were often written as occurring in either year, expressed, as here, with a slash between them.
2   London Metropolitan Archives, P69/JS1/A/002/MS07894/003; <http://joinermarriageindex.co.uk/results.php>, accessed 1 August 2020. I am indebted to Jane Card for the research on Matilda's marriage and her later life.

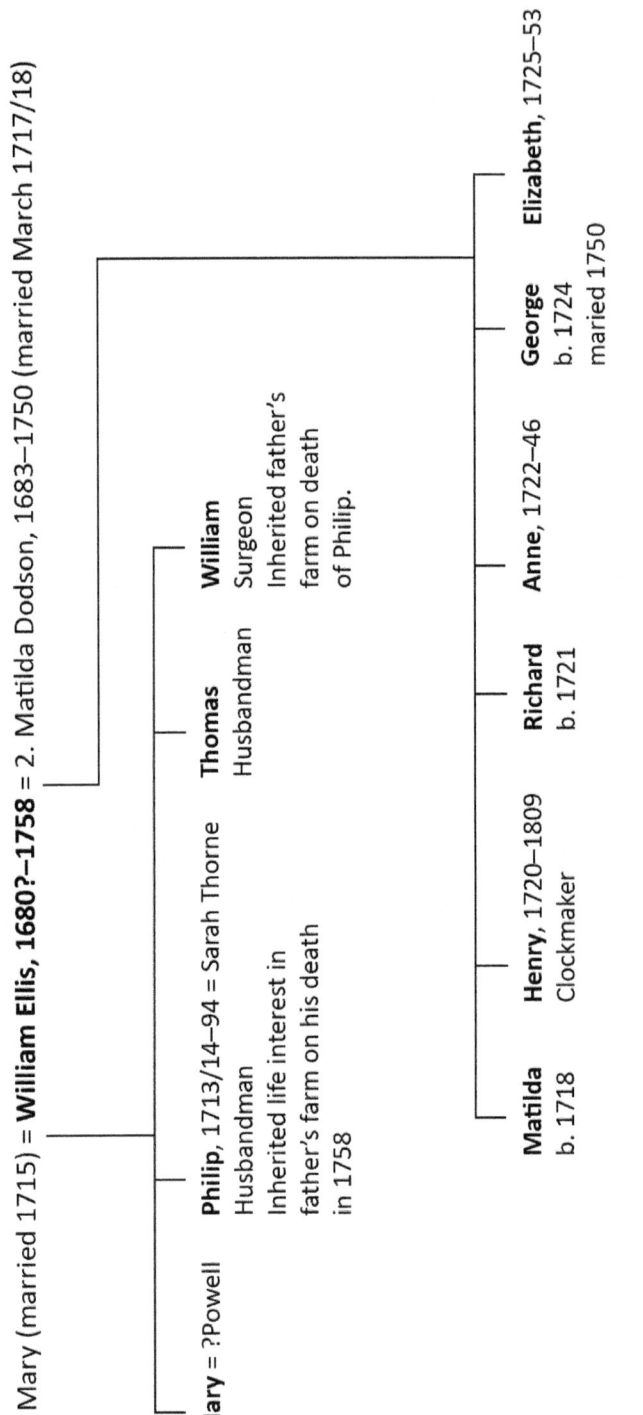

1. Mary (married 1715) = **William Ellis, 1680?–1758** = 2. Matilda Dodson, 1683–1750 (married March 1717/18)

**Mary** = ?Powell

**Philip**, 1713/14–94 = Sarah Thorne
Husbandman
Inherited life interest in
father's farm on his death
in 1758

**Thomas**
Husbandman

**William**
Surgeon
Inherited father's
farm on death
of Philip.

**Matilda**
b. 1718

**Henry**, 1720–1809
Clockmaker

**Richard**
b. 1721

**Anne**, 1722–46

**George**
b. 1724
maried 1750

**Elizabeth**, 1725–53

would have been 34 on marriage. The year of this marriage ties in with the earliest date William mentions working on his farm, 1718.[3] Rumour was that his second wife brought a substantial dowry to the marriage and that Ellis used much of this money to buy farmland and squandered the rest on unsuccessful agricultural experiments. She 'grieved so much over it, that she had not been able to recover herself'.[4] Her distress was certainly severe: she was admitted to the famous asylum of Bethlehem Hospital in London in October 1733 and discharged in May 1734, either cured or incurable but not dangerous. The fact that she went to 'Bedlam', where conditions could be primitive, rather than to a private institution, either implies parsimony on William's part or perhaps lack of funds, for Ellis was said to have been impoverished at the time.[5] In his numerous books Ellis makes no reference to either of his wives, although he frequently mentions recipes and the general household practices of neighbours' wives and those of his servants. Matilda may have been incapable of work on her return from the hospital.[6]

Yet the medical history of Matilda bears further scrutiny. Her admission to Bedlam in 1733 was *not* her first. She was admitted, on the recommendation of a London apothecary, in May 1715 and discharged in the following September. She was 32 at the time of this first admission, which was two and a half years before her marriage to Ellis.[7] Did Ellis know of Matilda's mental instability? Did her family wish to marry her off with as little fuss as possible (at 34, she was quite old for a first marriage at the time)? Was he induced to marry her by the dowry she brought with her? The marriage seems to have been rushed and neither Ellis nor his bride were resident in the parish where they were married. St James's, Duke's Place was at one time notorious for clandestine weddings: marriage there was made easier because it was not within the jurisdiction of the bishop of London. It may be significant that the marriage was by a licence issued only the day before the ceremony and no banns were read. Although Ellis may have gone through whatever fortune Matilda brought with her on marriage, the fact that he was already living at Little Gaddesden may indicate that he obtained money to set up as a farmer from another source at an earlier date. His farm eventually consisted of both rented and owned land, and he may have started with the rented fields and used his second wife's money to buy land (see below).

---

3   William Ellis, *The Timber Tree Improved* (London, 1742), pt 1, p. 45; London Metropolitan Archives, P69/JS1/A/002/MS07894/003.

4   Bell, *Mr. Ellis*, p. 151.

5   He may have been short of money for several years – in 1745 he paid nine years' back rent for use of an acre of land owned by the parish. *Little Gaddesden* parish records, Churchwardens' Book, 1676–1769.

6   Bethlem Museum of the Mind, Admissions Registers, ARA-04, p. 268.

7   Bethlem Museum of the Mind, Admissions Registers, ARA-03, p. 271.

Much of Ellis's life before he began farming at Little Gaddesden is a mystery. The *Dictionary of National Biography* puts his birth at around 1700, but this is ten to twenty years too late – other evidence points to a date probably around 1680–1690. When he talked with Pehr Kalm in 1748 Ellis put his age at 'somewhat more than 60 years old' and said he 'was born between 1680 and 1690'.[8] He tells us he 'had the pleasure to know ... Captain Savory [sic]', an innovator of the steam engine. Savery was made captain in 1702 and died in 1715, implying that Ellis was an adult for at least some of that period. In mid-1713 he was appointed executor by his uncle Richard in the matter of his will, an office with a minimum age requirement of 21.[9]

In the first edition of his book on brewing, in 1734, Ellis claims to have resided in the country for nearly twenty years. In the 1735 edition this becomes 'Twenty Years past', which implies that he acquired his farm in 1715. Certainly, soon after this time he was repairing the farm, renewing hedges and planting trees, for in *The Modern Husbandman* (1742–3) Ellis remarks that he has owned a pear tree in his orchard for 'these twenty-five and more years past'; this puts the acquisition of the farm at about 1717 or 1718.[10] The anonymous editor of *Ellis's Husbandry Methodized*, published in 1772, thought Ellis had spent fifty years farming, putting the date of his beginning to 1722. This is probably too late a date, for in 1723 he had sufficient experience in agriculture to advise a gentleman on buying a farm at Cheddington, Buckinghamshire. Most of these pieces of circumstantial evidence thus imply that he started farming at Little Gaddesden at about the time he married Matilda, which fits with her being the source of capital to start at, or expand, Church Farm. What Ellis does not tell us in his books, and which has not been found elsewhere, is why he started farming and why he decided to farm at Little Gaddesden.[11]

Pehr Kalm was told by neighbours that, prior to arriving in Gaddesden, Ellis had no knowledge of farming and '[h]e has also been for a time a Custom House officer, or Exciseman, also for a long time with a brewer in London'.[12] Little support for an early career as an Exciseman has been found: the theory appears to be based on the hearsay recorded by Kalm, some strong condemnations by Ellis of brewers who cheated the excise and some technical knowledge he had of levying excise duty. Some of his remarks on

---

8   Mead, *Pehr Kalm*, p. 42.
9   William Ellis, *London and Country Brewer*, Part 3 (London, 1742), p. 277.
10  William Ellis, *The Modern Husbandman*, September (Dublin, 1743–4), p. 106. Unless otherwise stated all subsequent references are to the 1743–4 edition of this work, published in three volumes: May to December in 1743 and January to April in 1744.
11  [Ellis], *Ellis's Husbandry*.
12  Vicars Bell, *Little Gaddesden* (London, 1949), p. 92; Joseph Lucas, *Kalm's account* of his visit to England (London, 1892), p. 192.

the subject are so technical as to be incomprehensible to those not expert in mid-eighteenth-century brewing. For example, talking about how duty was determined: 'If the excise man takes his Gage on the Floor, he allows ten to the score, but he sometimes gages in Cistern, Couch, Floor, and Kiln; and where he can make the most, there he fixes his Charge.'[13] He wished brewery workers were obliged to wear soft overshoes to avoid damaging malt, 'and it is a Pity the Exciseman is not obliged so too'. He gives examples of ways to cheat the Excise, writing: 'I once knew a Person that had only a Hogshead Copper in London, and entered himself at the Excise Office as a Common brewer, that he might have one in the Score allowed him free of Duty'; and he reproduces an undelivered letter written by his late uncle and found in his papers confessing to the authorities that he had cheated on paying the correct amount of duty. But some of his strongest remarks on Excise duty are from the standpoint of a brewer. There are the examples above on gauging and damaging malt, and he also complains of the high excise duty on beer, concluding that families should brew their own beer, 'and so save the great Expense of Excise that the common Brewer's Drink is always clogged with, which is no less than 5s for Ale, and 18d. per Barrel for small Beer'. He blames the Excise duty rather than the brewers for selling bad beer made up of the dregs of numerous barrels:

> I am incited to take Notice of the hardship, that such Public Brewers lie under of being forced to pay Excise on such excrementitious Drink, and thereby tempted to prejudice the Health of the ignorant Drinker, for the Sake of re-imbursing themselves of Duty, and which, I think, should be a moving consideration to an Officer to take Care of oppressing the Subject with Overcharges in Gauging. That I remember too frequently happened to me, when I was concerned in a Public Brewery.

On balance, it seems that Ellis was not an Excise man and that his knowledge came from his experience as a brewer.[14]

Ellis tells us nothing in his writings of his childhood years but he does mention that his father was a brewer in St James's Westminster, and there

---

13  *Oxford Dictionary of National Biography*, <https://www.oxforddnb.com/view/10.1093/ref:odnb/9780198614128.001.0001/odnb-9780198614128-e-8718?rskey=u6tMMz&result=5>, accessed 28 May 2020; Ellis, *London and Country Brewer*, p. 7. Marc Meltonville, a food historian with an encyclopaedic knowledge of brewing history, interprets this passage as follows: 'if the taxman takes his estimate from the malt on the *floor*, where it is still wet, or at least, not yet kilned dry, he assumes a weight of half of what he sees. Alternatively, he can take his measure for tax at the *cistern*, where the grains are being soaked, the *couch*, where it rests, or even the drying *kiln*, and whichever he thinks he can get the best rate (higher tax) he uses that measure to fix the rate.' Pers. comm.

14  Ellis, *London and Country Brewer*, pp. 92, 110, 127–30.

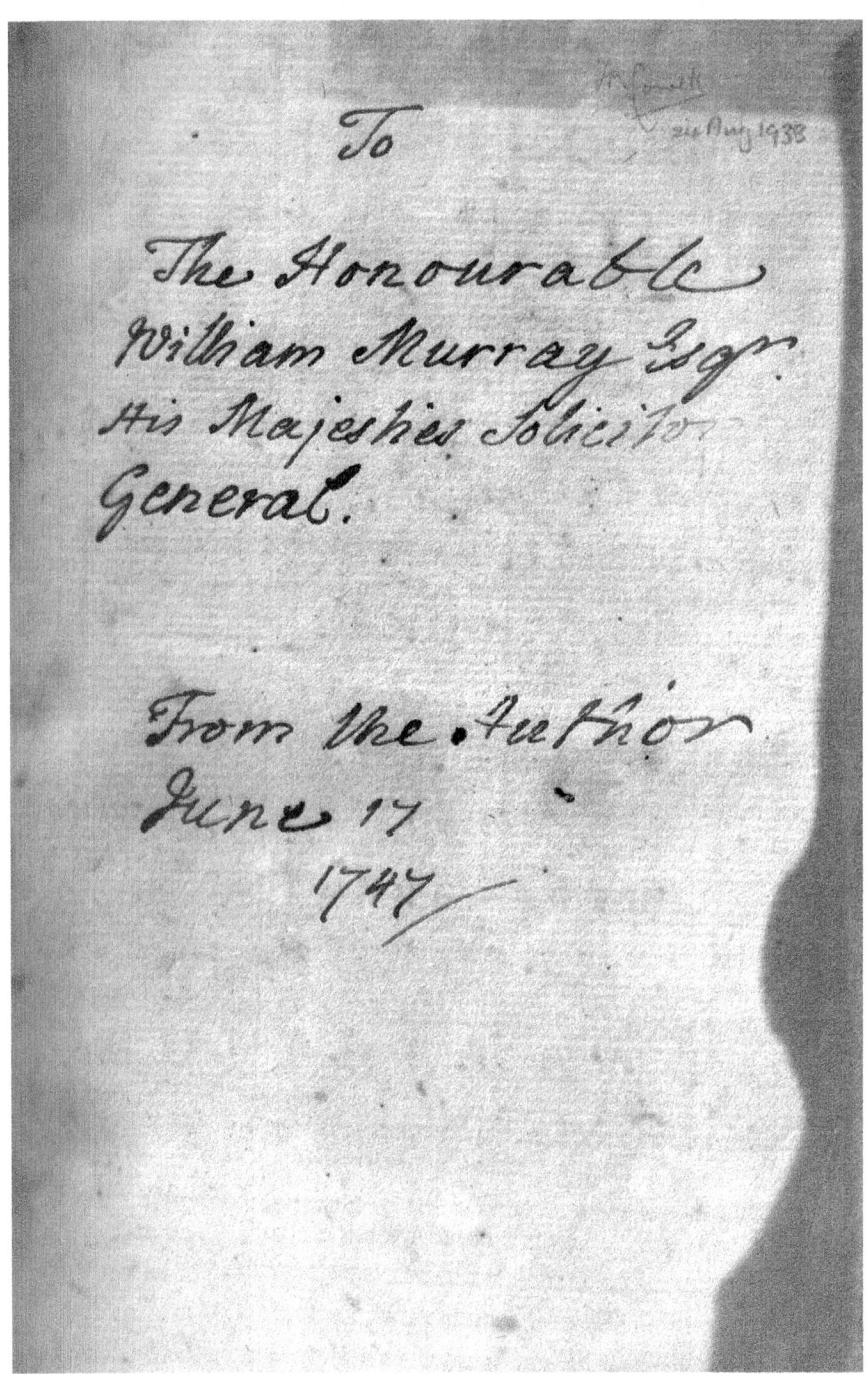

2. Dedication by Ellis of the 4th edition of *The London and Country Brewer* to William Murray, the Solicitor General.

is an intriguing offhand reference to Kent when discussing pork pickling methods there, which were 'well known to me, that have lived in three parts of this famous county'. He certainly did not live in Kent after 1718, but was he brought up there? In *The Practice of Farming* (1735) he informs his readers of 'many Parts of Kent and Essex that abound in low, wet Grounds where the Ague in particular is more rife than in other Places, as I have experienced to my Cost, when I lived at Upnor near Rochester'. Moreover, he hints that he once lived at Upnor Castle:

> But there is a Difference even in brackish Waters, occasioned by the Nature and Situation of the contiguous Earth; so in the Yard behind the Governor's House at *Upnor-Castle*, that lies on the River *Medway* about two Miles from *Rochester*, there is a Well out of which they pump a Water a little Brackish; and yet it makes both excellent Bread and Beer as I have often tasted.

A further early link to the area is his claim to have been acquainted with Colonel Gage, MP for Rochester.[15]

Ellis regards his first adult occupation to have been that of brewer, an occupation thrust upon him – although he may already have been in that trade – by his being appointed executor of his uncle Richard's will. Richard was a brewer who lived in St James's Westminster until he died in 1713, and confirmation that his nephew is our man comes from William, who wrote in his book on brewing, 'I had an Uncle, a common Brewer, in London' and 'I was Executor to my Uncle's Will, a Brewer in London'.[16] Richard describes his estate in his will as 'several leasehold messuages or tenements mortgages Exchequer Bills debts due on bond or otherwise household goods and other estate to a considerable value'. He had no living children and made specific bequests totalling only £65; William was left the residue of his uncle's estate, including the brewery. He was required under the will to pay his aunt Frances an annuity of eighty pounds a year, a substantial sum, and his late uncle must have envisaged that William would carry on the business to generate the income to pay the annuity. The estate included the brewery *business* but the premises were probably rented by Richard, as there is no brewery listed in his will as property owned. The brewery was in Stanhope Street, near Clare Market.[17] It is likely that Ellis was already in the brewery trade when

---

15  William Ellis, *The Practice of Farming and Husbandry in All Sorts of Soils* (Dublin, 1735), p. 191; Ellis, *London and Country Brewer*, p. 4. William Gage died in 1738. <https://en.wikipedia.org/wiki/William_Gage>, accessed 31 May 2020.

16  Ellis, *London and Country Brewer*, p. 460.

17  National Archives, Prob.11/533/269.

3. Upnor Castle, Kent (1781), New York Public Library, <http://digitalcollections.nypl.org/>, Creative Commons CC0 1.0 Universal Public Domain Dedication ('CC0 1.0 Dedication').

Uncle Richard died, because Kalm reports he was for a *long time* a brewer in London – was he apprenticed to his uncle (or his father)? His uncle trusted him to carry on the business and pay his aunt's quite large annuity, which probably exceeded the income on the bonds and securities owned by Richard on his death. Certainly, Ellis was expert enough to write a book which Pehr Kalm said was well received: 'The Treatise he has written on Brewing, is considered by several in England as the best of all his writings, because he relates therein his own experiences.' That Ellis's father was a brewer and his uncle thought him capable of taking over a brewery reinforces the likelihood that he was involved in brewing for some time before his uncle's death.[18]

The terms of his uncle's will pleased neither Ellis nor his aunt. Ellis had to continue his uncle's business to pay his aunt Frances's annuity each year. Frances was clearly not satisfied by her legacies under the will. She got no capital, only an annuity of £80, plus the family home and its contents, including the ready cash. She refused to hand over the bonds, Exchequer

---

18  Lucas, *Kalm's account*, p. 192; *London Gazette*, 15 September 1713. I am indebted to Dr David Drummond and Jane Card for tracing the members of William Ellis's immediate family and for details of his marriages and children used in this chapter.

bills, securities and bank notes that Richard owned at the time of his death (estimated by Ellis to be worth in total £2,000), saying that she did not have the keys to open the cabinet where they were stored. In this she was abetted by some friends and relatives. Ellis, as executor, started an action in the Chancery Court to recover the securities, alleging a conspiracy between Frances and her friends and relatives. In her reply to Ellis's deposition to the Court Frances hints at foul play – Richard went into the country in good health and some days later Ellis turned up, informed her of Richard's death, and proceeded to read a will which Frances had not seen before.[19]

In an effort to track down some of the securities William placed an advertisement in the *London Gazette* in September 1713: 'Lost or concealed, 4 Exchequer Bills lately belonging to Mr Richard Ellis, deceas'd viz 54717 for 100 l. 55536 for 100 l. 55556 for 100 22394 for 50l.l.' The Chancery case commenced in May 1713 but was all over by December: Frances accepted a lump sum payment of £600 and gave up the right to the annuity of £80. Presumably, this outcome was mutually beneficial: Frances got a large capital sum and Ellis was free to dispose of the brewery business and to take up farming at Little Gaddesden. There is no more mention of Richard's unexpected death and the previously unknown will – possibly this was merely a negotiating tactic on Frances's part. The settlement gave William capital with which to expand his farm, in the form of the proceeds of the sale of the brewery and the bonds and securities left by Richard, less the lump sum to Ellis's aunt, some minor bequests and the costs of the funeral and administration of the will.[20]

The sequence of events is somewhat hazy, but it is most likely that Uncle Richard's residual legacy gave him the wherewithal to move into the farm at Little Gaddesden prior to his second marriage. If his first wife was Mary, and he married her in 1713/14, there is just time for the birth of four children before her death. She first gave birth in 1715, so he probably married her as soon as his legal spat with his aunt was settled. His second wife's fortune was probably spent on buying land to enlarge the farm, as well as on machines and other experiments in husbandry, and financing his many journeys to view the agriculture of England and forward his business activities.

## *At Church Farm*

Ellis is often called 'William Ellis of Little Gaddesden' because in his books he firmly associates himself with the Hertfordshire village where he farmed for so many years. As far as can be ascertained, he had no family or other connection with the village prior to his settling there and there was nothing

---

19  National Archives, Prob.11/533/269; C6/406/47/B.
20  Ibid.

4. Little Gaddesden parish is on the western border of Hertfordshire, neighbouring Bedfordshire and Buckinghamshire. It is also relatively close to London.

special in the village to attract him from London. Writing of the village in 1949, local historian Vicars Bell starts his book on a downbeat note: 'At first glance our village seems to be diffuse, and lacking in character. Thirty miles from London, and high up on a wooded spur of the Chilterns, it has little to show the passer-by.'[21] Later he remarks, 'The village has no centre, no focal point, and no apparent reason or existence. It is on the route to nowhere.'[22] The same could be said of the village today, but it may now have established a reason to exist – to shelter many rich residents in substantial houses down long driveways off its leafy lanes. A recent search of the internet for houses sold in 2020 in the village yielded four properties, the cheapest of which was sold for £1,680,000. An unusual feature of the village is its proximity to Ashridge Park, seat of the Egerton family from the seventeenth to the twentieth centuries. The demand from the Ashridge Park estate for labour and goods may have been the major influence on the siting of the village.[23]

---

21  Bell, *Little Gaddesden*, p. 1.
22  Ibid., p. 1.
23  Ibid., p. 48.

Vicars Bell sums up the geography of the parish succinctly. The parish of Little Gaddesden is in the Chiltern Hills,

> very nearly at the northern edge of a great plateau which falls away gradually to the south-east, more suddenly into the Bulbourne valley [...] into the Gade Valley beyond the church, and steeply into the Vale of Aylesbury beyond Steps Hill. The top of the ridge is covered with a deposit of heavy yellow clay mixed with flints. Two parallel glacial valleys score the ridge from west to east. The clay cap becomes shallower as it approaches these valleys, the sides of which are of chalk. The bottoms are covered with patchy deposits of gravel.[24]

The relatively simple solid geology of Hertfordshire, mostly chalk, the rest Reading Beds and London Clay, has been much complicated over the centuries by the 'drift' of material over the surface of the solid rock caused by erosion and deposition. In 1967 H.W. Gardiner described the situation:

> Like a well-worn counterpane made up of many irregular patches and many holes, in some places hiding and in other places disclosing the mattress beneath, these drift deposits usually obscure, but sometimes leave exposed the solid rocks below. When the drift is taken into account much of the county's simplicity of structure is lost and the soils, derived mainly from drift, but partly from solid formations, are extremely variable.[25]

Arthur Young came to the same conclusion in 1804: 'the soils of this county mix and run together into each other in a remarkable manner.'[26] As we will discover, Ellis's farm was partially composed of scattered fields and he had to contend with this typical range of varied soils in the parish.

By 1750 all but 120 acres of the cultivated land at Little Gaddesden had been enclosed. At that time, Little Gaddesden had one long street of houses, most of them with vegetable or flower gardens. This pleasant rural scene was peopled by relatively well-off farmers such as Ellis but also by a fair number of poor landless labourers and itinerant beggars, whose plight had been worsened by enclosure. Their poverty was exacerbated by the custom in Hertfordshire of hiring men by the day, as needed, rather than on annual contracts. Such labourers did not 'live in' and so were not fed as part of their contracts.[27]

---

24  Ibid., p. 2.
25  H.W. Gardiner, *A Survey of the Agriculture of Hertfordshire* (London, 1967), pp. 93, 107.
26  Arthur Young, *General View of The County of Hertfordshire* (London, 1804), p. 8.
27  Bell, *Mr. Ellis*, pp. 15–18.

Ellis, for most of his adult life, lived and farmed at Church Farm, Little Gaddesden. He tells us: 'I occupy my own Farm and the Glebeland of our parish, containing in all twenty-four inclosed Fields of several sorts of soils.'[28] Fifteen fields had been purchased by him and the rest were the rented glebe, apart from one field, 'The Town Acre', which he rented from the parish; the rent was put towards relieving the poor.[29] In his publications he tells us about the condition of his various fields – the soil conditions, drainage and so on. Ellis clearly needed money to start farming but he may have only needed working capital to start with because he rented the glebe, which gave its name to the farm, from the rector: 'My landlord, the late Mr Colemar, rector of Little Gaddesden'.[30] At various times he bought land: in 1718 he bought a 'Copse-wood' and frequent mention of trees he has managed indicates that his farm was well-wooded. In 1735 he tells us that 'I formerly bought a six Acre Field', which may have been one of a parcel of fields, including at least one with chalky soil that he bought in 1730. In 1738 he owned a four-acre meadow adjoining his house.[31]

At the time of his death he owned freehold his farmhouse and outbuildings and 'Freehold and Copyhold Inclosed fields consisting of meadow and arable lands' in Little Gaddesden. After his death the manorial court of Little Gaddesden agreed to the transfer of copyhold land comprising seven fields containing twenty acres to his son William Ellis and a further three fields totalling seven and a half acres to another son, Henry Ellis.[32] The twenty-four fields that made up his farm may have been somewhat scattered: Ellis made his farm more convenient by swapping enclosed fields, exchanging 'a Field with my Neighbour for one of his, that joined this [...] to lay both Fields into one'. The scattered fields posed a challenge, as some were on high ground, others were not. Some low ground was in a frost hollow, and this 'spoiled my Cherries this last Season, 1732, that grew in my bottom Grounds, which lying more from the Sun's influence than the Hills, the Frosts, and these by their long Continuance in the Situation, prov'd destructive to the Fruit, tho' so late as in the Month of May'.[33] Kalm emphasised the amount of chalk soil on the hills at Gaddesden, but Ellis had a mixture of soils in his fields: 'As

---

28  William Ellis, *Chiltern and Vale Farming Explained* (London, 1745), A2v.
29  Little Gaddesden parish records, Churchwardens' Account Book.
30  Ellis, *Timber Tree Improved*, pp. 26, 76. Colemar was rector between 1730 and 1754. The glebe was land owned by the church and farmed by the incumbent minister.
31  Ibid., p. 26; Ellis, *The Practice of Farming*, p. 239.
32  Paul Stanbridge, *William Ellis, The Forgotten Improver* ([1984]), Appendix C, pp. 166–9.
33  Ellis, *Timber Tree Improved*, pt 1, pp. 75, 188. A frost hollow is an area of low ground, often at the foot of a hill, into which cold air drains at night and remains for a time the next day when the surrounding area has warmed up.

I am Owner of various Sorts of Earths; among the rest, I have some Fields of a gravelly and chalky Nature: These I have sown with Ray-grass, Trefoil, Saintfoin, and Lucern Grasses, as I have done my stiff Loams with Clover, &c.'[34] One field had topsoil of 'loamy Gravel' but not far below the surface was red clay. Another field, almost half a mile from his farmhouse, also had gravelly soil, while another 'inclosed Field, [was]of a gravelly loamy Soil' and he had 'fine loamy ground in [his] garden'.[35] Another field, of about three acres, was situated between two hills and benefited from rain running off them. Its soil was 'about six tenths loam, three tenths chalk and one tenths gravel', which he judged to be an excellent mixture. Ellis, therefore, seems to have rented or bought land with a good cross section of Gaddesden soil types.[36] The common where he grazed his sheep also had variations of soil and topography that he commented on:

> [In] our Parish of *Little Gaddesden*, [...] there is a Common on a high Hill, just before our Houses, that feeds my Flock in the Summer-time, and several others: Now this Common has two Sorts of Situations on it, some of it lies sloping, the rest lies flat; and all of it under a clayey Surface. That Part of it next to my Farm, and where my Sheep generally graze, lies mostly on a Hanging, which is so much in their Favour, that they never take the Rot here, because here the Waters run off before they can settle to wet the Ground much, or enough to make it dangerous to Sheep.[37]

We have no details of his farm buildings other than the barns, stalls, garner[38] and outhouses mentioned in his will. On the subject of his farmhouse, he casually informs his readers, when warning of the combustibility of furze,[39] of a 'woful experience, I can say, that great part of my dwelling-house was burnt down, in the year 1724, and also three of my neighbours' intirely consumed,

---

34 These fodder crops are still sown today, especially on organic farms. All are best suited to light, warm soils, the type of soil on which Ellis was sowing them. Ryegrass is a perennial suited for leys (temporary grasslands) of several years. The other three crops are all legumes that fix nitrogen via their roots and so can enrich soil for a return to arable cropping. Lucerne thrives in a light, non-acid soil. It lasts for up to four years; sainfoin and trefoil are also suitable for short leys on light soils. Clover does well in a loamy soil. Ellis, *Country Housewife*, p. 312.

35 Ellis, *Timber Tree Improved*, pt 1, p. 57; Ellis, *Chiltern and Vale Farming*, p. 34.

36 Ellis, *New Experiments in Husbandry*, pp. 2, 3.

37 William Ellis, *A compleat system of experienced improvements, made on sheep, grass-lambs, and house-lambs: or, The country gentleman's and the shepherd's sure guide* (London, 1749), p. 113. A hanging is a wood on a steep slope.

38 A garner is a granary.

39 Furze is gorse.

by means of a spark jumping from a smith's anvil through a crevice, among some furz'. One of his garrets, 'which unfortunately fired by a Neighbour's house', was damaged but repairable; 'several of the Beechen Boards [i.e. floorboards] were preserved and laid down again, since which they never stirred'. The scope of this disaster was limited, 'as my house was fortunately insured with the Sun-fire -office'.[40] The frontispiece of *The Country Housewife* shows a rundown farmyard and buildings, but it is not meant to be a picture of *his* farmhouse and outbuildings – the engraving is probably a Dutch one dating from the seventeenth century. Two of the cows in the foreground are from an engraving by Paullus Potter, *Two Cows Seen from Behind*.[41] In the background are hayricks, but they are not a type of rick used in Hertfordshire. Visiting Ashridge Park, which bordered Ellis's farmhouse, Pehr Kalm saw one of the ricks that seem to have long been common in the Hertfordshire: a square haystack built under a roof suspended from four pillars, one at each corner. When hay was taken from the stack, the roof could be lowered to fit snugly on top of the stack by moving pegs to a lower position in a series of holes in the pillars. Kalm gives much detail on this piece of equipment, making a sketch of it. At the risk of digressing 'Ellis-style', such structures were known in Hertfordshire in the late sixteenth century. Sir Hugh Plat, who had land at St Albans, saw one of these, 'a patterne whereof standeth to be seene nere unto St Albones not far from Parkmill; in the backside of one of my tenaunts howses there'. Plat comments that it was made 'as they use in the low Countries to make their barnes'.[42]

Ellis had a garden next to his farmhouse, apparently a pleasant spot that contributed vegetables and fruit to his kitchen. Although he proclaimed 'I am not a gardener', on the same page he could not resist giving a gardening hint:

> I take this opportunity to inform my reader of a most necessary cheap improvement that is to be made, by buying only a pennyworth of Welch onion seed at a London seed-shop, and sow it in a little square bed of earth about four foot long and two or three foot wide. I did this, I think, in 1742, and at this time [1749] they are in a flourishing condition.[43]

---

40  Ellis, *Timber Tree Improved*, pp. 33, 204; Hertfordshire Archives and Local Studies, 39 HW 37.

41  Ellis, *Country Housewife*, engraved frontispiece; Paullus Potter, *Two Cows Seen from Behind*, Harvard Museums, Cambridge, MA. Spencer Album 10., S10.92.8. I am grateful to Professor Christiana Payne for her identification of Potter as the origin of this frontispiece.

42  Mead, *Pehr Kalm*, p. 67; Sir Hugh Plat, *Diverse new sorts of Soil* (London, 1594), pp. 33–5.

43  Ellis, *Country Housewife*, p. 297.

Elsewhere he notes 'In my garden in this month, 1740, I had a most plentiful crop of the large white Nonpareil Pease.'[44] He also had vines and fruit trees in his garden: the waste 'nitre liquor'[45] from his seed steep[46] 'I put on the roots of my vines, and fruit trees [...] and it brought on their growth very expeditiously'. He also used waste blood as a fertiliser – a success in gardening terms, but rather unpleasant:

> And this last spring I apply'd to the roots of a young vine that grew against my house, the blood of a hog, but at the first coming of the hot weather, the blood began to be offensive: I therefore took a pail of wood-ashes, and covered the border all over, which being wash'd in by the rains [...] soon overcame the ill stench of the blood; and both these by emitting their several salts to the roots, made the vine shoot more in one summer than it had done, I think, in three before.[47]

The present Church Farmhouse is near the church, some distance away from the village, and what Ellis tells us of his farmhouse indicates that the present building is not the house he lived in. Ellis mentions that there were several houses near his, that he owned his house freehold and that he lived next to the entrance to Ashridge Park. Therefore, he must have owned and lived in a house in the long street which then constituted the village, some distance from the present Church Farm.[48]

The size of Ellis's household at Church Farm varied considerably over the years. On his first occupancy his immediate family was just himself and his first wife, but he may, contrary to local custom, have had some farm hands as well as domestic servants living in from the start. His ploughman and his boy apparently lived in because, in *The Country Housewife's Companion*, he tells how his serving maid makes a baked pudding 'against my plowman and boy com[ing home] from the plow' to dinner, and the household dined together: 'I assure my readers that with such a pudding and a piece of pickled pork my family makes a dinner to their satisfaction.'[49] He favoured live-in employees because, as he remarks: 'The keeping of servants at home must redound to their masters and mistresses profit' because they can be better

---

44  Ellis, *Modern Husbandman*, April, p. 66.
45  An infusion of water and saltpetre.
46  See below, pp. 41–2.
47  William Ellis, *The Practical Farmer: or the Hertfordshire Husbandman* (London, 1732), p. 154.
48  Hertfordshire Archives and Local Studies, 39 HW 37; William Ellis, *Agriculture Improv'd* (London, 1746), vol. I, p. 127.
49  Ellis, *Country Housewife*, p. 82. 'Family' in this context means all who live in the farmhouse.

controlled than if they live out. At its most numerous, William's household would have numbered about sixteen: ten children (all under the age of 12), a maid, a ploughman and ploughboy, maybe a shepherd, Ellis himself and his second wife Matilda. She may have been unable to do any housework because of her mental state, for, if she was capable of housework, one would have expected her to be the source of recipes and so on. When Matilda was admitted to Bedlam in 1733 there were still six or more children at home, three of them 12 or under.[50] It may be relevant to the relapse in her mental state that between 1718 and 1725 she had given birth to six children, almost one a year, and also had children from Ellis's first marriage to look after. In addition, because of Ellis's frequent trips to London and tours of southern England, she would have been in sole charge of the household for much of the time. In October 1743 he had two sons working hard for him. He explained:

> I bring them up to work as soon as they are able to do any Thing [...] I have a Boy but sixteen Years of Age, that thrashes me Wheat, Barley, Oats, Pease, Beans [...] and, tho' he is my Son, I favour him not [...] I have another Son, my Ploughman, that is so naturalised to Fatigue [...] that, if he is kept idle but one Day in the House, he protests it is more disagreeable to him, than Labouring all that Time.[51]

This latter youth was probably the son he placed in employment with a gentleman farmer:

> I sent a son of mine, at eighteen years of age, into a gentleman's service, to be his ploughman, and look after his great farm in the Vale country; and, as he was then accounted a good workman at the plough, and at sowing, mowing, reaping, houghing Turneps and carrots, felling timber trees, plaishing hedges, and at most other rustic business, he had the care of all his master's country affairs, and lived with him until he died in 1739.

In 1741, when his son was 20, Ellis sent him to work for another farmer, sixty miles to the north, where 'he gave his master great satisfaction, till he was overtaken with the small-pox' and had to come home. Ellis concluded: 'it is well known, I bring up my boys to work as soon as they are able, and continue them as close to it as possible I can, which makes them workmen at an early age.'[52] By 1748 he had living with him '[b]ut one girl and a boy,

---

50 Ellis, *Country Housewife*, pp. 37, 81–2; Ellis, *Compleat system of experienced improvements*, p. 304. My thanks to Dr David Drummond for research on Ellis's children.
51 Ellis, *Modern Husbandman*, April, p. 48.
52 Ellis, *Modern Husbandman*, October, pp. 143–5.

other than his son and daughter'.⁵³ The son was then 21. Ellis also hired labourers, as was the Little Gaddesden custom, as required; these were the 'Day-Workers' he mentions.⁵⁴

Before his death in 1758, Ellis's immediate family may all have left the farm, with the possible exception of his son Philip, who inherited the farmhouse, outbuildings and some land at Gaddesden; this may indicate that he was still living with his father and took over what remained of the farm after, under the terms of the will, land was sold to redeem mortgages and other debts.⁵⁵ Philip may have been mentioned by Ellis in 1736 as the son 'whom I have brought up from his Infancy to farming and is now twenty-one years of age'. Philip was living at the farm in 1746 when 'my least son' (probably George) was paid two pence a dozen for killing sparrows and Philip was living in Little Gaddesden in 1752, when he was appointed Overseer of the Poor for that year. After Ellis's death he could occupy the farm until he died, after which, under the terms of Ellis's will, the farm passed to his son William, a London surgeon. In 1759 Philip is described as a husbandman in manorial court records, as is another son, Thomas, who was farming at Chingford.⁵⁶

Ellis's second wife had died in 1750. Two daughters were married by then and one more, Anne, had died in 1746. Another, Elizabeth, died in 1753. The eldest son by his second marriage, Henry, a clockmaker, probably also living in London, was bequeathed several fields in Little Gaddesden. This bequest was 'in lieu of discharging my Contract with Richard Shelburne Deceased whom I appointed Trustee for seeing invested the value of the summe of four hundred pounds By way of Jointure on my said late wife Matilda Ellis and her heirs for ever'.⁵⁷ This is interpreted to mean that his second wife protected some of the wealth she brought to the marriage, namely £400, and, she having since died, Ellis was leaving property to this value to her eldest son. But the fact that he invested his wife's jointure in land for his own farm rather than, say, government bonds in her name may be a reason for the distress which caused her to be sent to Bedlam. To sum up, even without the distractions of journalism and journeys collecting information, Ellis would

---

53  Mead, *Pehr Kalm*, p. 41
54  Ellis, *Modern Husbandman*, April, p. 50.
55  Hertfordshire Archives and Local Studies, 39 HW 37.
56  Ellis, *New Experiments in Husbandry*, Preface; Ellis, *Agriculture Improv'd*, p. 129; Little Gaddesden Parish Records, Overseers' Book; Stanbridge, *William Ellis*, Appendix C, pp. 166–9.
57  Hertfordshire Archives and Local Studies, 39 HW 37. Ellis, *Chiltern and Vale Farming*, p. 243. A letter from William Hayton to son William, clerk of the peace at Ivinghoe, published by Ellis, includes: 'I understand he [Ellis] is related to Dick Shilburne, by Marriage'. Richard Shelburne was a relative of Matilda.

have found life on the farm a struggle when faced with a large number of children below working age and a mentally ill wife to provide for. Once the children were capable of work life was much easier and it is no wonder that he insisted on putting his boys to work as soon as they were able. As a rule, large families were a sensible strategy for farmers – once the children were capable of work life was a lot easier and farms could be more productive.

# Chapter 3
# Agriculture

Ellis's general books on agriculture are organised very much like others of his time. They cover ploughing and cultivations; observations on soils and how to improve fertility; the major grain and other food crops; farm animals; new crops, especially fodder crops; and timber and fruit trees. In his discussion of grains, wheat is always the first to be considered; cows come first among the animals; and the oak has pride of place among the trees. In his periodical writings he also keeps to a well-worn path. The monthly parts of the *Modern Husbandman* invariably start with wheat, very often followed by barley and then other grains and crops, but these periodicals also contain much of his more idiosyncratic writings, including his descriptions of new agricultural machines, his advertisements for them, and correspondence with customers.

This chapter will broadly follow the outline of his general books set out above, discussing his writing on agriculture and considering the sources of his ideas. We will tease out references to his own farming practices, those of his neighbours and those prevalent in Hertfordshire, plus some observations on the farming activity in the various counties he visits. In addition, we will note the examples of innovations and experiments he provides – those of his neighbours, those he came across in his travels, those reported to him by letters from gentlemen and, perhaps most interesting, those he claimed to have done himself or advocated in his books – the latter category often wrapped up with the many means of increasing agricultural productivity he sought to sell. Such practices were usually presented together in any one chapter of his books, especially in his periodicals. Take, for instance, the opening chapter of the *Modern Husbandman* for January. It is on wheat, and begins with a discussion of good and bad reasons for sowing wheat in January, including his own experience and local custom in Gaddesden. Then follows an extract from the *Gentleman's Magazine* upon an award-winning method of sowing wheat in Ireland, with Ellis's comments on this. Several methods of breaking up sward and sowing corn on it gleaned from

Hertfordshire and adjacent counties are discussed, followed by examples of methods and experiments carried out by specific farmers.

*Ellis's farming, and that of his neighbours in Chiltern and Vale country*
'Those who can – do, those who can't – teach': so goes the witticism attributed to George Bernard Shaw. Pehr Kalm concluded as much about Ellis after his visit. On his first arrival in Little Gaddesden, before he met Ellis, Kalm walked the fields to examine the local agriculture. He found some fields in good order but others 'which deserved our pity. The moss had there so got the upper hand that it had almost entirely extirpated the beautiful hay which had previously been sown there.' Meeting an old farmer, Kalm pointed to a field and asked, 'And who is the cultivator of this field, which to a great extent stands under water, and is so ill cultivated?' He was told that both this field and the one full of moss belonged to 'Mr Ellis'. Kalm asked if this was a relative of the man he had travelled to meet but he was assured only one Mr Ellis farmed at Little Gaddesden. In Kalm's later conversations with Ellis's neighbours he was told that Ellis's farming methods were essentially the same as theirs and he had similar yields to theirs.[1]

On another occasion Kalm questioned Gaddesden farmers on Ellis and his farming and summed up their answers thus:

> When he first came here to Little Gaddesden, he was very unskilled in rural economy. Most of what he knows he has learned here. They did not consider him to be so good a farmer as many others and said that he never used and arranged his arable land as well as other people. He acquired a rich dowry with his present wife who is his second wife. He bought the property that he now occupies with her money. At first, he engaged in various experiments in rural economy as a result of which he frittered away a large amount of his money, so that he became impoverished. His wife grieved so much over this that she went mad. He had her taken to London to live but this did not help, so he had to take her home again.

When Kalm visited, Ellis's second wife Matilda had been mad and incapable for fourteen years and much of what was then 'women's work' on the farm had to be done by his youngest daughter.

Kalm continued:

> After he had squandered his money in this manner, he began to write books, to sell different kinds of implements etc. for which he obtained considerable money. Yet he would never be particularly wealthy, because as a result of writing so many books

---

1  Bell, *Mr. Ellis*, pp. 148–9.

he has no time to look after his fields and Meadows. He depends on his sons for this and his ploughlands etc. are consequently worse than those of his neighbours.[2]

It is against these unpromising remarks that we will try to measure Ellis's own husbandry at Little Gaddesden. One could say of the answers Kalm was given, to use a phrase popular in the 1960s, 'they would say that, wouldn't they?' Ellis's neighbours would be unlikely to endorse him as an agricultural expert, given his remarks on several occasions that they were backward-looking and set in their ways. Taken with Kalm's own observation of Ellis's fields, we must consider whether his agricultural theory as expounded in his books was sound but just not put into practice by him, or was practised by him but was not a success. Note also the remark of a neighbour above that when he first came to the village he was 'very unskilled in rural economy'. It is likely that he had *no* knowledge of agriculture when he started at Church Farm and had to learn the rudiments of farming from his neighbours. If so, it is an indication of his ability to absorb and use information that he began writing books on the subject after only a few years' farming. Some of the scepticism about his abilities on the part of his fellow farmers may stem from his apparent conceit, after a few years' experience only, in writing books on the subject and trying to persuade them to adopt new methods.

That Ellis kept a close eye on what went on in his own fields is evident; he is constantly referring to specific instances of crop successes and failures, to the weather and to incidents on his own farm or locally, and to recall this amount of detail he must have kept a farm diary. References to a particular month or year might be dredged from memory, but he gives specific dates for many occurrences. For example, on '[t]he 18th Day of November, 1747, I had a Wether sheep that had two loose teeth', while in an early book, *The Practical Farmer*, he gives a detailed summary of the weather and its effect on his crops during the summer of 1734.[3]

### *Hedging*
When Ellis entered his farm it may have been in a run-down state, because soon after he took it over he was busy renovating hedges, and this was probably one of the first agricultural skills he acquired. He was particularly pleased with a beech hedge: 'It was about the year 1718, that I planted above fifty Poles [just over 90 yards] of Ground with Sets, and was esteemed by proper Judges to be as fine a Hedge as ever they saw; for it

---

2  Mead, *Pehr Kalm*, p. 100.
3  Ellis, *Modern Husbandman*, September, p. 10; August, p. 97; Ellis, *Practical Farmer*, pp. 215–19. A wether is a castrated ram.

was in some Parts of it eight Foot high.'[4] Beech hedges were particularly appropriate for chalky grounds. It was, Ellis writes, formed of sets pulled 'out of woods about two feet long [...] it will return much wood, as being of the tree kind'.[5] He goes on: 'I planted one about fourteen years ago [i.e. in 1718] with cherry trees in the same hedge, at a considerable distance',[6] and the hedge and trees 'thrive to admiration'.[7] To start a hedge from scratch, he recommends throwing up a bank with soil taken from a corresponding ditch, planting whitethorn on it and in the spring sticking in two-foot long pieces of 'sollar' (i.e. willow) in the bank on a slope. These 'truncheons' would in time root and thicken the hedge. In wet ground such hedges should be made of alders, willows, poplars and the like. To discourage livestock from eating the new hedge he recommends painting it thickly with a mixture of cow dung and water or lime and water. He was planning, in 1731, to use this method of hedging to enclose, perhaps by agreement, some of the remaining open-field land of Little Gaddesden: 'by taking in a piece of common field-land'. He adds that in his time at Gaddesden 'we commonly make our hedges once in nine years'.[8]

Arthur Young, writing in 1804, thought hedges were usually renewed every twelve years in Hertfordshire. Young was impressed by the standard of hedging in the county, especially by the 'plashing' – cutting not quite through the stems of bushes or young trees near the ground, then laying them almost horizontal and supporting them by weaving them in and out of vertical sticks at intervals. The plashed stems produce new growth, thickening the hedge. Young also comments on the number of trees allowed to flourish in Hertfordshire hedgerows: he explains that the cost of transporting coal to this county was high, so the hedgerow trees were periodically cut for fuel.[9] Ellis also emphasises that a well-made hedge is a source of fuel that, if sold, will yield as much profit as if the land on which the hedge stands was sown with corn. In a hedge of sallow (willow) and thorn, the faster-growing sallow

---

4 Ellis, *Timber Tree Improved*, p. 45.

5 He sets his hedge with beech tree saplings, hoping they will eventually grow into trees. Ellis, *Practical Farmer*, p. 129.

6 Ibid., p. 130.

7 Ibid., p. 130.

8 Ibid., pp. 128–30, 192. Ellis was very much in favour of enclosure, which allowed a farmer to sow 'what he thinks fit, and when, which open fields generally debar him from'. Temple H. Croker, in *The Complete Dictionary of Arts and Sciences* (London, 1765), vol. II, fol. L7, considers 'The best hedges made anywhere in England, are those made in Hertfordshire; for they are plashed in a middle way between the two extremes' (i.e., neither too high or too low).Top of Form

9 Young, *Hertfordshire*, pp. 49–54.

can be cut close to the ground after six years and made into faggots sold for fourteen shillings per hundred. After another six years both species might be cut back and sold as faggots, leaving enough growth for renewed plashing.[10]

## Soil management

Ellis often begins his agricultural works with a chapter on soils; his farm, as we have seen, had a variety. He was conscious of the need to work *with* the soil in successful farming (as true today as in the mid-eighteenth century):

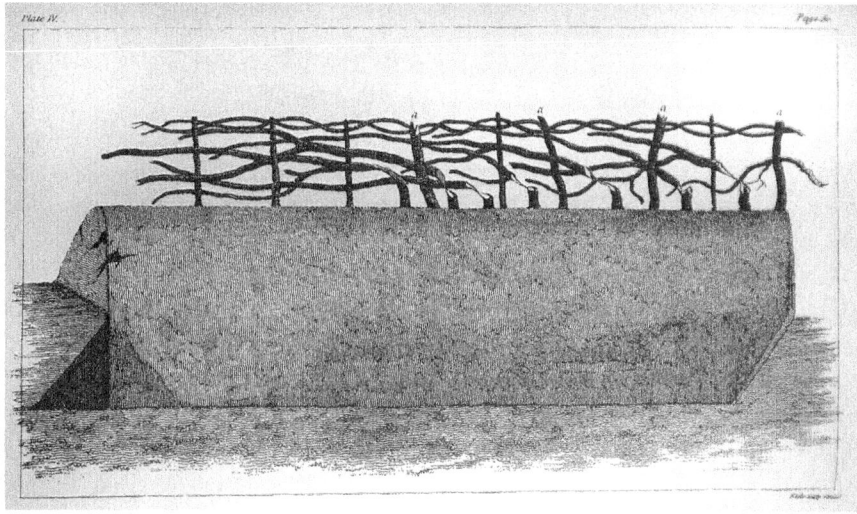

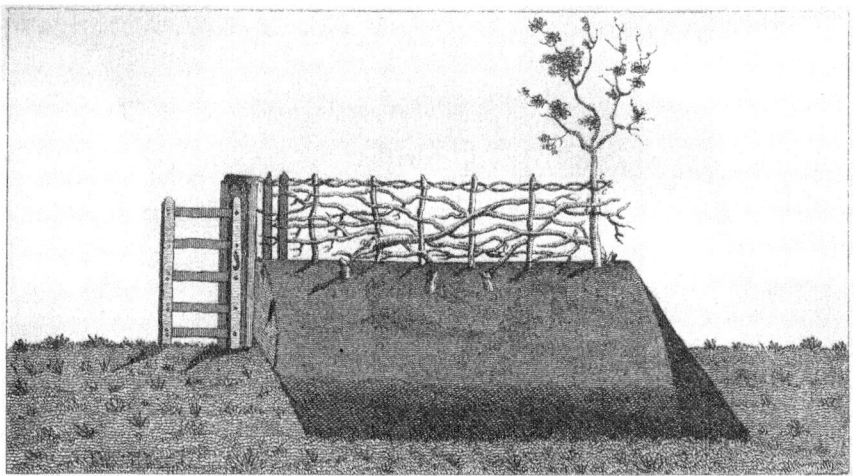

5. Methods of plashing hedges in Hertfordshire, recorded by Arthur Young in 1804 (Young, *Hertfordshire*, Plates iv and v).

---

10  Ellis, *Modern Husbandman*, January, pp. 90–1.

'the very best of husbandry, which I think is justly concluded in the several terms of the nature, culture, melioration, and improvements of soils; as therein lying the chief foundation of after-success, in the growth of corn, grass and trees.'[11] In *The Practical Farmer* Ellis sums up what a farmer can do to make soils as productive as possible:

> The melioration of soils may be otherwise called an alteration of Earths, or Improvement of them, by mixing their several Sorts of Bodies, with Dungs, Chalks, Lime, Sand, &c. or else by manuring them with Hand-dressings; as with Soot, Ashes, Hornshavings, Coney-clippings, and Rags, at proper Seasons; or else by the several Sorts of sowed Grasses, which gives the Earth an Opportunity of enjoying a Rest, a longer or shorter Time, as the Owner thinks fit.

Rags – almost all woollen in his day – improved the soil structure and released nitrogen. Soot, ashes and hair are also sources of nitrogen as they decompose in the soil.[12]

On another occasion he gives a summary of 'Four ways of preparing and meliorating the ground' – good ploughing, mixing earths, 'dungings and dressings' and resting the ground. These are sound principles, endorsed by Gardiner in 1967. To facilitate the first precept, Ellis recommends offering a premium for a good ploughman: £10 a year for a good one is better than paying £5 for a mediocre one. He thought that '[p]loughing of Ground is of such absolute Necessity in all Lands ... that whoever is wanting in this Work to get the Earth into a fine, hollow, sweet Condition when it is sowed, may depend on it, that they stand a sorry chance of having a plentiful crop.' Invariably he gives details of the amount of tillage required for each crop and soil condition he describes, and no farmer would fault his general observation that wet loams and clays 'can't be ploughed too often, when sands, chalks, and gravels can't be too seldom'.[13] In his introduction to ploughing in preparation for wheat, he gave the sound advice that April was the month to first plough land:

> both in the Vales and hilly or Chiltern Countries; and is so necessary to be done in April, that whoever neglects it, is justly accounted a slothful Farmer, and is certainly very much wanting to his own Interest, even to a Proverb. – Better an April Sop, than a May Clot, because in this Month the Ground is generally soppy wet, when

---

11 Ellis, *Practical Farmer*, pp. 5–6; D.H. Robinson (ed.), *Fream's Elements of Agriculture* (London, 1949).

12 Ellis, *Practical Farmer*, pp. 5–6.

13 Gardiner, *Hertfordshire*, p. 122; Ellis, *Chiltern and Vale Farming*, pp. 186–8.

May is so dry as to clot: But the exact Meaning is; that it is better to fallow in this Month than the next, by reason the Earth has a longer Time to be got into a true Tilth against the next Wheat Season, than if it was later plowed.[14]

Ellis offered to supply many different ploughs in his publications, and he saw many in action on Hertfordshire farms. For the initial ploughing described above he said 'it may be performed with the two Wheel single Fallow-Plough, with the two Wheel double Plough, with the Turnrise Plough, and with three Sorts of one Wheel Ploughs. In the Vale, or low Grounds they use but two Sorts, the Swing-Plough, and the Foot Plough.'[15] The Hertfordshire wheeled plough he classifies as one of the several sorts of two-wheeled single-fallow ploughs currently in use. He describes it in detail: the

> Ashen beam is 9 foot long, its iron share 4 foot 4 inches in length, and made with two mortices, weighing about 50 lb. which by the help of a broad board so fortifies it, that it is strong enough, with its pecked point, to plow through the most stony land in this country, whose dry gravels, tenacious clays, and large flints, very often try its strength, and sometimes break it; for which reason we are frequently obliged to draw four, five, and six horses, who find work enough to manage an acre and a half in a day, in dry seasons.

He adds that this plough needs a strong and able ploughman to guide it.[16]

George Fussell traced the origin of this plough, a heavy instrument dragged through the soil by a large team, originally of oxen, to Saxon England. Its use became widespread in midland England.[17] A century before Ellis, Walter Blith wrote a chapter on ploughs in his book of agricultural improvements, and included a plate of ploughs, one of which is the 'Harfordshire wheeld plough'. Blith wrote that, for heavy soils, it

> is of most constant use in Hartfordshire and many up-Countries, and is very useful upon all flinty, stony, or hard gravell, or any other hard Land […] and very necessary for al great Corn-masters have one of these for strength, that so he may not force his other plows which are made on purpose for other lands in a Tillable condition,

---

14  Ellis, *Modern Husbandman*, April, p. 9. Confusingly, 'fallow' means both letting the soil rest for a period with no crop sown in it and the initial ploughing-up of land that has been so rested. Fallow here refers to the initial ploughing-up.
15  Ellis, *Modern Husbandman*, May, p. 1.
16  Ellis, *Modern Husbandman*, May, pp. 1–2.
17  George Fussell, *The Farmer's Tools* (London, 1985), pp. 35–6.

& so are made more light & portable than these will bear to be, but these will go and work well with a great strength, when other ploughs will not to any purpose.[18]

Arthur Young, in his *General View of Agriculture of the County of Hertfordshire* in 1804, found Hertfordshire farmers 'much prejudiced' in favour of this implement. He found it well suited, with its long beam, sole and share, for breaking up 'strong flinty fallow [...] this plough will do such work, at times when few others would stir in such land at all'. But Young could not understand its use in any other context, for its 'faults are numerous; heavier than necessary for every other work', it did not produce a neat furrow, it needed the constant attention of a ploughman and, in short, it was 'a heavy, ill-formed, and ill-going plough'. Young had farmed for some years in Hertfordshire and knew of the soil conditions there. He and Ellis are agreed that the Hertfordshire plough was necessary to break up land that had lain fallow for some time, and Young probably underestimated the limited resources of small farmers who, if they needed a strong plough to tackle their harder soils, could not afford another for more general use. Although Ellis makes no criticism of the Hertfordshire wheeled plough during his long description of it in the *Modern Husbandman*, on other occasions he acknowledges that it is heavy and unwieldy for general use.[19]

In an early work, *The Practice of Farming*, Ellis gives a straightforward account of the ploughs then used by Hertfordshire farmers in the Chilterns, describing the Wheel-fallow plough (i.e. the Hertfordshire Wheel plough); the Creeper or Bobtail plough; the Lent-seed plough; the Wheat-seed plough; the Swing plough; the Foot plough; the Newmarket or 'flat sharr'd' plough; and the trenching plough.[20] He details how each is used and makes the sensible general point that '[t]he many sorts of ploughs now in use in this our Nation, shew the necessity there is of employing a right one in a soil proper for its working'. He explains, however, that many ploughs in use in Hertfordshire originated from outside the county:

although some ploughs have been made use of time out of mind, in certain places, as the best sort that could be got and employed [...] yet time, ingenuity, and experience have proved such their assured opinion to be wrong founded, and

---

18  Walter Blith, *The English Improver Improved* (London, 1653), pp. 200, 202.

19  Young, *Hertfordshire*, pp. 36–7. Ellis, *Modern Husbandman*, May, pp. 1–2; Blith, *English Improver Improved*, p. 202. The beam of a plough is the long piece of wood on the top. The sole is a piece at the bottom that keeps the plough running straight. The share is a pointed piece of iron at the front of the plough that slices through the ground.

20  Ellis, *The Practice of Farming*, pp. 244–60.

convinced many farmers, that others, lately discovered, have better supplied the room of the old ploughs.

Moreover, some ploughs enjoying success were new inventions. He was particularly taken with the Hertfordshire Double Plough. '[T]his transcendent instrument', invented in 1732, 'hath obtained such a reputation, as invites the farmers more and more to come into the use of it'. He describes a ploughing match organised by a large farmer near him where this implement ploughed almost twice as much as any of the other ploughs. At first the other farmers threatened to destroy it, then some took it up: 'it soon got footing among many of the best of husbandmen, who now say they never will be without it as long as they live.'[21]

In various publications Ellis works his way through the many soil types in his area, with remarks on how to handle each one. He begins with clays – Red Clays, Black Clays and White Clays: difficult soils, but potentially fertile if carefully handled and appropriately mixed with additives such as chalk, sand, gravel and manures.[22] Applying heavy dressings of chalk to clay soils was a practice common in Hertfordshire for many centuries, from before Roman times to the early twentieth century.[23] Some chalk was carted from

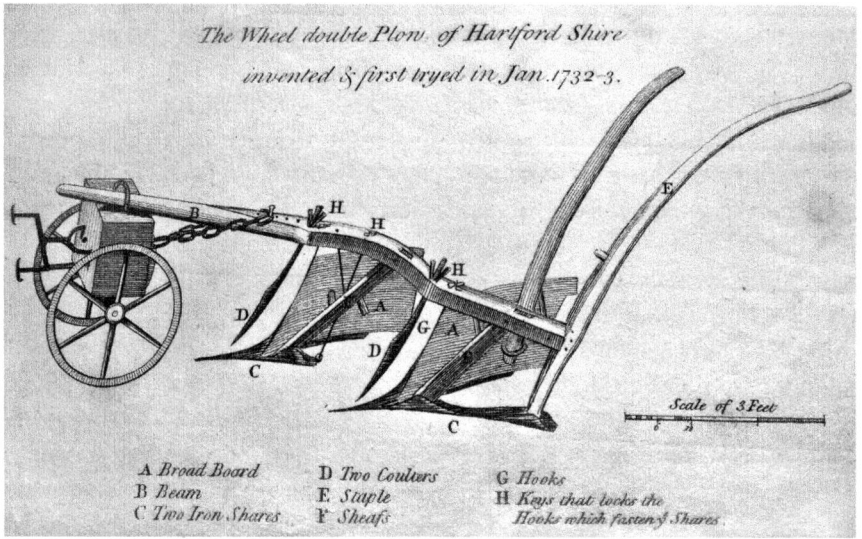

6. *Husbandry Methodized* (1772), vol. 1, engraving of the Hertfordshire double-wheeled plough.

---

21  Ellis, *Modern Husbandman*, April, pp. 15, 106–9.
22  Ellis, *Chiltern and Vale Farming*, pp. 9–13.
23  Gardiner, *Hertfordshire*, pp. 127–33.

open chalk pits, but another method, employed where the clay overlay chalk at convenient depth, was mentioned by Ellis and, in 1804, described in some detail by Arthur Young. Gangs of so-called Chalk Drawers contracted with farmers to dig a shaft in the middle of a field:

> here a pit, about four feet in diameter, is sunk to the chalk … . The earth and chalk is raised from the pit by a jack rowl[24] on a frame [...] The pit is sunk from 20 to 30 feet deep and then chambered at the bottom, that is, the pitman digs or cuts out the chalk horizontally, in three separate directions [...] One pit will chalk six acres, laying 60 loads to an acre. Eighteen barrowfulls make a load, and the usual price for chalking is 7d. per load.[25]

Ellis described how, by ploughing around the pit, it would in time be filled in. There is no doubt that this practice did, as Ellis suggested, much improve the structure and fertility of clay soils.[26]

Ellis continues through all the soil types in his area – loam, gravels, sands and chalks – discussing the characteristics of each and how they can be improved. He mentions that he has carried out experiments on loams, but gives no details.[27] He does, however, describe an experiment a farmer near him carried out that involved chalking a gravelly soil. This was a success, improving the soil structure, making it 'more loamy' and easier to plough, as well as improving fertility. A similar experiment, but using lime, was carried out in 1931 on gravelly soil on a Hertfordshire farm. The treated land was sown with sugar beet which came up ten days earlier than on a control plot.[28] Ellis's emphasis on good ploughing was also sound advice. The many variations of soil types in Little Gaddesden's fields sometimes made it feasible to mix the soil of adjoining fields to produce a more productive loam. Ellis tells of two neighbours, one with a sandy field, the other a field of yellow clay. By carting topsoil between the two fields, they doubled the value of their fields and enjoyed a succession of good crops.[29]

On several occasions Ellis mentions that large quantities of waste materials were carted from London to fertilise the soils of Hertfordshire, mostly being applied as top-dressings (i.e. spread on the surface of the land). He describes these fertilisers as 'great mellowers of Earths, by warming and hollowing

---

24  A hand-operated winch or windlass.
25  Young, *Hertfordshire*, pp. 158–60.
26  Ellis, *Chiltern and Vale Farming*, pp. 24–8.
27  Ibid., pp. 29–67.
28  Gardiner, *Hertfordshire*, p. 129.
29  Ellis, *Practical Farmer*, p. 104.

AGRICULTURE

7. Photographs of digging chalk for the very long-established Hertfordshire practice of 'chalking', which was in decline by the early twentieth century (Gardiner, *Hertfordshire*).

their parts in the frosty or watery seasons', and recommended human urine ('stale') as a top-dressing, encouraging his maid to empty chamber pots into a barrel for use in the fields and composting human dung from his privy.[30]

Ellis was convinced, too, of the benefit he derived from folding:

> It is Sheep that return every Evening to pay for their cheap Keeping, by being confined in a Fold, to dress our Land with their Dung and Stale, a Dressing that is so agreeable to it, that were it not for them, there would not be half the Grain that yearly [there] is [...] In short, the Dressing of Land, by Folding of Sheep, is one main Support of the Country, as it is next to the Land itself, and the Ploughing and Sowing of it, the chief Means of our plentiful Crops of Grain and Grasses.[31]

Folding involved grazing a flock of sheep, supervised by a shepherd, on common land during the daytime – grazing sometimes supplemented by fodder grown for them, such as vetches or turnips – while at night they were folded on a small part of an arable field, bounded by hurdles staked out each night, where they digested their food and dropped their dung. The next day the process was repeated, the fold being moved to another part of the field in the evening. Ellis comments that less manure is now brought from London than previously, because of the adoption of folding: 'under that incomparable dressing of the Fold' chalk soils yield the best returns because sheep dung, he finds, readily yields its fertilizing qualities to this type of soil. Sheep treading on the soil also makes it firmer, 'more fit to hold the seed, and preserve it from droughts and frosts'.[32]

Interestingly, Arthur Young in his survey of Hertfordshire agriculture in 1804 does not share Ellis's high esteem of folding. He writes of

> the general predilection for the application of the sheep-fold, which is more universal in this county than in any other with which I am acquainted. What a system of waste, both of time and labour, must it be, to set a fold for 20 or 30 sheep! In proportion, therefore, as folding is necessary, a large farm is necessary; for it cannot be practised advantageously on any other.[33]

A contemporary commentator, Edward Lisle, was more nuanced in his opinion of folding. Taking soundings among many farmers in his county of Hampshire, he found many advantages in folding, but there were also

---

30  Gardiner, *Hertfordshire*, p. 138; Ellis, *Practical Farmer*, p. 8. 'Stale' is urine.
31  Ellis, *Compleat system of experienced improvements*, f. iv.
32  Ellis, *The Practice of Farming*, p. 53; Ellis, *Modern Husbandman*, vol. VIII, 1750, p. 57.
33  Young, *Hertfordshire*, p. 24.

complicating factors, such as the composition of the flock and, most importantly, the timing of folding. If employed too early after winter sowing the richness of the dung was washed away before it could do any good; folding in frosty weather was useless, because the cold would not allow the dung to be absorbed by the soil; and folding on dry soil recently sown with corn risked the sheep scratching out the seed. On the other hand, farmers told him that folded land was less apt to produce smutty wheat than dunged ground, i.e. land fertilised by dung carted from a farmyard dung heap.[34]

Presumably writing of his open-field lands, Ellis describes a three-year rotation of wheat, fallow, and finally oats, peas or beans. Edward Lisle noted the same rotation in Hertfordshire. He also writes that in the open fields of the Vales everyone 'generally plows and sows as his next neighbour does'. Summing up the differences in rotations between the enclosed Chilterns and the open-field Vales, Ellis explains:

> we in the Hill-Country have sometimes three crops in less than a Year and a Half; as Clover, Turnips, Wheat or Barley &c. by means of our convenient Inclosures; whilst they in their valley open Fields are confin'd to lose a Year and a half before they must set on a Barley-Crop after their Beans.[35]

This remark highlights a major problem with open-field agriculture – the need to act collectively slowed down the pace of farming and restricted the choice of crops. Under the three-field open-field system each farmer worked a number of small strips of arable land in three large open fields. In the instance described here every farmer sowed beans in an open field in October or the following February. They were harvested in high summer, after which the land stood idle until spring barley was sown in the following February. So almost a year and a half was taken up by a crop of beans and a period of fallow. In contrast, farmers with enclosed fields could follow one crop almost immediately with another, so that, for instance, clover might be sown in barley stubble and harrowed in, or a crop of quick-growing turnips, taking four months from sowing to harvest, could be squeezed into a rotation. Farmers in the common fields have to grow the same crops as their neighbours and, more importantly, harvest them at the same time. This is because, after a crop has been harvested, the animals of all farmers in the manor or village are allowed to graze on the stubble and eat the weeds, often until the next crops are sown. So crops must be cleared by an agreed date

---

34  Lisle, *Observations*, vol. I, p. 248; vol. II, pp. 178–91. 'Smut' is a fungal infection which greatly reduces the yield of wheat.
35  Ellis, *Practical Farmer*, p. 221.

by all. To maintain soil fertility, one field in a three-field open-field system was left uncropped each year to 'rest'; that is, it was left fallow. Farmers with enclosed land could avoid this enforced idleness of one-third of their arable land and restore fertility by rotating their grain crops with plants such as legumes, which deposited nitrogen in the soil via nodules on their roots. They could grow what they chose, without having to avoid crops that would not be ready to harvest before the open field was thrown open to grazing animals. Farmers could more easily fold sheep on enclosed land. They could also respond to the market, growing what would sell well. This is a very simple explanation of open-field agriculture. In practice the system might be more flexible – Eric Kerridge, in his comprehensive 1992 study of open-field agriculture, found that the dates when fields were thrown open for grazing were generally strictly enforced, but there was considerable flexibility over what crops were grown. On occasion crops could be grown when an open field was fallowed with the agreement of the rest of the farmers as long as hurdles were placed around it to keep animals out.[36]

Ellis contrasts what he considers to be the limited choice of crops in the open fields with the freedom of the enclosed Chiltern lands, where some farmers had sown weld, woad, French wheat, cole seed, coriander, caraway, hemp, flax, liquorice, potatoes, hops, saffron and other crops. He thought that big improvements in agricultural productivity per acre in recent years had come about because farmers had inserted various improvement crops into the fallow year. However, he exaggerated the constraints on individual farmers' freedom imposed by open-field agriculture. He saw for himself how saffron-growing fitted into open fields and he must have been aware of farming in Fulham where the farmer–gardeners grew patches of vegetables for human consumption in their open-field holdings and had been doing so successfully since the early seventeenth century.[37]

Ellis does not provide us with a neat rotation that he followed on his enclosed lands. Clover and some new grasses, increasingly recognised as useful fodder plants, were incorporated into his rotations. Clover grew fast after being mowed or grazed. The main virtue of grasses and clover, he believed, was that when animals were turned into the field to feed on them, their dung and urine added goodness to the soil. He does observe that some plants themselves improve soil fertility, but his explanation of this process is muddled. Appreciating that a grass or clover ley benefits the soil, he attributes this to a 'certain crust or grass-clover, which prevents the ground being

---

36   Eric Kerridge, *The Common Fields of England* (Manchester, 1992), pp. 70–3.
37   Joan Thirsk (ed.), *Agrarian History of England and Wales* (Cambridge, 1984), vol. V, pt 1, p. 518.

exhausted by the sun's attracting heat and power'.[38] He does, however, say in a later work that clover itself enriches ground: it 'is justly called the Mother of Corn, for its breeding in the ground those several enriching qualities, that have often been the chief means of producing good crops of Wheat'.[39]

In his book *Chiltern and Vale Farming Explained*, he gives several sequences of crops over a two-year period. For instance:

| | | | |
|---|---|---|---|
| Year one | barley or wheat | Year two | Peas |
| Year one | Vetch | Year two | Wheat |
| Year one | Turnips | Year two | Wheat |
| Year one | 'corn' | Year two | Trefoil |
| Year one | Barley | Year two | Clover |
| Year one | 'corn' | Year two | Sainfoin |
| Year one | Clover | Year two | Lucerne |

In addition, in the Vale they sow oats 'for a change in the ground, lest it degenerate under constant growth of certain particular crops'. This last remark is an acknowledgement that a rotation can improve or restore fertility. He similarly advocates sowing trefoil and clover on 'worn out' land. Some crops are ploughed in as green manure – rye sown in the spring for animals to feed on was later ploughed in and followed by peas or oats, and vetch was treated the same way before wheat was sown.[40]

In his enclosed fields Ellis grew lucerne as a fodder crop and he shares his experience of it: 'I have it now [in 1732] growing in four fields on two sorts of soil', both loams, one moist with red clay two feet under it, the other a dry loamy gravel. The latter was sown with lucerne after a crop of clover. It was well harrowed between late October and May to produce a fine tilth. On 15 May it was sown with steeped oats, three bushels an acre, harrowed in. The next day he sowed a pound of lucerne an acre 'by throwing it from between two fingers, in broadcast manner, and rolled it immediately'. The oats proved a good crop, and the lucerne came on after.[41]

---

38 Clover or trefoil are common names for plants of the genus *Trifolium*, which are part of the legume family. They are low-growing plants, some biennial, others slightly longer-lived.

39 Ellis, *Practical Farmer*, p. 6; Lisle, *Observations*, vol. I, p. 167; [Ellis], *Ellis's Husbandry*, vol. I, p. 503. Clover has the additional advantage that nodes on its roots fix nitrogen, greatly aiding soil fertility, a mechanism not known in Ellis's time. A ley is a piece of land temporarily sown with grass or fodder crops such as clover for several years, before being used to grow grain again.

40 Ellis, *Modern Husbandman*, September, pp. 6–7; Ellis, *Chiltern and Vale Farming*, pp. 197, 251, 261, 269.

41 Ellis, *Chiltern and Vale Farming*, pp. 280–1.

Preparations for sowing wheat on broken-up sward[42] in various home counties are reviewed: in Hertfordshire Ellis says the usual course is to break up the sward, ploughing the sods well into the ground then sow with a crop of black oats to take off some of the richness (an acknowledgement of the increased fertility brought about by the ley) before sowing wheat in the next year. Some in the county sowed wheat after clover. This information in one instance leads into a long discussion of wheat sown directly after the sward is broken up using the three-wheeled drill-plough, which he offered for sale. Emphasising that grain is the major arable crop on his farm and wheat is the grain of most importance to him, he observes:

> Wheat is with good reason called the King of Grain, as gold is the King of Metals. Wheat is named the Golden Grain, not only for its being nearest in colour to that most valuable ore, but also for bringing in the greatest profit to the farmer's pocket, as being the best corn for the support of life, and selling beyond, or surer than, all others for ready money.[43]

Presumably writing of the lands he has in the open fields, he says, 'The profit of our wheat is generally reckoned to have two years rent dependant on it', because one year in three was fallow. It was therefore important for the farmer to choose the right sort of wheat from the many strains available – if, that is, he had a choice, for many farmers saved part of their harvest as seed corn for the next sowing and in this way local strains were perpetuated.[44] Ellis reviews what he considers to be the best options for those who could choose their seed wheat. The White Wheat, or Yellow-Lammas, was a high yielder, performing well on lean soil, and 'grinds to a most excellent flour'. It was, however, more likely to sprout in wet weather and was also prone to mildew. Red Lammas was not suited to Chiltern soils, and the Dugdale was hardy but yielded coarse flour. The White-Brown and Red Pirky Wheats grew well on poor soils and were not susceptible to mildew, but Ellis predicted that it was the White Wheat that would be much sown in the future in his neighbourhood. Arthur Young, writing in 1804, found Pirky Wheat grown in Hertfordshire, as well as red and white Rivets. He mentions red and white Lammas but does not give these any particular prominence.[45]

In his enclosed fields, Ellis could follow his own rotation of crops. He considered that 'wheat is the properest grain to follow clover of any, because

---

42  Sward is land that has for some years been grassland; ley is another term for this.
43  Ellis, *Modern Husbandman*, February, p. 3.
44  Ellis, *Chiltern and Vale Farming*, p. 197.
45  Young, *Hertfordshire*, pp. 82–3.

it will bear with sour tilth' (i.e. acidity in the soil) caused by the clover. His remark is surprising, as today wheat is considered to be sensitive to soil acidity.[46] He proceeds to sow wheat as follows:

> after the ground has been sufficiently harrowed, I sow three bushels of wheat on every acre, and harrow in the seed once, twice, or more in a place, as the ground requires it. When all is thus far done, I spread rotten dung all over the surface as equally as I can, and thus let it lie the rest of the year.[47]

On one occasion he sowed wheat after peas and on another he obtained '[a] good crop of wheat got by sowing on a Barley Stubble'.[48]

The barley sown by Ellis and his neighbours was of two types: common barley and raith-ripe.[49] Raith-ripe seed barley was purchased at Fulham, where the farmer–gardeners who cultivated the open fields there, alternating grain crops with market-garden vegetables, produced a superior grain and 'most of our curious farmers hereabouts send their wagons to Fulham to buy the same every third year, it declining its virtue after twice sowing'. This seed had long been prized: in 1716 John Mortimer thought it 'the best for rank Land, because it doth not run so much to straw, as the Common sort, and yields much better. It will also grow on cold wet stiff land.' Ellis explained that 'the Chelsea and Fulham farmers are thought to have the whitest, most thin-skinned, and mellowest barley in England, from off their loamy land, that always fetch the greatest price for seed and malt'.[50] He tells us little of the place barley held in his rotation in his enclosures but in one year he sowed barley after wheat and fallowed the land between the summer wheat harvest and the following March. He cautioned against dunging young barley: 'amongst the several methods that I have practised in dressing of Barley-ground, I do not approve of laying long litter, or dung, on top of new-sown barley.'[51]

Oats were accustomed to poor soils: 'oats are a grain that best agrees with lean Chiltern ground, and least with rich Vale earths.' In November 1739 he ploughed up a bean stubble intending to sow it later with wheat, but instead he 'harrowed in black oats about the beginning of March, without plowing

---

46  Ellis, *Practical Farmer*, p. 10. Soils vary from the strongly alkaline to highly acid. A neutral soil is best. Ian Moore (ed.), *Primrose McConnell's The Agricultural Notebook*, 16th edn (London, 1976), pp. 64–5.
47  Ellis, *Modern Husbandman*, July, p. 9.
48  Ibid., September, p. 42.
49  Raith-ripe means early ripening, ready to harvest before other varieties.
50  John Mortimer, *Whole Art of Husbandry* (London, 1717), pp. 130–1; Ellis, *Practical Farmer*, p. 28.
51  Ellis, *Practical Farmer*, pp. 27–9, 32.

any more, and had an excellent crop at harvest, because the violent frosts had so crumbled and hollowed the surface, as to let in the harrow tines deep enough to make it fine and cover the seed'.[52]

Ellis sowed 'thetches' (vetch) as a fodder crop for horses, cattle and sheep. He fed it green to horses and cows and folded sheep on a small part of the field each day, bringing them in from the common at about two or three o'clock in the afternoon. The effect on soil fertility of the nitrogen-fixing quality of this plant he noticed when he sowed two acres of a large field with vetch. In the following year, after ploughing and dunging, the whole field was sown with wheat, which grew better on the part where the vetch had previously grown than on the rest of the field.[53]

Ellis recognised that clover 'is now become the most general artificial grass sown in England'. As we have seen, it was often sown with barley or, in this case, with oats: 'I harrowed in four bushels of oat seed on one plowing up of a barley-stubble, in which, as soon as done, I harrowed in ten pounds of clover, on the same acre.' He found letting large cattle feed on clover 'hollowed out' the soil and made it the 'better for harrowing in of wheat on one ploughing'. There was much resistance by local Vale farmers when clover was first introduced on the Chiltern lands because they feared the increase in output on those lands would cause agricultural prices to fall and their rents would be burdensome:

> Vale farmers used (on clover seed's being first sown in England) their utmost endeavours to suppress its propagation in the Chiltern country, and accordingly petitioned the Parliament to stop its growth, for that it would prove so detrimental to the Vale farmers, as to disable them to pay their old rents. But all their efforts, on this score, proved abortive.[54]

Initially, Ellis grew several varieties of peas, and was perhaps experimenting to find the best variety for his soil: 'some of the best of Field pease which I sow myself are the Great Blue Union, The Double Maple, The White Non-Parrel, The most hardy Horn Grey, and The Carolina Large Pease.' He later narrowed the list: 'but for my part, I sow at present only three [...] the Horn-Gray, Maple, and Blue Pea.' In 1742 he used just two types: 'I sowed the horn-grey pea, and common maple hog-pea.'[55]

---

52 Ellis, *Modern Husbandman*, August, p. 32; William Ellis and Samuel Trowell, *The Farmer's Instructor or, The Husbandman and Gardener's Useful and Necessary Companion* (London, 1747), p. 32.

53 Ellis, *Modern Husbandman*, May, p. 47; September, p. 57.

54 Ellis, *Modern Husbandman*, January, pp. 68, 73; February, p. 75; Ellis, *Practical Farmer*, p. 10.

55 Ellis and Trowell, *Farmer's Instructor*, p. 51; Ellis, *Chiltern and Vale Husbandry*, p. 218;

Turnips were grown by Ellis and his neighbours – the youngest and earliest were sent to London for human consumption, whereas the main crop was fed to cattle and sheep. He tells us that in 1742 he transplanted some of the best-growing turnips into fresh ground to feed his sheep. On another occasion, after a crop of peas, he ploughed and harrowed a field, then in June harrowed in turnip seed. The summer was very dry and the turnips did not appear, then, on Sunday, 20 July, 'a shower of rain falling the same night, on the morrow a fine thick crop was seen, and which proved a good one indeed'.[56] Turnips could also be fed to the fancy fowl he advertised for sale.

In the 1744 *Modern Husbandman* for June Ellis devotes a chapter to turnips, declaring: 'I shall here remark the transactions of my Neighbours and others, besides my own, as they relate to the obtaining of a good crop of turneps.' He covers soil preparation – giving many local examples – sowing, hoeing, combating the fly and saving seed, and describes the varieties of the root available.[57]

Ellis grew sainfoin on gravelly/chalky land to feed his cattle and he also grew lucerne and a fodder crop called 'Ladyfinger', sown as part of a sward. He was particularly enthusiastic about this latter plant, the more so because he offered to sell the seeds.

## *Seed steeps*

Ellis was convinced of the efficacy of treating seeds before sowing them, especially brining wheat and steeping (i.e. soaking) barley. In order to prevent smut, a disease of wheat, many of Ellis's fellow farmers at Gaddesden soaked seed wheat in brine and mixed it with lime before sowing. His neighbours all had slightly different recipes for their steeps and brines, which Ellis reviews, with apparent if not explicit approval. He then introduces his own seed steep for barley:

> Take a quantity of the grain you are to sow, a bushel, more or less, and boil it in a copper (to a bushel put five pails-full of water) till the grain bursts, and the water thereby becomes impregnated with the essential salt of such grain; strain your liquor [...] While the liquor is hot, put in three pounds of nitre, [saltpetre] that it may dissolve, and add four or five pails-full of nitre which drains from the dunghill, or urine of any sort.[58] And in this prepared liquor, steep the grain about

---

Ellis, *Modern Husbandman*, February, p. 41.
56  Ellis, *Modern Husbandman*, July, p. 25.
57  Ellis, *Modern Husbandman*, June, pp. 17–33.
58  Nitre is potassium nitrate, $KNO_3$, also known as saltpetre. This was formed naturally in dung heaps.

twenty-four hours [...] then take the grain, and let it dry in the shade, or sift lime over it, which will dry it sooner, and sow one third less than usual, and you will assuredly find the benefit by twenty-fold; I have actually tried it with barley, and had commonly thirty ears from one root.

Ellis claimed his steep saved on seed, produced a high yield, made up for any inadequacy in fertilising the soil and combated drought early in the seed's growth. He first tried it in 1731, when it caused even germination and yielded 50 per cent more grain than he had ever had before; the crop aroused 'the admiration of the beholders'.[59]

Ellis repeats this recipe several times in his publications, once describing it as 'the most fertile liquor in the world'. By the 1740s he had discovered 'a most cheap ingredient' (which he said he would reveal in due course – he did not), to replace the nitre, reducing the price of using the steep to six pence an acre.[60] Another relatively cheap way to enhance the sowing of grain, invented by a gentleman but exploited by Ellis, was a sieve, or series of sieves, which riddled out the smallest seeds, leaving the largest for sowing. It was especially recommended for wheat.[61]

Ellis and his neighbours were by no means pioneers in brining to prevent smut and steeping to enhance yield. Many literate gentlemen in the sixteenth century noted that Virgil steeped his corn before sowing and many afterwards wrote of steeps. Sir Hugh Plat advocated brining wheat and tells a tale of how brining was first discovered when a 'silly wench' dropped some seed-corn in the sea. In the 1720s Richard Bradley had heard that a sinking grain ship led to the discovery of brining. Sir Francis Bacon carried out experiments with many steeps and experiments were still being made in Arthur Young's time. Ellis does not comment on how his drill-ploughs coped with steeped seed – one would guess that steeping would make seeds sticky and less likely to flow evenly into the drills.[62]

## *Drilling*
Once a farmer had extracted the best seed he had to decide when and how to sow it, and here we come to discussion of drill-ploughs and the horse-breaks or horse-hoes, controversial innovations in Ellis's time and for some time after him. There is no doubt that Ellis regarded seed drilling as

---

59 Ellis, *Practical Farmer*, pp. 20–7.
60 Ellis, *Modern Husbandman*, June, p. 45.
61 Ellis, *Modern Husbandman*, March, p. 113.
62 F.A. Buttress and R.W.G. Dennis, 'The Early History of Cereal Seed Treatment in England', *Agricultural History*, 21/2 (1947), pp. 93–103.

8. Engraved frontispiece of *The Farmers Instructor*, showing Ellis's four-wheeled drill plough in operation.

a distinct improvement on the traditional method of broadcasting seed, but he had an ulterior motive in championing drilling because drilling and weeding implements were heavily advertised by Ellis in his books. He was initially most proud of his four-wheeled drill-plough, which is depicted in the frontispiece of *The Farmer's Instructor*, where it was said to have been invented by him in 1745.[63] With its large central hopper and four wheels it looks not unlike the drill that John Worlidge had invented in the previous century, but in both cases we can compare them only from a sideways view; the internal workings of each were not displayed. Ellis made extravagant claims for this machine, the purpose of which was to sow seeds at a steady rate in rows evenly spaced apart. Despite heavy advertising he opined that 'I am persuaded many would send to me for this plough, if they were sensible of the several advantages belonging to its uses.'[64]

Ellis first encountered the *three-wheeled* drill-plough, which he eventually seemed to favour over the four-wheeled, on the farm of 'Farmer Clements' near Bath. This plough was invented by James Godden, who sent details of it to Ellis in January 1738 – Godden apparently had no objection to Ellis's sales of his invention, although he may have supplied only ready-built ploughs to Ellis.[65] The plough could be modified to sow 'wheat, barley, oats, beans,

---

63  Although he was drilling peas in 1742 and 1743.
64  Ellis and Trowell, *Farmer's Instructor*, p. 32; John Worlidge, *Systema Agriculturae* (London, 1681), facing p. 18.
65  Ellis, *Modern Husbandman*, June, pp. 7–8.

pease, thetches, tills, St. Foyne, clover, trefoil, turnep, cole, canary, woad' and other seeds. In the *Modern Husbandman* for January, Ellis gives very detailed instructions both for the use of this machine and how it works but he does not say he himself has used it. In no publications does he describe his experience using this instrument, but he must have used it for he was drilling seeds before he developed his four-wheeled plough. Ellis explains the mechanism that regulates the flow of seed into the drill using the three-wheeled plough thus:

> [the] plough is to have its hopper charged with wheat seed, and then drawn along for making a drill, and dropping out the seed, as the large third wheel turns a little wheel or box about three inches in breadth, which, by its notches or circular cavities, lets out the wheat perfectly regular, at equal distances in the drill.[66]

In a more detailed description of the use of this drill to sow wheat he explains:

> This excellent Plough, lately invented, seems to supply in a great Measure Mr. Tull's Machines for sowing Corn in Drills, but at a vast cheaper Rate, and with Abundance of less Trouble, and with much more Assurance of a Crop; however, I am of Opinion, that this serviceable Three-wheel Plough was first contrived from the Models of the aforesaid ingenious Gentleman's Mathematical Sowing and Hough-Ploughs, for this one Drill-plough can be and is often so ordered as to supply both these Uses. This Drill-plough performs its Work in Chilturn, gravelly, chalky, sandy, and loamy Soils, and even in dry, stiff Grounds and, in short, wherever a Drill can be conveniently made, after they have been reduced and brought into a fine Mould by other common Ploughs; then in this Month we sow Wheat-seed out of it in our dry Loams, by putting near a Peck into the Hopper of the Plough, which drops regularly out of it into a Drill that the Share makes, by Means of a small, round, wooden, notched Box, about six Inches long, and three or four broad, that is turned in an exact Manner by a long iron Spindle, that is also turned by a third Wheel, so that this Spindle serves as an Axle-tree both to the third wheel and Box, and, as the Plough is drawn along, the Drill may be covered by two Sticks fixed to the Arse of the Plough, made so as to close the Drill and leave a small Ridge of Earth upon the Corn.

The 'notched box' for regulating the flow of seed was the vital part of a drill-plough – Ellis's four-wheeled plough had a similar device, but, on the evidence of Kalm, it did not work at all well. Godden's drill was

---

66  Ellis, *Modern Husbandman*, June, pp. 8–9; January, pp. 22–5.

apparently much less complicated to build than Tull's, and apparently was more robust.[67]

Ellis used his drill-ploughs first to sow peas: 'in March, 1742, I drilled hog-pease in one of my fields.'[68] He applied one of his secret fertilisers to the drilled seed via a separate hopper on the plough. The following year he drilled rouncival peas – 'In this month, 1743, I drilled in for the first time some of these pease, and by houghing the intervals in due time, I had in return a desired quantity.'[69] He carried out a trial 'before some persons', again drilling fertiliser along with his peas. His onlookers 'desired that three rows or drills might be left unmanured for a trial; I acquiesced, and it was not long before they had a glaring proof of the difference.'[70] He delayed using the drill-plough for grain: 'the first barley crop I ever sowed in drills out of the four-wheeled drill plow was in May 1746' and 'it made so fine an appearance, as highly pleased all beholders'. Significantly, when talking of wheat either drilled or sown broadcast he says: 'For my part, I sow wheat both ways, according to the nature of the ground'. When he carried out his demonstration of drilling before Kalm in 1748 he was probably still ironing out problems with his plough (see below).[71] Ellis also used, on occasion, a horse-hoe to weed his drills and he sold these and a variety of other types of plough that he could commission on request. But he had to put up with ridicule bordering on hostility from his neighbours when trying to use these new machines, which

> raises a resentment in me, against my brother farmers, for slighting, and even ridiculing new inventions, that do not correspond with their sordid humours, and thus make it a most difficult work for an author, to give such a description of any new, though ever so serviceable an instrument, as to introduce it into use with common farmers, in any reasonable time.[72]

In 1746 Ellis put forward Tull's controversial theory of soil fertility – that frequent hoeing not only kept down weeds but also mixed air with the soil; nutrients were absorbed into the soil from this air and in turn were absorbed

---

67 Ellis, *Modern Husbandman*, September, pp. 38–9. 'Mr. Tull' is a reference to Jethro Tull, who invented a seed drill and horse-drawn hoe that he described in *The New Horse-Hoeing Husbandry*, first published in 1731. His was the first seed drill to work effectively, but it was very complicated (and expensive) to build.
68 Ibid., August, p. 46.
69 Ibid., March, p. 53.
70 Ibid., September, p. 40.
71 Ibid., September, pp. 22–3, 31.
72 Ellis, *Modern Husbandman*, January, p. 50.

by the roots of plants; therefore, manuring the soil was unnecessary. By the use of his drill-plough 'Wheat, and other Corn crops, may be got for many Years together, without the Help of any Dung whatsoever'. Ellis did not repeat this theory in later books and he may have been dubious about it, but he told of a gentleman who sowed wheat according to Tull's theory on a 'lean, gravelly, loamy Soil' in drills one foot apart. Dutch hoes were used

> to earth up the Mould in the Interspaces to the Roots of the Wheat, that will vastly nourish it, even as much or better than Dung, and destroy all manner of Weeds besides. With this Help, and with the Help of the fine Mould, that the Drill – plough leaves in the Posture of a little Ridge on the Drill, as soon as the Wheat is dropt out of the Hopper of the Plough, the Land is made to produce as much or more Grain than usually grows, where Wheat-seed has been sown out of a Man's Hand in the broad-cast way.[73]

If this method of farming had been successful it would have saved the considerable expense of a flock of sheep and a shepherd, as well as that of a dairy. To the question 'How can Land be made to produce great Crops of Corn, without Dung or Manure?' he answered:

> That the little Ridge of fine loose Earth, that lies on the Seed, will prove a sufficient Dressing to the Corn, by the Salts that wash down on the Seed out of this little Ridge of Earth; and the Dews beside, that fall from time to time afterwards on the same, and likewise are wash'd down to the Roots of the Corn. This is Nourishment enough, in the wettest or driest Seasons, to force on its Growth; and the more, because all the Earth is kept free and clear of Weeds.[74]

This was Tull's theory: that nutrition passed from the earth to plant roots and much earthing up and stirring of the soil passed fertiliser from earth to plant. Fertility itself came from the air and was absorbed by the soil. Tull's ideas were disputed by many at the time and are now known to be totally without foundation, and it is interesting that Ellis put them forward in only one book – he may have believed them but thought it best not to engage in the controversy surrounding them or, just as likely, he simply put them forward as another benefit derived from buying his drill-plough.[75]

Ellis gives the impression that drilling was inevitable in the future but experiments with drilling were carried on by Hertfordshire farmers in the

---

73 Ellis, *Agriculture Improv'd*, vol. II, pp. 129–30.
74 Ibid., p. 131.
75 Ibid., pp. 129–33.

half century after Ellis's death and they were by no means convinced of its efficiency by the end of the century. Arthur Young interviewed many who had tried drilling and reported, in 1804,

> upon the whole, they leave the subject pretty much as I found it: a conclusion, however, is fairly to be drawn, that a method of putting in crops which has failed with several intelligent cultivators, and only partially succeeded with some others, cannot be generally necessary as a means of profit.[76]

### Kalm's observations on Ellis's farming

It is with Ellis's resentment over the local reception of his machines in mind that we will examine Pehr Kalm's reports of the demonstration of drilling given to him by Ellis and the answers to Kalm's questioning of Ellis's neighbours about his husbandry. Kalm came to see Ellis principally to examine his new machines and probably went to Little Gaddesden eagerly anticipating viewing each one closely. His first disappointment was finding that Ellis did not have the machines on display. He explained to Kalm that he commissioned machines as they were ordered by customers. Kalm obviously wanted, nonetheless, to see them in the making, but Ellis told him the manufacturers lived some distance away (whereas his neighbours said they were made locally).

On 2 April 1748 Kalm was shown the four-wheeled drill-plough in action. He examined it with interest, noting that at the front a share made a furrow, a funnel dropped seed into this, another funnel behind channelled compressed fertiliser into the furrow and a harrow at the back covered over the seed. Kalm initially annoyed Ellis by claiming that his instrument had already been invented by a Swedish pastor, Zacharias Westbeck, a few years before.[77] Kalm records in his diary Ellis's extravagant claims for the drill-plough: 'When Mr Ellis showed me the characteristics of his four-wheeled drill-plough he sought to add to his own renown in some degree by saying

---

76 Young, *Hertfordshire*, pp. 131–2.
77 Kalm cites an article in a Swedish learned journal of 1741 describing and illustrating Westbeck's machine. Ellis's and the Swedish machine look somewhat similar, but Ellis's was more sophisticated. Westbeck's drill had just one hopper, presumably for seed. The seed was dropped by a regulator that opened and shut a hole in the bottom of the hopper and this was operated by a pivoted lever, one end of which was tripped by a ratchet on the inner side of the machine's wheel. There was no ploughshare to make a drill for the seed, no manure hopper and no harrow to cover the seed. It was, in essence, a modified wheelbarrow. In the journal Kalm cites the pastor is surnamed Welbęck. Zacharias Welbeck, *Kongl. Wetenskapsacademiens Handlingar* (January–March 1741), pp. 78–90. I thank Matti W. Leino for this reference and advice on Westbeck's drill.

that since Adam was created, no implement had been invented so useful as this' and he considered it 'worth its weight in gold'.[78] He continued:

> I should too much weep for human-kind if this were true, for after Mr Ellis had, with two carls, devoted the whole afternoon to using this plough, he had not succeeded in sowing a pint of seed. Scarcely half a furrow sowed before one was obliged to stand and attend to the plough. Now, the seed would not run; now, the mould [i.e. fertiliser] stuck fast in the hole at the bottom of the funnel; now the corn was not harrowed well down, so that there were here *frictiones frictionum* [rubbing and friction]. Had man for all time past not been able to sow in a better manner than was done here to-day, mankind would long before this have died of hunger. I do not deny that if this plough is rightly worked and used, it may for some kinds of seed have its great service, as with peas etc.[79]

After this disastrous demonstration, Ellis locked the plough away and Kalm complained that Ellis was generally not forthcoming in imparting knowledge about English agriculture. Kalm asked Ellis's fellow farmers if he actually *used* his advertised new machines:

> The answers were unanimous; that he never used other or more than they and that the ploughs that he uses are the same as those used from time immemorial. But they imparted that he may occasionally have used for his amusement several others perhaps for a short while. They concurred that he sells to various gentlemen a number of the same implements that he has described in his books.[80]

Another seed-drill inventor, John Randall, bought one of Ellis's drills. He found it temperamental, sowing one row only at a time and sometimes not working. He summed it up as 'rather like a child's go-cart'.[81]

The Gaddesden farmers also told Kalm that Ellis used no special manure, cultivated his arable the same way they did and had the same average yields as they did. Kalm had already been shocked to see, when he first arrived at Little Gaddesden, that some of Ellis's fields were ill-tended: one was full of moss and another flooded.[82] Despite what his fellow farmers said, the drill-ploughs and hoes were, according to Ellis, demonstrated to others in the same way that Kalm was shown them, and he claims that these other

---

78  Bell, *Mr. Ellis*, pp. 90–2; Mead, *Pehr Kalm*, p. 42.
79  Bell, *Mr. Ellis*, pp. 91–2.
80  Mead, *Pehr Kalm*, p. 40.
81  Fussell, *Farmer's Tools*, p. 103.
82  Ibid., pp. 40–1; Bell, *Mr. Ellis*, pp. 148–9.

demonstrations were successful, both in drilling in the seed and, at harvest time, in the yields achieved. Was Kalm just unlucky to have hit a bad day? After all, Ellis did successfully sell his drills and horse-hoes, no criticism of his machines by dissatisfied customers has been found in contemporary publications and his neighbours did not mention to Kalm any unhappy customers visiting Ellis. On the other hand, if Ellis did not habitually use the machines he advertised, was he selling machines he had no confidence in?

## Fruit trees

> What a charming sight is a large tree in blossom, and after that, when loaden with fruit, enough perhaps to make a hogshead of cyder or perry! A scene of beauty, hopes, and profit, and all! It may be on less than two feet diameter of ground. And above all, what matter of contemplation does it afford, when we let our thoughts descend to a single kernel of an apple or pear? And again, how heightened, on the beholding so great a bulk raised and preserved, by Omnipotent Power, from so small a body.[83]

This lyrical passage is so uncharacteristic of Ellis's writing that this author immediately suspected he had plagiarised one of the books he consulted on fruit trees, but it seems to be his own words. Rather like William Lawson over 150 years before him, Ellis was captivated by fruit trees, but he also saw their economic potential, in supplying both food and the raw materials for drinks. Ellis was an advocate of the planting of fruit trees in fields and hedges and had fruit trees dotted around his farm. He was by no means the first to do this and to encourage others to do likewise. Leonard Mascall in 1572 covered planting trees in hedges and fields in his book on tree-growing. Arthur Standish, in a 1612 pamphlet, suggested 'That there may bee a certaine number of fruit-trees planted in all the Hedges' to ameliorate the 'extreme price of Victuals'. A correspondent of Samuel Hartlib in 1655 sought to encourage planting in hedgerows, especially of plum and damson trees. A year later John Beale, a Herefordshire parson, found that hedgerow fruit trees were common in his county but wanted to encourage this nationwide. He suggested hedgerow planting, especially for cider apples, in a pamphlet that was reprinted in 1724 by Richard Bradley. In 1696 T. Langford, in his book on fruit trees, devoted a chapter to planting them in fields and hedgerows. In response to those worried about thefts from isolated trees, he considered that if enough farmers planted fruit trees in fields collectively they could stand some losses and still be in profit (Ellis was of

---

83   Ellis, *Practical Farmer*, p. 163.

a similar opinion). John Evelyn, in *Pomona* (1664), saw apples and pears as raw material for cider and perry, which he believed could rival Continental wines. Interest in these drinks is shown by John Worlidge's book on cider of 1676 and John Philips's didactic poem *Cyder* of 1708. In short, Ellis was one of a long line of English writers who sought to encourage farmers to grow fruit trees in their fields and hedgerows.[84]

Ellis was particularly fond, and proud, of local varieties of fruit that he had growing on his land. Time and time again he promotes the Parsnip Apple, which seems to be a truly local variety.[85] He championed the Orange Bell pear. This was more known in his time: the 1768 edition of Philip Miller's *Dictionary* describes it as: 'Orange Rouge, i.e. the red Orange Pear. This Pear hath been the most common of all the sorts in France, which was occasioned by the general esteem it was in some years since.'[86]

In his book on cider Ellis gives information on his trees and his garden. He tells us his beloved Parsnip Apple tree is in his garden and that he has hundreds of cherry trees on his land, many planted on grass baulks at the edges of his ploughed lands 'in single rows'. He plants fruit trees 'high', digging only shallow holes for them. This is still a method of planting trees today, employed especially when planting bare root trees in grasslands. Despite having trees in fields both on hilltops, where they might be buffeted by winds, and in the Vale, where frosts might linger, he had respectable yields. Some trees in fields were dunged by animals which rested under them. His Parsnip Apple tree has its roots shaded by 'Rows of Currants and Gooseberries'.[87]

One of his favourite cherry trees, which grew in his home close, an arable field, 'was one of the largest trees in these parts; and tho' a wild cherry, I have sold the fruit for a Guinea upon the tree, clear of all charges [...] and

---

84 Leonard Mascall, *A book of the arte and manner, howe to plant and graffe all sortes of trees* (London, 1572); Arthur Standish, *The Commons Complaint* (London, 1612), pp. 34–5; Samuel Hartlib, *Samuel Hartlib his Legacy* (London, 1655), pp. 16–17; John Beale, *Herefordshire Orchards, a Pattern for all England* (London, 1656), pp. 2–3; T. Langford, *Plain and Full Instructions to Raise all Sorts Of Fruit-Trees* (London, 1696); John Evelyn, *Pomona* in *Sylva* (London, 1670); John Phillips, *Cyder* (London, 1708).

85 *The Journal of the Royal Horticultural Society* in 1898 (p. cxxxi) records that 'Mr Lyndsey, Waltham St. Lawrence sent an apple very like the old "Parsnip Apple"'. But this seems to be the only mention of the variety since Ellis.

86 Alexander McDonald, *A Complete Dictionary of Practical Gardening* (London, 1808); Philip Miller, *Gardeners' Dictionary* (London, 1768), Pyrus, para. 16.

87 In 1750 he more modestly claims of his Black Keroon Cherry trees, 'I believe I have above fifty of these sort of improved cherry-trees in my plow and meadow fields'. Ellis, *Country Housewife*, pp. 89–90; William Ellis, *The Compleat Cyderman* (London, 1746), pp. 3–5; <https://www.woodlandtrust.org.uk/plant-trees/advice/how-to-plant/>, accessed 12 December 2020.

the buyer gather'd the cherries'. His neighbour was even more fortunate, receiving 'ten pounds in one season' for cherries, 20 per cent of the yearly rent for his farm.[88] Young, in 1804, notes many orchards in the south-west corner of Hertfordshire, principally of apple and cherry trees.

> Every farm has an orchard; but the larger the farm the smaller the orchard. Orchards are found chiefly in farms of from 20 to 50 acres. The apples are most profitable; but cherries very beneficial to the poor, in the quantity of employment which they require in gathering the crop, for which the poor are paid from 4d. to 8d. per dozen pounds [...] A full-grown tree will produce 50 dozen pounds in a good year.

Clutterbuck commented in 1864 on the cherry orchards in the west of the county; their fruit was usually bought by dealers 'on the tree'.[89]

Ellis's Orange Bell pear tree was one 'of the highest and biggest pear trees in our country, so high that we have hardly a ladder that can thoroughly reach its top'. It yielded twenty or thirty bushels of fruit a year, 'the bite soft and juicy; it is of taste so pleasant, that it temps to gluttony. Its flavour has a small share of that of the China orange.' As well as being eaten raw, the pear was delicious baked in pies or pastries, and, 'in short, serves the farmer and his family, in some degree, so well as to save meats, bread, and drink, and this in harvest time, which makes this pear of double value'. This pear 'dressed, in the shape of a two-cornered turn-over pasty', made the 'harvest men rejoice' and willingly eat it instead of bread and cheese. The pear also made excellent perry with an orange perfume. As usual, there was a commercial reason for these hearty recommendations, for Ellis was 'ready to supply any person with scions or grafts for increasing, and furnishing their orchards with this noble necessary, and pleasant fruit'.[90] Moreover, he had been able 'to raise a nursery of these very sort of pear-trees' that he would sell for 'one shilling each, and send them to any part of England, Wales, Scotland, Ireland, or any of our plantations abroad'.[91] Ellis seems to have been a compulsive planter of fruit trees, especially in his fields. He breaks

---

88   Ellis, *Practical Farmer*, p. 140; Ellis, *The Timber Tree Improved*. In Ellis's time, London fruiterers roamed the Home Counties in spring looking for fruit trees with potentially good yields. They offered owners a discounted fee to return and harvest the crop to sell in their stalls and shops in London. See Malcolm Thick, 'The Sale of Produce from Non-commercial Gardens in Late Medieval and Early Modern England', *Agricultural History Review*, 66/1 (2018), p. 11.
89   Young, *Hertfordshire*, pp. 143–4; Rev. J. Clutterbuck, *Agricultural Notes on Hertfordshire* (London, 1864), p. 14.
90   Ellis, *Modern Husbandman*, October, pp. 109–10.
91   Ellis, *Country Housewife*, p. 89.

# THE TIMBER-TREE IMPROVED:

### OR, THE

Best PRACTICAL METHODS of Improving different LANDS with proper TIMBER.

### AND

Those FRUIT-TREES whose WOODS make the most profitable Returns to their OWNERS, according to the newest Inventions, by the *Plough*, *Harrow*, and other Methods most approved of.

CONTAINING,

I. Seven different Ways of improving the Oak, with REMARKS on the same.
II. The Nature and Improvement of the Beech.
III. To raise a Beech Wood from Seeds and Sets.
IV. Transplanting large Beeches.
V. To raise a Beech Hedge by Seeds or Sets.
VI. Of the Nature and Improvement of the Elm, Witch-Elm, Ash, Pollard-Ash, Ashen-Stems, Standard-Ash, Walnut, Black-Cherry.
VII. Reasons humbly offer'd for the common Use of the Black-Cherry.
VIII. Of the Horn-Bean, or Horn-Beech, Lime-Tree, Horse-Chesnut, Maple, Hazel, Firr-Tree, Sycamore, Sallow, Aps, White-wood, Poplar, and Abel, Alder, Withy and Willow, Oziers, White-Elder, Pear-Tree, &c.

*By* WILLIAM ELLIS,
Of *Little Gaddesden*, near *Hempstead*, in *Hertfordshire*.

The FOURTH EDITION.

### LONDON:

Printed for, and Sold by T. OSBORNE in *Gray's-Inn*, and M. COOPER, at the *Globe* in *Pater-noster Row*.

M.DCC.XLV.

9. Frontispiece of *The Timber-Tree Improved*, 4th edition, 1745.

off discussion of elms to inform his readers: 'I planted a Burgamo, Standard-Pear-Tree, that I bought of a Gardener for one shilling, ... about four years ago, on a gravelly soil, on the baulk or hedge-green of a ploughed field, near half a mile from my house.'[92]

Ellis's nursery also contained quantities of 'timber trees', but, although he wrote a book on this subject, *The Timber Tree Improved*, he tells us little in this or his other works about timber trees on *his* land.[93] He did buy a four-acre coppice wood in 1718, probably to secure a source of fuel, for coal was expensive in his area because it had to be transported some distance by land. The part of Hertfordshire where he lived was known for its thick hedgerows in which timber trees were carefully nurtured. A gentleman commented in 1769 that he knew

> [n]o part of England more beautiful in its stile than Hertfordshire. Thru'out the oak and Elm hedgerows appear rather the work of Nature than Plantations generally extending 30 or 40 feet Broad growing Irregularly in these stripes and giving the fields the air of being Reclaim'd from a general tract of woodland.[94]

## *Ellis and livestock: raising animals*

The agriculture of Hertfordshire was predominantly arable but horses were needed for draught, cattle for dairying, pigs for domestic consumption, fowls for eggs sent to London, young animals for some specialist branches of farming such as calf-rearing and house lambs, and for dung in the case of sheep folding. Many of these creatures, especially when raised for domestic consumption, were the province of farmers' wives in this part of the world.

Ellis advertised that he could supply various kinds of fowl to customers, but if he kept fowls for eggs or to sell at market he does not mention it in his writings – this was housewives' work.[95] Notwithstanding that pig-keeping was also women's work, Ellis provides some information on the management of his sows and piglets. It is his practice 'never to let a stye be littered with much straw, when a sow is going to pig because, if it is, the pigs are apt to be smother'd'. He scatters wheat straw on the sow which helps to nourish the piglets. Feeding sows boiled turnips or bran in water he finds helps to prevent constipation. He goes into detailed speculation as to exactly what poisoned a pregnant sow

---

92 Ellis, *The Timber Tree Improved*, p. 53.
93 His book drew heavily on contemporary and past writers on the subject, notably Evelyn's *Sylva*, which was the source of much of part two of the book.
94 Journal of Sir John Parnell, quoted in Anne Rowe and Tom Williamson, *Hertfordshire: A Landscape History* (Hatfield, 2013), p. 166.
95 Ellis, *Agriculture Improv'd*, vol. I, p. 51.

of his on 26 August 1746, when his 'silly maid-servant' gave her a pail full of 'yeasty wash' in the evening. The next day she was dead, swollen and frothing at the mouth. He has no doubt that sows will eat anything they can find and he provides pages of more anecdotes on pigs poisoned by various foods.[96]

Despite saying that raising calves 'comes under the care of farmer's wives, maid servants, and others', Ellis recognised that 'this oftentimes proves a profitable branch in the farming business' (because of the size of the London market for veal). For this reason, Ellis interested himself in calf-keeping and had hands-on experience of dairying and calf-rearing. He knew that what cows consumed affected the quality of their milk and butter: 'Turneps, cole or rape, green or dry thetches or vetches' gave milk a rank taste. In contrast, carefully selected meadow grass seeds (which he sold) made a sward from which the cows produced fine milk. Lady-finger grass was, he thought, particularly efficacious. It

> is a true hardy natural grass of English growth, exceeding in sweetness and goodness all other grasses whatsoever. When cows feed on it, they yield a milk that makes the finest of yellow-colour'd butter and cheese, and which is prefer'd for being drank from the cow, as conducing the more to the health of the drinker.

Rather than farmers 'lay down their plow'd ground with a promiscuous mixture of common grass seed' when they rest the ground by putting it under grass for some years, he exhorts them to buy his Lady-finger grass seed to produce a fine sward.[97]

He did not, as some did, wean calves in the winter, instead beginning in April or May, either with his own calves, or week-old ones purchased at Leighton Market. The latter he suckled on milk or milk and water for a month or six weeks, teaching the calf to drink from a bucket, then turned them out to grass. 'In this cheap manner I wean my calves without any cow near them.'[98]

Calves born to his own cows he managed thus:

> as soon as it falls from the cow, we strew a handful of salt all over its body, to be taken by the cow as she licks her calf, which we think tends to her health, and causes her to glean[99] the sooner. When the cow has calved, we generally let the calf suck what it will, and milk the cow besides, giving her the milk to drink, and for two days after water made lukewarm. As to the calf, we let it lie with the cow the

---

96  Ellis, *Country housewife*, pp. 187–8, 190.
97  Ellis, *Country Housewife*, pp. 394–6.
98  Ibid., pp. 428–9.
99  To 'glean' here means a cow consuming her afterbirth.

first night and day, and while the maid is milking one side, she lets the calf suck on the other: For by this the cow gives her milk the freer, and therefore the maid continues this practice all the first week, and throughout the next she allows the calf short of a bellyful, because their nature is too weak to be gorged with a full quantity of milk till they are about a fortnight old.[100]

Over-fed calves might die of scouring[101] and Ellis provides remedies to cure this. He also gives advice on bleeding calves (to make the flesh pale) and mixtures of feedstuffs to cram calves. The length of time calves should be suckled depended, thought Ellis, on the market they were to be sold at: Smithfield required 'the largest and whitest calves', suckled for nine to twelve weeks; those sold at a country market could be suckled for six or seven weeks.[102]

The demand for veal in London is reflected in the recipe books of the time. In John Farley's *London Art of Cookery*, first published in the 1780s, there are twenty-two recipes for beef 'made dishes' and thirty-eight for veal. Eliza Smith lists six for beef and five for veal in her cookery book of 1753. Other cookery books similarly rank veal alongside or of more importance than beef, whereas today many books have no veal recipes, reflecting unease about veal production methods or simple squeamishness about eating very young animals. Ellis provides recipes only for the garbage of the veal trade, the 'Chauldron or Guts' of calves slaughtered for London consumption. He explains that so many calves sold at Tring market were slaughtered there that the town had become notorious for pies made of these entrails, which the butchers were pleased to be rid of. Ellis's recipe for such a pie does not sound appetising. The guts were first thoroughly washed to remove 'slime and foulness', then soaked in brine for two days before being parboiled and cut into small pieces, spiced and seasoned, then baked. A sauce was poured into the pie made with nutmeg, vinegar, butter, sugar, egg yolks and sherry.[103]

Other 'minor' livestock covered by Ellis's pen are rabbits and pigeons. Rabbits were quite commonly kept in Ellis's time, both in London and its suburbs, and were often raised in hutches by poor people as a by-occupation to supplement a meagre income. Ellis comments that they are 'Creatures that not only supply the markets, but also serve a family for variety, and in time of necessity'. Rabbit keeping was for many a marginal occupation

---

100 Ellis, *Country Housewife*, p. 433.
101 Scouring is a rather vivid synonym for diarrhoea.
102 Ellis, *Country Housewife*, pp. 428–37.
103 John Farley, *The London Art of Cookery* (London, 1793), pp. 101–8, 109–19; E. Smith, *The Compleat Housewife* (London, 1753), ff. i–xii; Ellis, *Country Housewife*, pp. 372–3.

and most, he claimed, did not know how to do it: he thought not one in ten breeders knew how to feed them correctly. Pigeons are another minor part of Ellis's animal farming (he thinks they are more profitable than rabbits – and less trouble). Some breeders did not feed them, making them roam far for their food. This is a false economy, thinks Ellis, for they are more prone to attack by hawks or huntsmen with guns and their dung is dissipated. Ellis mentions a neighbouring woodturner who rents a cottage and orchard for five pounds a year. On his smallholding he keeps forty pairs of pigeons and twelve breeding doe-rabbits in hutches, plus a number of fowls. He goes to market almost every week to sell young animals or eggs and, Ellis implies, uses his skill in raising these animals to make a decent living.[104]

Sheep were an integral part of Ellis's farming and he gave this animal much prominence, devoting an entire book to the subject. The animal was unique in supplying dung to the arable farmer, wool to keep a major English industry going, skins for parchment and other leather goods, and meat for the table. We have noted Ellis's approval of folding. He devoted a chapter of his book on sheep to wool, discussing the weight and quality of the fleeces of various breeds. He notes that Gaddesden sheep, principally kept for folding, yielded fleeces of two or three pounds each, whereas those bred for their wool might yield six or seven pounds. Sheep meat was, according to Ellis, at best not inferior to venison, especially the succulent flesh of house lambs bred locally for the London market. He also describes the meat at its worst – tainted lamb and mutton disguised as good by unscrupulous butchers who also sold 'mutton dressed as lamb'.[105]

He employed a shepherd who supervised his flock; they grazed on the common daily and were folded at night on a small area of fallow or fodder-growing land. He provides little detail about his own flock, such as the numbers and breed of animals, but from his general remarks about sheep in his area we can get a good idea of its likely composition. The native Hertfordshire sheep

> is generally of a larger Size than the West Country Sheep, yet not so large as the Oxfordshire, Leicestershire, or Lincolnshire Breed. It is a horned Sheep that has black Spots on its Face and Legs, or what we call speckled; is a hardy profitable Sheep, but not quite so well qualify'd to get a Living on a very short Bite of Grass on Commons, as the smaller West-Country Sheep are; nor is their Wool so good; therefore they are mostly kept by those Farmers who have not the Conveniency of

---

104 Ellis, *Practical Farmer*, pp. 190–2; Malcolm Thick, 'Intensive Rabbit Production in London and Nearby Counties in the Sixteenth, Seventeenth, and Eighteenth Centuries', *Agricultural History Review*, 64/1 (2016), pp. 1–16.
105 Ellis, *Compleat system of experienced improvements*, pp. 159–62, 218–19, 358–9.

feeding Sheep on Commons, but are forced, for this Reason, to keep them always within Ground; and where they do this, their Profit lies in breeding and fatting Lambs on Clover or Ryegrass, or Trefoil, and on their fallow Grounds.[106]

Ellis also described the characteristics of Oxfordshire, Leicestershire, Lincolnshire, Welsh, Scotch and Romney Marsh sheep, but the West Country breed most impressed him:

> This Sort of Sheep, of all others in England, we in Hertfordshire, Buckinghamshire, Bedfordshire, and Middlesex, account the very best, for Soundness of Body, for living on our short Grass, for folding to dress our Land, for fatting on Turnips, for suckling House and Grass Lambs, for driving to and from our Fields and Commons, for not straying, and for yielding the very best Staple of Wool.[107]

A great many were bought up in the West Country by 'Sheep jobbers' and sold in the Spring at the market at Tring, three miles from Gaddesden, to local farmers. Ellis's detailed description of various sheep breeds is indicative of the fact that the overwhelming proportion of sheep in Hertfordshire in his time were not Hertfordshires. This was still true in 1804, when Arthur Young found many sheep farmers favoured the South Down or Wiltshire breeds, although there were many other breeds to be found on Hertfordshire farms (Young makes no mention of a Hertfordshire breed). He makes the general remark that livestock are not much regarded in the county: 'It is merely an arable country' and there is more profit, in 1804, to be made sending fodder crops to London than feeding animals at home.[108]

Ellis and his neighbours fed their sheep on turnips during winter and spring, hastening their fattening; in April, when the turnips were exhausted, rye, vetches or clover were ready to succeed as sheep fodder. Many farmers in Hertfordshire and other counties near London made, according to Ellis, a considerable profit by raising house lambs for the London meat markets. John Laurence in 1727 mentions that Middlesex graziers produce house lambs 'so as to become a dainty to great Men's Tables long before Christmas; and care is taken to have a Succession of them all the Winter'. Ellis claimed: 'In Hertfordshire and Middlesex [...] the Suckling of House-Lambs is perhaps more in Practice, than in all England beside.'[109]

---

106 Ibid., p. 43.
107 Ibid., p. 42.
108 Ibid., p. 42; Young, *Hertfordshire*, p. 182.
109 Ellis, *Compleat system of experienced improvements*, pp. 209, 251–2, 258; John Laurence, *A New System of Agriculture* (London, 1727), pp. 99–100.

He may have raised house lambs himself because he knows the husbandry of it in detail, giving full instructions on all aspects of this system. The 'Hertfordshire Method of suckling House-Lambs' involved a complicated system of moving lambs between pens:

> the Farmers employ four several Coops or Pens, and one large Suckling Room, for the Ewes to stand in, till they are sucked; the four Coops, or Pens join each other in a Row, with a Door to every one of them, to open and let out the Lambs, by Degrees, into the Suckling Room. Three of these Pens are each of them about ---- Feet square; the fourth as big as two of them, and the Suckling Room bigger than all of them; now the Use of all these four Pens, and Sheep-Room, is as follows, viz. One Pen is for the oldest Lambs, the second Pen, for the next eldest, and the third Pen is for the youngest Lambs; but the fourth Pen is for two Uses, one of which is, that as the Shepherd, and his assistant Boy, suckles four Lambs at a Time, when these of the oldest Sort are suckled from out of their little Pen, they are for the present put into the large fourth Pen; and when four more, of the oldest Lambs, are taken out and suckled, they are likewise put into this large Pen, and so on, till all the oldest Lambs, out of one Pen, are suckled, and then return'd into their own little Pen, from whence they were at first taken out. Then the Shepherd begins to take four Lambs out of the second Pen, and suckles them, and when suckled they are put into the large Pen, and so on, till all out of the second Pen are suckled, and returned into their own little Pen; and thus the Shepherd serves the Lambs of these two Pens, by which Mode of Suckling, every Lamb is kept to its own Pen.[110]

Ellis does not state why this complicated system was employed but the separate pens were presumably to keep lambs of the same age together so that they were sent to market when they were ready for the table: Richard Bradley advised that 'the House for lambs ought to be divided into stalls'. Bradley also advocated the use of 'Bastard Ewes', those who have lost their lambs or suckle lambs which are not their offspring, to help suckle the lambs.[111]

## Animal health

Ellis had an antipathy to calling in doctors for human aliments, and he was equally wary of seeking professional help with sick animals. He anticipated that farriers would be used in the last resort for horses but that he and his neighbours would mostly cure their own animals. The job of spotting disease in cattle 'belongs to the Country Housewife', because they milk morning

---

110 Ibid., p. 251.
111 Richard Bradley, *A General Treatise of Husbandry and Gardening* (London, 1727), November, pp. 95–7.

and evening and 'they have an opportunity to espy the cause and beginning of distempers [...] and in some cases administer medicines for the cure of the same'. They are usually at home (whereas their husbands are often not), ready to administer medicines or send for help.[112]

An almost universal remedy Ellis advocated for livestock was oil of turpentine. Anyone, 'whether he be Farmer, Grazier, Shepherd, or any other Person that is concern'd in keeping Sheep or other Beasts', should not be 'without some Oil of Turpentine by him'.[113] Sometimes this was administered as a drink, but it was most frequently advocated by Ellis as a rub or ointment for sores and bruises. The ointment was a mixture of turpentine and oil of vitriol.[114]

Ellis firmly believed that giving cows a 'tonic' prevented illness and 'those fatal distempers, the murrain, the garget, the blain, and the yellows, and many other foul maladies incident to these most serviceable creatures'.[115] He recommends drinks to give to cows: 'The 3rd day after carving I give 3 pints of piss out of a horn to a cow, and about a week after repeat the same; for this cleanses her body and blood, creates an appetite, and prevents the breed of diseases'.[116] As an alternative, 'sweep half a Pint of that Soot as lies over the Oven's Mouth, and boil this Quantity in three Points of strong Beer or Ale, about fifteen Minutes; then add and mix a Quartern of Butter with it, and, when almost cold, put in a Penny worth of Flour of Brimstone; then let one Man hold the Cow by one Horn, and her Nose, and the other give the whole Drink at several Times out of a Horn.'[117] He claims this disgusting mixture cures inflammation of cows' udders and prevents the Garget. This mixture was good for the most frequent problems associated with cows – disorders as a result of giving birth and common infections of the udder – but he is silent on cures for most of 'those fatal distempers' that he lists above.

In the preface to his book on farriery Ellis acknowledges that some farriers are competent but he nevertheless believed it was good for a farmer to have some competence in veterinary matters because a farrier might live at some distance away and animals might die before he attends, he might be away from

---

112 Ellis, *Country Housewife*, p. 439.

113 Ellis, *Compleat system of experienced improvements*, p. 102. Turpentine can still be used to alleviate the pain of strains or sprains, swollen udders and so on, and it also can be used internally as an antiseptic or treatment for bloat (gas in the stomach caused by an excess of rich green fodder).

114 William Ellis, *Every Farmer his own Farrier* (London, 1769), pp. 15, 28, 100, 106.

115 Garget is inflammation of the udder of a cow; blain is an inflammatory swelling or sore; the yellows is jaundice.

116 Ellis, *Country Housewife*, p. 440.

117 Ellis, *Modern Husbandman*, May, p. 106.

home, he might charge too much for his services or he might 'be ignorant and headstrong, administering Medicines to the Destruction of the Beast'.[118] Like his writings on human medicines, Ellis's recipes for horse cures are mostly homely, country medicines and most originate from non-specialists, although he did include cures taken from books, going as far back as Gervase Markham for some recipes. His many stays at inns in London and the home counties are reflected in the cures for sick horses he obtains from ostlers and innkeepers. Other men whose profession involved horses gave him recipes: waggoners, pack-horse men and several grooms, including one from the royal stables and the ex-groom to the king of Sardinia. This latter man was connected with horse racing, and some others similarly involved with racing gave him recipes.[119]

Farm horses needed to be carefully looked after – they provided the power on a farm and the means of transport to and from markets. Moreover, they were expensive pieces of farm equipment. In 1754 a neighbour's horses caught the 'yellows' and three farriers failed to cure them – the horses were worth £12 apiece. Ellis at one time had at least nine horses on his farm, over £100 worth of capital investment.[120] He cured his own horses of disease or injury – 'One of my cart-horses took up a nail in August, 1756 that ran into his hind foot an inch and an half deep, and stuck so fast in, that I was obliged to have it pulled out with a pair of pincers.' On another occasion 'my till-horse had his hind foot cut'.[121]

To maintain horses in the peak of fitness Ellis recommends Antimony, describing it as 'the best general Medicine for a Horse'. Repeated doses of 'Crocus Metallorum, or as it is called in common, Liver of Antimony', given in powder form at a rate of two ounces a day with feed will work wonders on a horse:

> it will relieve his Appetite, destroy Worms, help the Cure of Wounds, or Farcin, or Mange, sweeten the Blood against all Obstructions, open the Passages, improve tired and lean Horses to a great Degree, and is a Sovereign Medicine in Coughs, and Shortness of Breath [...] it prevents the Staggers, Yellows, Pole-Evil, Cankers, and all other Distempers proceeding from the Blood; for this neither Purges nor makes a Horse Sick, but the more you work him the better it is. To prove which, let the Horse you give it to be curried with one particular Comb, and you'll find it stink, when another shall not, by Reason it throws out all the foul Humours of the Body through the Pores of the Skin, by Perspiration, in a Scurf. And how valuable

---

118 Ellis, *Every Farmer*, Preface.
119 Ibid., p. 86.
120 Ellis, *Practical Farmer*, p. 17.
121 Ellis, *Every Farmer*, p. 12.

such a Catholicon will be to Farmers and others, I will leave them to judge on Tryal. In my humble Opinion, some had better give ten Pounds than be without the Knowledge of this Medicine.[122]

Nowadays it is regarded as a very old-fashioned and dangerous equine medicine, but it was still much used in the mid-nineteenth century.[123]

Another medicine Ellis thought beneficial for horses was fenugreek seed. Modern veterinary practice concurs with his view. In 2015 an article in the *Farmers Weekly* explained:

> Fenugreek seeds contain protein, Vitamin C, niacin, potassium and diosgenin (which has similar properties to oestrogen). It is high in L-tryptophan and makes a wonderful tonic to elevate depressed horses (and owners). It also contains steroidal saponins. If you have a horse that is recovering from an illness or has just come down with an illness, fenugreek can speed up the recovery of the animal.[124]

Ellis devoted the largest number of written words on veterinary matters to the care and management of sheep. These creatures, which Ellis thought vital to the fertility of his and his neighbour's farms, were highly efficient converters of fodder into dung, but they were also prone to many diseases. Ellis claimed his book on sheep contained remedies against the most common (and fatal) diseases of sheep, foremost of which was the rot – a liver infection picked up by grazing in wet ground. 'No author whatsoever, has hitherto published one, or more Remedies, that will infallibly prevent it, in so cheap, and in so ready a Manner, as to encourage Farmers, and others, to attempt the Prevention of the Rot.' He claimed also to have cures for 'those common, fatal Maladies, the White, or Red Water … if they are given to the Beast in due Time'; and, 'as the Ingredients are very cheap, the poorest Farmer must be induced to make use of them'.

An example of his cheap remedies is that given

> *To recover a sucking Lamb that is sick*; By this Author. – Boil some Southernwood and Rue, chopt small together, in Half a Pint, or more, of Ale, and with the Liquor mix a little Syrup of Marygold, which give the Lamb by a Spoon, a little Quantity at a Time, and repeat it as you see Occasion. Southernwood and Rue are two Plants, that grow about two Feet high, which every Farmer ought to keep always by him, either green or dried, for their excellent Virtues, as they relate to Sheep and

---

122 Ellis, *Modern Husbandman*, April, p. 105.
123 <https://www.scientificamerican.com/article/antimony-1869-06-12/>, accessed 4 May 2021.
124 Kim Dyson, 'All about Fenugreek', *Farmers Weekly* (5 June 2015).

Lambs Health. Marygolds, also, I keep ready in my Garden for these and other salubrious Occasions.[125]

An even cheaper remedy was his own

> Receipt to cure an aged sick Lamb.
> If a Lamb is taken sick, when it has got into an Age of Strength, it is practised by several Shepherds in Hertfordshire, to set the Lamb upon its Arse between their Legs, and rub its Mouth with a little Virgin Mold, which is the next Earth under a thin Grass Turf; and when he has so done, he pisses into the Mouth of the Lamb, or puts a little Piss out of a Pot, or Vial, into its Mouth.[126]

This remedy was used in Roman times; both Columella and Palladio recommend it for lambs with excess bile and, in the seventeenth century, Gervase Markham also used this medicine on horses. Whether it did any good or not is another matter; there are many minerals and trace elements in human urine and it is possible that some, such as potassium and sodium, may have benefited sheep.[127]

A gentler way of avoiding the death of a lamb, which Ellis used

> to recover a new-wean'd Lamb, almost dead with Cold, is, to put a little Straw into an Oven, to light it, and give the Oven such a moderate Heat, as will only just serve to revive the Lamb; and when it is come to itself, by such Heat, we then take it out, and feed it with a Tea-Spoonful, or more, of warm Milk from the Ewe, or from a Cow; and this we do for a Day or two, or more, afterwards, while we keep the Lamb in the Chimney Corner, till it gets strong and able enough to be put to the Ewe, in an Outhouse, or Barn, where, if we cannot make the Lamb suck the Ewe, we feed it with a Spoon, or out of a Sucking-Bottle, till it will.[128]

### *Farming beyond Little Gaddesden*

So far we have largely concentrated on what Ellis tells us of his own farming, that of his neighbours in Little Gaddesden and that observed in Hertfordshire in general. He wrote a great deal about his own county – two of his early

---

125 Ellis, *Compleat system of experienced improvements*, p. 85.
126 Ibid., p. 60.
127 *Columella of Husbandry* (London, 1745), p. 319; John G. Fitch (trans.), *Palladius, The Work of Farming* (Totnes, 2013), p. 248; Gervase Markham, *Cheap and Good Husbandry* (London, 1664), p. 62; <http://www.fao.org/ag/aga/agap/frg/tap31/3_1_13.pdf>, accessed 6 February 2021.
128 Ellis, *Compleat system of experienced improvements*, p. 85.

books on agriculture were specifically on the husbandry of Hertfordshire and the Chilterns and clay vales that he and his neighbours worked. Time and time again he refers to the 'Hertfordshire way' or the 'Gaddesden way' of doing things agricultural and he is forever contrasting the best method of cultivating the light soils of the Chilterns with the heavier ones of the Vales, but he often went further afield – frequently citing farming methods in neighbouring counties, Bedfordshire and Buckinghamshire in particular but also Middlesex, a county he must have often travelled through on his way to and from London. This county gets close attention – Ellis is fascinated by the intensive agriculture he witnesses there.

In Ellis's role as agricultural advisor, seller of agricultural machinery, seed seller and book seller he went on many expeditions to counties further afield in southern England, as far as Cornwall and south Wales to the west and East Anglia and Kent to the east, and he draws on these journeys to provide examples of good and new methods of agriculture. In the *Modern Husbandman* in particular this material is woven into dense chapters on individual topics. Take, for instance, the discussion of sowing beans in the *Modern Husbandman* for February. He begins with a general description of the best soil for beans – a rich soil. Linking this with his own area, he tells his readers that all Chiltern and Vale stiff clays are suitable for bean cultivation. In the Vale beans generally came after a wheat or barley crop and were sown in February, broadcast after one ploughing and harrowed in. It was becoming increasingly common for peas and beans to be sown together in the Chiltern country. The peas defended the beans from the dolphin fly and provided the bean shoots with shade. If one crop failed, the other usually succeeded. In Little Gaddesden's open fields beans were also sown broadcast, harrowed in to kill weeds, and later rolled to earth up the seed beans and leave the ground smooth for the scythe. Elsewhere in Hertfordshire and in nearby Bedfordshire, black sands found about Leighton, Brickhill, Woburn and Hockley produced good bean crops, as did some Chiltern loams. Between Watford and Hempstead Ellis had seen beans sown in loamy soil in individual holes made by men with dibbers. Going into Middlesex he finds dibbers employed also at Harrow and Ruislip – although here the beans are set by women who use a garden line to keep the holes for the seeds in straight rows. Beans are dibbered in rows also in Kensington, Fulham and Chelsea, where the strong pull of the London market results in the production of crops of beans earlier than anywhere else in England. Vast amounts of dung and other refuse are dug into the soils here and the beans are picked green for human consumption in London. The amount of information Ellis includes in his books on Middlesex agriculture reflects the frequency of his visits to London on business. Plotting on a map the many places in Middlesex he mentioned in a chapter on beans in the *Modern Husbandman* produces a probable itinerary for a journey to the capital.[129]

In his extensive travels on horseback he was accompanied by a servant who also rode. In this way he visited prospective and existing customers, soliciting new orders for the variety of goods and services he offered,[130] delivering small items – seeds and probably books – and no doubt reminding slow payers that debts were outstanding. He could also 'wait on any Gentleman in any Part *of England* or *Wales*, that thinks fit to consult his Advice in the Improvement of his Estate, according to the ancient, or the newest Methods of Husbandry'.[131] Collecting information was also a major reason for these trips: 'I yearly travel hundreds of Miles, on Account of several Sorts of Books, I have, and intend to publish, whereby I have an Opportunity of acquainting myself with the Methods used in several different Counties.'[132] In 1748 Kalm reported

> He has travelled around most places in England to see and write up their husbandry. Often, when he heard that someone well-versed in rural economy lived at a particular place and was renowned for a special insight in some special branch of husbandry, he would journey there even if it lay 20, 30 or more English miles out of his way.[133]

He could not have pursued his occupation of agricultural journalist without these journeys; nor could he have written his book on brewing, which is full of references to beer and ale he has consumed and discussed with brewers in inns, breweries and private houses up and down the country.

In undertaking these journeys he was imitating London seedsmen and nurserymen who commonly took to the road in the summer months – men like George London, partner in the vast nursery at Brompton Park, who, a few years before Ellis's time, was an indefatigable traveller who journeyed up to sixty miles a day:

> he made his Northern Circuit in five or six Weeks, and sometimes less, and his Western in as little Time: As for the South and East, they were but three or four

---

129 Ellis, *Modern Husbandman*, February, pp. 7–22. For market gardening generally around London at this time see Malcolm Thick, *The Neat House Gardens: Early Market Gardening around London* (Totnes, 1998). Ellis's route to London was: Little Gaddesden, Hemel Hempstead, Watford, Harrow, Ruislip, Fulham, Kensington, Chelsea, London.

130 See below p. 62 et seq.

131 Ellis, *Practice of Farming*, p. 5; Ellis, *Compleat system of experienced improvements*, p. 8.

132 Ellis, *The Timber Tree Improved*, f. a2.

133 Mead, *Pehr Kalm*, p. 42.

Days Work for him; most Times Twice a Year visiting all the Country Seats, conversing with gentlemen and forwarding the Business of *Gard'ning*.[134]

It is doubtful whether Ellis was as swift in his travels as George London: on one of the few occasions when he mentions dates he was returning home through Surrey on 13 June 1749 and two days later he was still in Surrey, putting up for the night at an inn in East Grinstead.[135] The sparsity of travel dates or details of itineraries make it difficult to reconstruct in detail his 'circuits'. He does make reference to observations made 'in my travels' in 1732 and I have extracted from his books references to travels in at least the years 1736, 1737, 1738 and 1749. In 1736 he went to East Anglia, Kent and the West Country. The following year he visited the same areas with the exception of Kent, and in 1738 he went to the South of England and Kent. In 1749 he visited Surrey. Many references in his books to people and places visited in Hertfordshire, Bedfordshire and Buckinghamshire show that he often went on short excursions. On one long-distance jaunt he ventured as far as Cornwall, visiting a gentleman with a 'great Estate in Cornwall, near Callington', and he tells us: 'in my journey along the Sea-Coast of South Wales, I observed the great Maple at Morgam a Seat of Lord Mansels, near the sea.' He went as far north as Nottinghamshire, and he intended to go further, replying to a correspondent in 1742 that he hoped to travel to Yorkshire in the summer. In all, Ellis mentions travelling through Berkshire, Buckinghamshire, Carmarthenshire, Cornwall, Devon, Dorset, Essex, Hampshire, Hertfordshire, Kent, Middlesex, Norfolk, Northamptonshire, Nottinghamshire, Rutland, Somerset, Staffordshire, Suffolk, Surrey, Sussex and Wiltshire.[136]

In his travels Ellis notes the normal agriculture of different regions, as well as peculiarities in local husbandry and experiments done by gentlemen and farmers. Indeed, without this extensive travelling his books would be a lot thinner. He praises Kentish husbandmen for their perfection of the use of the scythe for grain harvesting. He is dismayed at seeing fields of oats infested with weeds between Godalming and Haslemere in Surrey, and in Wiltshire he visits a farm taken in hand because the young former tenant neglected to manure it properly.[137] He notes the use of old sailcloth to cover haystacks

---

134 Stephen Switzer, *The Nobleman, Gentleman and Gardener's Recreation* (London, 1715), pp. 60–1.
135 Ellis, *Country Housewife*, p. 205.
136 Ellis, *Practical Farmer*, p. 131; Ellis, *Complete Cyderman*, p. 9; Ellis, *The Timber Tree Improved*, p. 81; Ellis, *Modern Husbandman*, December, p. 495.
137 [Ellis], *Ellis's Husbandry*, vol. II, pp. 125–6.

near Rotherhithe. He spends some time on the good qualities of Romney Marsh sheep and he is convinced, from his travels, of the great benefit of fodder crops to feed sheep: 'The prodigious number of sheep, fatted every year on turnips and rapes, shews the great improvements that are made by sowing fields with their seeds, but more especially with those of turnips, as the counties of Cambridge, Suffolk, Norfolk, Essex, and Hertfordshire etc. will attest.'[138] On the sandy lands of Suffolk and Norfolk he finds farmers who buy in Welsh and Scots cattle from drovers and fatten them on turnips for the London market. He is full of praise for what these farmers have done with their sandy soils:

> it is in these two counties, beyond all others in England, that some fine improvements in husbandry may be seen, to the infinite profit of both landlords and tenants, which have been brought to pass within these fifty years, ever since they learned the way of sowing and hoeing turnips in their open, common, sandy fields, which has not only proved a preparative to their succeeding crops of barley, but such turnip crops give them a vast first profit besides, by feeding their horned beasts with them to a degree of fatting, so as to fit them in a compleat manner for a Smithfield market, where thousands of them are sold in a year and by the cooling fat dung, and fertile urine that their runts, oxen, and cows leave behind them in the land, they so dress and prepare their dry, husky, hungry, warm, sandy grounds, as to cause them to return more plentiful crops of barley, of late years, than they had formerly.[139]

He finds a gentleman feeding carrots to fatten an ox in Gloucestershire. In Kent he notes the long-established growing of canary seed to feed caged birds. Many pages in his books are taken up with wheat and, although most of his examples are sourced from his own locality, he does note that in Somerset more grey- and blue-poll wheat is sown than elsewhere in England. The use of oil-cake as fertiliser is discussed: he has seen it being made at Hauxton, near Cambridge. He has also seen French Wheat grown as green manure in Norfolk, Suffolk, Surrey, Kent and Berkshire. Peat ashes are, he believes, a good fertiliser and he visits the 'greatest peat ground in England', near Newbury.[140] While probably not the largest area of peat in England at this time, there was then a substantial amount of peat in the Kennet valley near Newbury. Pits were dug to exploit the peat, some of which was burnt and the ashes used as fertiliser. The extent of the peat deposits were described in 1767:

---

138 Ellis, *Compleat system of experienced improvements*, p. 212.
139 Ellis, *Modern Husbandry*, March, p. 16.
140 [Ellis], *Ellis's Husbandry*, vol. I, pp. 184, 482; Ellis, *New Experiments in Husbandry*, p. 28; Ellis, *Modern Husbandman*, September, pp. 64–70, 82–91.

The town of Newbury lies north and south, in the shape of a Y, across a valley; which valley runs east and west, and is here about a mile broad, the river Kennet running along the middle of it. The peat is found in the middle of this valley, on each side of the river, extending in all from between a quarter of a mile to about half a mile in breadth; and in length, along the valley, about nine miles westward, and about seven eastward; and I believe much further, tho' not yet discovered, and perhaps with some intermissions.[141]

On his travels he came across local specialities. At Saffron Walden his visit coincided with the harvesting of saffron, mostly by women and girls, who undertook the painstaking work of extracting the filaments of saffron from each flower. At Kesteven, two miles from Walden, he saw the clay ovens, powered by charcoal, in which the saffron was dried.[142] In fields just west of Dover Ellis discovered hemp growing. In August 1736, when he visited, hemp that had been pulled up at the beginning of the month was set up in bundles to dry. He saw female hemp, which had seeds attached – often, he was told, the seed (from which oil was extracted) would be as valuable as the rest of the plant. In September Ellis observed the hop-picking season in Kent. A successful crop returned a handsome profit, but hops were a chancy crop:

> Happy are they, whose large plantations have escaped the damage of flies, lice, bugs, blights, fen or mould, storms, and other pernicious incidents, and who at last enjoy a dry mild time for gathering or picking them in this month: for it is the notion of some concerned in hop plantations that they are liable to fifty accidents in a year, and to the charge of twenty pounds an acre.

He describes in minute detail how hops are gathered, dried, bagged and used in brewing.[143]

Another specialised crop Ellis described was liquorice, then grown principally at Pontefract in Yorkshire and, where he observed it, at Godalming in Kent, both areas with deep sandy loams suitable for the crop. He passed through Godalming in June 1738, when he saw 'a fine liquorice plantation' behind the Kings Head inn, where no doubt he stayed. He describes in great detail the preparation of liquorice beds, the planting of the runners from which the plant grows and, after three years, the digging up of the mature roots from which edible liquorice is extracted. During the three years when

---

141 John Collet, 'An Account of the Peat-pit near Newbury', *Philosophical Transactions*, 50 (1767–8), pp. 109–15.
142 Ellis, *Modern Husbandman*, September, pp. 58–9.
143 Ibid., pp. 94–104.

the liquorice was maturing, salad crops and garden vegetables were grown in the intervals between the beds. Ellis claimed one acre at Godalming had produced 400 stone of roots.[144]

These locally important crops shared common characteristics. They were high-cost crops, somewhat risky and, in the case of hops and saffron, best undertaken by substantial farmers, but they also yielded high returns if the harvest was good. Ellis claimed that many Kentish gentry families had 'got estates by hop plantations'. Growing hemp commonly made ten pounds per acre. Saffron was potentially a most valuable crop; in 1735 the price of dried saffron was thirty-five shillings a pound but in the subsequent year a better harvest was expected to make a guinea a pound. Ellis calculated the total cost of producing an acre of saffron to be £14, and the profit on average was £20. As to liquorice, Ellis conceded that the market price was variable, but said it was possible to sell the product of one acre for £60.[145]

Another common thread running through the description of these four crops was that they were labour intensive, employing many poor people. In the case of saffron, liquorice and hops the employment was mostly in growing them but hemp was used to create a material that could be worked by many with no other means of support. Hemp was made into a wide variety of cloths, including sailcloth, and it was also used for many types of rope. Many things today made of plastic or wood would, in Ellis's time, have been made of hemp. Drawing on the writings of John Houghton fifty years before, and Sir Richard Weston a century ago, Ellis supports measures to make growing of hemp compulsory for large farmers in order to produce a stock of raw materials in each parish to set the unemployed poor to work on. 'By this means ... the poor would not be so numerous, nor chargeable, but, instead thereof, made to become a very great benefit to the Nation.'[146]

All these products were, to some extent, imported from abroad and so more widespread growing of them would lessen imports. Ellis emphasises this 'mercantilist' view of foreign trade in particular with reference to hemp. He quotes Houghton: 'many thousand pounds, nay hundreds of thousands, which are exported in cash, or good commodities' could be saved by growing hemp (and flax) in England, 'nor should we be beholden to Holland for their fine linen and cordage, nor to Flanders for thread; because at our own doors, we may supply our-selves with these commodities in an abundant manner.'[147]

---

144 Ibid., pp. 172–6.
145 Ibid., pp. 62, 65, 75, 99.
146 Ibid., *Modern Husbandman*, September, pp. 64–70.
147 Ibid., pp. 69–70. The Mercantilist theory of trade, put simply, was that countries that exported less than they imported were drained of gold and became impoverished. Anything

On the whole, Ellis seems to have enjoyed his journeys. He liked meeting and talking to people of all classes; during the day he could talk to gentlemen and in the evening gather information from ordinary folk who frequented the tap rooms of the inns at which he put up. His offer to Kalm of an escorted fourteen-day tour of the counties of England to observe the agriculture in return for the keep of himself, his horse, all expenses and twelve or fourteen guineas shows that his appetite for touring was undiminished in 1748, when he was in his sixties. Kalm coldly rejected the offer, which was not cheap – Ellis would have made a profit of around £1,575 at today's prices.

As well as recording the usual mode of agriculture in his own county and in many parts of southern England, Ellis reports specific experiments made by gentlemen, farmers and himself, such as the cultivation of beans, which we have touched on already. A dog breeder at Dagnall manures a one-acre field of beans with dog dung and has a fine crop. A gentleman farming in the Chilterns tried to drill beans on fallow ground in rows wide apart, so that he could plough between the rows and keep down weeds. He was not successful in controlling weeds but Ellis praises his effort, commenting that

> the country is much obliged to [him] for trying new projects in husbandry: I say, obliged, because, if one new improvement hits or is found out, after several such attempts, it, very likely, may compensate his time and charges; for as the farmer is the farthest of men from, and most averse to, the tryals of new inventions, I know not how any good ones should be brought to perfection, unless gentlemen attempt them first with their more rational conceptions and endeavours, and their larger purses.[148]

Smut was a major problem that disfigured and devalued many wheat crops in Ellis's time. In a chapter devoted to this disease he described nineteen instances where farmers and gentlemen tackled the problem by various means, indicating that many were prepared to experiment.[149] Ellis carried out experiments himself, contrary to his neighbours' assertions that he did little on his farm that was unusual:

> I have also a new Sort of foreign Grass sowed this Summer for a Trial, which, if it answers my Expectation, I shall venture to sow it in common, and publish its Effects: And indeed, it is a great Pity, that Trials are not more made to naturalize

---

that lessened dependence on imports was therefore to be encouraged.
148 Ellis, *Modern Husbandman*, February, p. 16.
149 [Ellis], *Ellis's Husbandry*, vol. I, pp. 216–25.

Exoticks in our Fields by those whose Abilities are capable of doing it, that our Ground may be more employed in Variety of Corn, Grasses, Fruits, Trees, &c.[150]

He experimented with novel strains of wheat that came his way, such as the 'Sicilian Wheat, that one of the Royal Society was so good to make me a present of a peck, that I have now growing' and Smyrna Wheat.[151] In 1733 he sowed another parcel of 'foreign wheat, that was given me by a member of the Royal Society, on a hungry gravelly soil', another part of the field being sown with English wheat. His foreign wheat came up a different colour from the native sort and had strong stalks and bearded ears, like Dugdale wheat, a variety quite widely grown in Ellis's time but now obsolete. This foreign variety grew much faster than English wheat, being ready to harvest a month before the English variety. Ellis hopes this new wheat might be suitable for northern England, where the growing season is short, and will make it possible for him to sow wheat after a turnip crop. In May 1734 the same FRS gave him more foreign wheat to experiment with.[152] Another experiment growing an exotic crop involved a small amount of 'Indian wheat' – presumably maize. In 1736 he describes experiments with a new type of roller he has apparently invented.[153]

Ellis welcomed visitors to view the results of all his experiments:

> Any Person that pleases shall be welcome to view my Proceedings in Farming, after the several Methods that are publish'd in my Books, and be satisfy'd of the same by ocular Demonstration, and the Declaration of the Neighbourhood, particularly of the great Efficacy of the *French* Wheat that this Summer I ploughed in, in three several Fields, and other Ways of cheap Manuring; for where these and other Dressings may be had cheap, it would be very absurd Management of any to let the Ground want Assistance, according to those plain Directions that I have published, which, if duly regarded, by the Blessing of God, no Person need fear a good Crop on the Ground.[154]

Did Ellis have any scientific methodology behind his experiments? He was, we have abundantly observed, a 'hands on' writer on agriculture; he condemned 'writing on Agriculture in a London Chamber; because all the

---

150 Ellis, *Practical Farmer*, p. 209.
151 Ellis, *Modern Husbandman*, June, p. 36.
152 Ellis, *Practical Farmer*, p. 212. The Royal Society in Ellis's time was the foremost scientific society in England.
153 Ellis, *Practical Farmer*, pp. 214–15; Ellis, *New Experiments in Husbandry*, p. 17.
154 Ellis, *Practical Farmer*, p. 212.

Philosophy that it can furnish, will never come up to the Information of Field Experiment'.[155] But did his experiments have any scientific rigour? He was fortunate, firstly, in occupying a farm composed of many types of soil:

> as I occupy my own Farm and the Glebe-land of our Parish, containing in all twenty four inclosed Fields of several Sorts of Soils; I have had a very favourable Opportunity, almost twenty years together, in a Country where Farmers are allowed in the general to excel all others in this Kingdom, to make my Observations, Collections and Experiments.[156]

Whereas 'Observations' and 'Collections' are essentially passive actions – he is just recording what he sees and hears, even if he often collects several different ways of carrying out an activity – we have seen above instances when he does something new on his own farm, sowing exotic seeds or using newly invented equipment. Was he just acting on a whim or had he a scientific method? There *is* some evidence that he was approaching new ways of farming in a scientific manner. Take, for instance, an experiment with wheat in 1722. He gives no details of this, wanting someone to sponsor him before revealing the secret of his method, but he does explain, by way of preface, that he was inspired by the success of gardeners in forwarding crops:

> this Consideration brought me under a Propensity of finding out an Improvement in the Field, that might in some measure answer in the forwarding of Grain [...] and therefore this Winter, 1722, I ploughed up an Acre of Clover Lay into broad Lands, and harroughed in three Bushels of Wheat Seed, half of which I prepared after a Method, I hope will answer my Expectation; the other half I sowed in the common Way; I also managed one half of the Ground accordingly, and the other I did nothing to: This Experiment I have now under Trial, and was invented by me, in order to find out a way to prevent Wheat, Barley, and Rye suffering by Wets and Frosts, causing them to overtake and be as forward at Harvest, as that sowed at the usual times; and if I can bring this to bear, then may a Crop of Turneps be got, besides a Crop of Wheat, the same Year, to the great enriching of the Ground, lessening the Charge of Dressings, and to the Benefit of the Kingdom in general.[157]

Ellis also carried out controlled experiments in small plots in his garden, on a loamy soil: 'I have by several Trials on Loams, this Summer, found out what will improve an Acre of Ground to a high degree for the Charge

---

155 Ellis, *Modern Husbandman*, May, p. 83.
156 Ellis, *Chiltern and Vale Farming*, Preface.
157 Ibid., pp. 370–7.

of the Acre which I would gladly publish for the Benefit of the World, if I could meet with reasonable Encouragements.'[158] We have noticed above an instance where his neighbours introduced a 'control' to an experiment, asking for several rows of beans to be sown without manure to judge the effectiveness of Ellis's drill. This intervention by neighbours is interesting – it shows they too were not unversed in scientific methods.

Even when Ellis is just collecting information there is, on occasion, evidence of a methodical approach. The most notable example is his assembly of nineteen experiences of smut in wheat by various farmers. He does not discover the cause of smut but he does pull together these experiences and draws eleven conclusions from them:

> First. It may be occasioned by the Weakness of Brine, that ought to be strong enough to bear an Egg.[159] Secondly. By the Weakness of the Lime, which is beyond the Brine, for securing a Wheat-crop from Smut. Thirdly. By sowing one Sort of Seed in the same Soil too often. Fourthly. By a very frosty Winter, a very cold Spring, a very wet or a very dry Summer, or by infectious Winds. Fifthly. By Wheat growing very thin among many Weeds. Sixthly. By a rough, sour, bad Tilth. Seventhly. By infected Seed, that grows in the smutty Ear, and yet appears to the Eye sound and clear, or by sowing Pepper-wheat, or that damaged by Insects, or burnt in the Mow, or of too great an Age, or too small Wheat-seed. Eighthly. By the Heat of Dung that lies along with the Seed in the Ground. Ninthly. By the Use of Stale or Urine in the Preparation of the Wheat-seed. Tenthly. By a small red Worm that is very apt to gnaw the Kernel or Blade of young Wheat, and thereby causes the Ear to be smutty, or kills it entirely, as I have known it do in a chalky gravelly Soil in the Years 1740 and 1741, about the Month of November before the Frosts came on. Lastly. In very low Vallies great Floods and their Continuance often corrupt the Roots of Wheat, and cause Smuttiness, as well as great Rains do that fall about the Blooming and Kerning-seasons, so that the Ears as well as the Roots of this Golden Grain may be damaged by too much wet Weather, and brought into a smutty Condition; for undoubtedly all those Causes, that hurt either Root, Stalks, or Ears in their green Growth, tend towards infecting this Corn with that stinking black Sickness called Smuttiness.[160]

How do we sum up Ellis's writings on agriculture, which are at the heart of his books? Did these writings add up to a good survey of the agriculture of his time and a sensible programme for improvement? The editor of

---

158 Ibid., p. 35.
159 Ellis is talking of the brine used to steep grain before sowing. By bearing an egg he means that the brine should be strong enough to allow an egg to float at the top of the brine.
160 Ellis, *Modern Husbandman*, September, pp. 63–9.

*Ellis's Husbandry, Abridged and Methodized*, having explained that he has excluded Ellis's advertising 'puffs', his asides about rural life, his writings on medicine and food and what he considers to be 'rubbish' to fill out his monthly requirement of copy is impressed by the agricultural material that remained and was included in the abridgement:

> we then plainly perceive that he knew what he wrote of; he speaks clear, sound, good sense, and so much to the purpose that I will venture to assert no writer has in this path exceeded him: but the public have paid so little attention to his works from the quantity of rubbish they contain, that Ellis's real merit is little known. It is not at present recollected, that all the spirited practices of excellent common husbandry, which have of late years made so much noise, are clearly ascertained by him, their merit stated, and their conduct explained. The best turnip and clover husbandry are in particular set forth, as practically as they can be at this day: the whole conduct of manures, though not philosophically handled, yet are stated with practical precision; and the common management in them fully explained. A full knowledge of the use of soiling cattle with tares, clover, &c.—saving the drainings of the farm yard—forming composts—the variations of soils which require corresponding variations of manure and tillage (an article of great importance, and fully treated by no other writer), and the whole management of sheep—are among many other instances of Ellis's thorough knowledge in common husbandry.[161]

Reading the abridgement, today's readers would probably come to the same conclusion as Ellis's anonymous editor. Gathered together in thematic chapters, Ellis's agricultural works cover the major operations of farming – soil amelioration, including mixing soils and fertilisation; the use of new fodder crops and nitrogen-fixing plants; observations on the best ways to grow the major food crops; the care and exploitation of farm animals, timber and woods; and particular local crops which Ellis thought could be grown more widely.

What effect did Ellis's experiments, trials of machinery, writing and particularly his travels have on his farm? The answer seems to be a disastrous one. We have seen how Kalm, on his way to meet Ellis for the first time, was shocked at the condition of some of his fields. The farmer who told him Ellis owned the fields was of the opinion that, if Ellis did not make a reasonable living from his books, he would be in financial difficulties, for he would not make much from farming. 'Mr Ellis mostly sits at home in his room and writes books, and sometimes goes a whole week without going out into his ploughed fields and meadows to look after the work, but trusts mostly to

---

161 [Ellis], *Ellis's Husbandry*, Preface, f. xi–xii.

his servant, and young son, who is still a boy.'[162] If we consider his time writing, his slow circuits around England in the summer months for many years, the time taken to meet visitors and demonstrate his machines, and the frequent trips he made to London to deliver copy, meet his publisher and visit seed-shops and nurseries, we see the scale of the problem – Ellis did not have the time to farm properly. The burden of running the farm fell on his ploughman and his sons. The tradition of hiring labourers by the day in Gaddesden compounded the problem – there may have been no live-in agricultural labourers to help with the farm on a day-to-day basis. Moreover, Ellis told Kalm that he always travelled with a servant, leaving for some time only a boy and a maid at the farm during his absences. Add to this the possibility that some of the land he bought may have been already neglected and waterlogged (he describes how he drained one field with a stone-filled gutter in 1735), and it is no wonder that Kalm found some of his fields in bad condition. This inconsistency between his writings and his farming has bedevilled Ellis's reputation over the years since his death.[163]

---

162 Bell, *Mr. Ellis*, pp. 148–9.
163 Ellis, *The Practice of Farming*, p. 167; Bell, *Mr. Ellis*, p. 153.

## Chapter 4
## Advertising and trading

In his book *More Old English Farming Books, 1731 to 1793*, George Fussell heads his chapter on the period 1731–50 'The Age of Jethro Tull and William Ellis'. It was Tull's age because of the controversy his system of row cultivation and horse-hoeing, and his theories of soil science, stirred up. It was Ellis's because he was the most prolific writer on agriculture in this period. His books were an attempt to make money by writing, mainly about agriculture, but they were also vehicles for his attempts to sell a wide variety of agricultural goods and services, many by mail order. As he got into his stride, his books were more and more filled out with advertisements, often, as we shall see, subtle ones, for the various agricultural goods he sold. Pehr Kalm reports that when he asked local farmers about Ellis's writing, 'They said that Mr Ellis's principal object in writing books was to sell to gentlemen the ploughs and implements, that he praised therein; though he seldom used them himself.' This may have been an over-cynical view of Ellis's motives, but there is no doubt that he was a skilled and pioneering advertiser. This chapter will examine Ellis's advertising techniques, discuss the various things he sold and review the time and effort he devoted to trading activities.[1]

In a fascinating article Sandra Sherman has analysed Ellis's advertising in *The Modern Husbandman* and *The Country Housewife* and is impressed by the novelty of his approach. She finds that his presentation of information regarding both new methods he used and his own status as an innovative farmer using new techniques, implements and materials was so closely linked to an invitation to buy the products he advertises that it would seem that a reader was being informed rather than induced to buy, what Sherman calls 'cognitive muddling'.[2] He frequently uses novelty as a justification for his

---

1  Mead, *Pehr Kalm*, p. 100.
2  Sandra Sherman, 'Advertisements for Myself: William Ellis and the Reinvention of the Puff', *Prose Studies*, 24/2 (2001), p. 66.

writings, whether it be about new meadow seeds, new types of implement or something seemingly as mundane as sausage making: 'many authors', he writes, have written about sausage-making, 'but not one of them has told his readers how to prepare the skins for them; which deficiency I here undertake to supply'. That he has tackled topics others have neglected is a frequent justification for his books – in the *Country Housewife* some aspects of cow keeping he describes 'have slipt the notice of many authors'; pigs were similarly neglected by earlier authors and the problem of mites 'has escaped the pen of most or all authors'.[3] He cunningly embedded his advertisements in his text, making them extensions of the (new) facts he was imparting, rather than pure advertisements. By Ellis's time, London newspapers were full of advertisements and their readers were increasingly cynical about the claims they made. In Sherman's words:

> By 1750, papers were so crammed with adverts that the jostle of claims for books, medicines, real estate, employment opportunities, razor strops and hats was a bricolage of adverts traducing other adverts, the whole making one's head swim. In *The Idler*, Johnson commented on 'filling the Newspapers with Advertisements [...] now so numerous that they are very negligently perused' and have to 'gain attention by magnificence of promises'.[4]

One way to circumvent this growing cynicism about advertisements was to dress them up as an article on the item advertised – say, a comment on a particular disease that concluded that a certain potion was bound to cure it. It was such 'puff' that Ellis took and refined as his advertising medium in a manner described by Sherman as 'renovated puffing'.[5] She sums up her conclusions about Ellis's advertising thus:

> Both *The Modern Husbandman* and *The Country Housewife's Family Companion* are finally puffs: commercial vehicles 'passing for something else,' but they are not puffs in the conventional sense. They harness the didactic mode, hugely popular in the eighteenth century, to a commercial enterprise that engages readers in complex relations with a self-declared author/seller.[6]

---

3   Cited in Sandra Sherman, 'Printed Communities: Domestic Management Texts in the Eighteenth Century', *Journal for Early Modern Cultural Studies*, 3/2 (2003), p. 48.
4   Sherman, 'Advertisements for Myself', pp. 65, 71; R.B. Walker, 'Advertising in London Newspapers, 1650–1750', *Business History*, 15 (1973), pp. 112–30.
5   Sherman, 'Advertisements for Myself', p. 66.
6   Ibid., p. 83.

Her statement that these books were essentially 'puffs' is too strong a conclusion – there was a good deal of solid information in them and it would not be tenable to suggest that the main motive for the 379 pages of *The Country Housewife's Family Companion* was to advertise his wares – it is interesting that Sherman and Ellis's neighbours shared the same opinion of his motives for writing. It is certain that Ellis makes his readers feel that he understands their needs and is there to help them. Readers would have considered the books as self-help manuals, with new solutions addressing familiar problems. Unlike the many advertisements in print that were obviously aimed at selling, Ellis's words were ostensibly those of a 'disinterested expert'.[7]

Ellis was a small part of the 'Consumer Revolution' that transformed economic growth in the eighteenth century. This, in essence, was an expansion of demand for goods and services, based on fashion and whim: goods were purchased because other consumers had them; new goods were introduced by retailers for sale; no longer were durable goods purchased for a lifetime, for fashions might change and consumption patterns with them. Although it can be argued that Ellis was not primarily in the fashionable goods market, he sold gun dogs, 'fancy fowls' (peacocks, pheasants and ducks), domestic pets such as guinea pigs and new types of fruit tree, all of which were subject to fashion, and his agricultural machinery was largely sold to gentlemen, some of whom might well have purchased it to put on ostentatious display on their home farms.[8]

We can trace the progress of Ellis's non-farming business activities through the amount of advertising of it contained in his books. We can date the start of his trading activities to about 1732, when he was in his early forties. In that year he published the first edition of the *Practical Farmer*, probably his first book. This book was published in two parts, although the second part, with a separate title page, is also dated 1732 and so must have been issued in the same year; probably it was issued with the second edition of part one.[9] The first part of this book contains no advertisements, either overt or 'puffs' in the text. In contrast, the second half does have some. For instance, he offers to demonstrate his farming methods to interested parties[10] and to sell wheat seeds, recommending white Pirk wheat seed:

---

7   Ibid., p. 83.
8   Neil McKendrick et al., *The Birth of a Consumer Society: Commercialization of Eighteenth Century England* (London, 1984); Ellis, *Agriculture Improv'd*, pp. 156–7.
9   Ellis, *Chiltern and Vale Farming*, p. 248.
10  Ellis, *Practical Farmer*, p. 212.

It is near alike to Sicilian Wheat, that one of the Royal Society was so good to make me a present of a peck, that I have now growing: And if any person think fit to be furnished with this true genuine seed, that I had the year before last from about Aylesbury, they may have it sent up to London, or elsewhere, at a reasonable rate, Sending a letter (post paid) direct to me at little Gaddesden near Hempstead in Hertfordshire, twenty-seven miles distant from London.[11]

He mentions his early book on brewing:

the further particulars of this management in brewing see in the London and Country Brewer, published by an experienced hand; a book far exceeding all others for its ample accounts of the several methods of brewing malt liquors etc. and is truly necessary for all persons whatever, concerned both in public and private brewings, also all drinkers of malt liquor.[12]

He also advertises forthcoming monthly books on agriculture at one shilling an issue, with a discount for those who subscribe for six in advance.[13] The advertisements are mostly for existing or proposed books; he was cautious about starting other forms of trading. Three years later, in *Chiltern and Vale Farming Explained*, he advertises hayseed for sale, as well as seeking 'encouragement' to explain a new way of cropping wheat and turnips in the same year. But in this book, too, the advertisements are few and restrained. Promoting hayseeds from the Vale of Aylesbury, which 'are the best of all others to sow first' on ground put down 'to a lasting sward', he simply adds, 'and which I can furnish any person with, that is desirous of so great a good'. He spends many pages discussing various types of plough, including one, invented in January 1732, 'that will perform just double the work with the same number of horses as the common wheel or foot-plough will'. But he modestly concludes 'If any person wants to be further informed in this particular, this author is ready to give them satisfaction.'[14]

It is not until the early 1740s, when the part work *The Modern Husbandman* was published, that the 'hard sell' appears in Ellis's books, and the range of products and services he can provide is fully exhibited. His advertisements were enticing enough for Kalm's patron to decide to send him to England in 1747 specifically to meet Ellis and view his advertised machines. The insertion of advertisements within instructional text was by

---

11  Ellis, *Practical Farmer*, p. 179.
12  Ibid., p. 211.
13  Ibid., p. 214.
14  Ellis, *Chiltern and Vale Farming*, pp. 293–324.

no means Ellis's only method of displaying his goods and services, although, because of the survival of his books, it is the most obvious. In the *Country Housewife*, wedged between a section on medicine and one on the dairy, is an article of three pages headed ADVERTISEMENT which, together with a similar advertisement in the front of his book on the management of sheep, is reproduced here in the Appendix. These are almost certainly copies of flyers informing prospective customers of Ellis's business. He probably deposited these with friendly innkeepers (carriers' London depots would be an obvious choice), and perhaps the seedsmen he dealt with might also have been persuaded to stock them – seedsmen themselves produced flyers promoting new agricultural seeds. The advertisements neatly set out much, but by no means all, of what Ellis was offering the public in 1749/50: ploughs, drills and horse-hoes of various types; plants of his local apple, pear, cherry and other fruit trees; seeds of new types of fodder plant; useful and ornamental fowls; rat and other vermin poison; secret fertiliser recipes; his latest agricultural book, on sheep; a consultancy service; and a bird scarer. Were there other such flyers which have not survived?[15]

Ellis, or his publishers, also advertised in other print media such as newspapers. An advertisement for one of his books 'which is allowed by all Judges of Husbandry, to be the best ever published on this Subject' was printed in February 1742 in the *General Advertiser*, and the *Modern Husbandman* was advertised in the same paper in December 1745.[16] A correspondent mentioned seeing 'a printed advertisement, containing the general Scheme of the Contents of your monthly books', no doubt another newspaper advertisement.[17] Publishers of Ellis's works took the opportunity to publicise his other books – in the rear pages of *Chiltern and Vale Farming Explained* (1745), the publisher Thomas Astley advertised the *Modern Husbandman* in five volumes, giving full descriptions of the contents of each volume. The set, bound, cost £1 7s 6d, a considerable outlay (equivalent today to around £2400).[18] Despite the cost of books, some gentlemen were firm fans of Ellis's writings; one gentleman hoping for advice from Ellis claimed, 'I have constantly purchased every book you have published.'[19]

A disadvantage of advertising forthcoming books before publication was that authors (and publishers) then, as now, were optimists, usually promising

---

15   Ellis, *Country Housewife*, pp. 303–6; Ellis, *Compleat system of experienced improvements*.
16   *General Advertiser* (London, 1742, 1745).
17   Ellis, *Modern Husbandman*, p. 48.
18   Roderick Floud, *An Economic History of the English Garden* (London, 2019), p. xii (facing).
19   Ellis, *Modern Husbandman*, February, p. 56.

# THE
# Modern Husbandman:

OR, THE

## PRACTICE of FARMING:

As it is now carried on by the most Accurate FARMERS in several Counties of ENGLAND.

## For the MONTH of *MAY*.

Containing the following Particulars;

*VIZ.*

I. Of PLOUGHS and PLOWING.
II. Of BARLEY, WHEAT, TURNEPS, &c.
III. Of WEEDS, and their Cure.
IV. Of MANURES and DRESSINGS proper for this Month.
V. Of Artificial GRASSES.
VI. Of BULLS, COWS, and CALVES.
VII. Of CHEESE.
VIII. Of BUTTER.
IX. Of HOGS.
X. Of SHEEP.
XI. Miscellaneous Matters in HUSBANDRY.
XII. Of TURNEPS; a farther Account of them.
XIII. Of Making and Repairing ROADS.
XIV. Of HORSES, MARES, and COLTS.
XV. Of TREES and INSECTS.

*By* WILLIAM ELLIS,
Of *Little Gaddesden,* near *Hempstead,* in *Hertforshire.*

### DUBLIN:

Printed by and for GEORGE FAULKNER.

M, DCC, XLIII.

10. *The Modern Husbandman,* for May. *The Modern Husbandman* was the most successful of Ellis's attempts at monthly periodicals.

new books' arrivals earlier than they actually appeared. And, sometimes, they did not appear at all. In *A compleat system [...] made on sheep, etc.* of 1749 Ellis advertises that he will say more on drill husbandry of turnips in 'my next Work on Husbandry, designed to be wrote in twelve monthly Books more, to be intitled – *New Discoveries and Improvements in Husbandry*. Each Book to contain five Cuts of new Instruments of Husbandry'. By 1750 this proposed book had a modified title: *Treasure of New Discoveries in the Improvements of Instrumental Husbandry*. No such books appeared – possibly the cost of 'five Cuts' in each volume put the publisher off.[20]

Another intriguing form of product promotion is glimpsed on the flyleaf of a fourth edition of the *London and County Brewer* (1742). It is an ink inscription:

> To
> The Honourable William Murray Esqr.
> His Majesties Solicitor
> General
> From the Author,
> June 17
> 1747

Murray (now better known as the First Earl of Mansfield) was then an up-and-coming lawyer and politician, with clients that brought him into the London elite. Was this a case of Ellis promoting his books by sending them to influential people? If so, who else did he send copies of his book to and why did he send one to Murray? He could hardly expect him to recommend a book on brewing to his important clients, and it was the fourth edition, hardly a new book hot off the press. Most likely he met Murray in London.[21]

## Mail order

We have seen the extent of Ellis's travels on horseback, one of the end products of which he hoped would be sales or consultancy work. Unless they lived near Ellis, purchases were transported to customers, who usually paid an agent appointed by Ellis in London. A good example of such a transaction is found in a letter of February 1735/6 from an Oxfordshire gentleman ordering some nursery trees:

---

20 Ellis, *Compleat system of experienced improvements*, p. 60; Ellis, *Country Housewife*, p. 221.
21 This inscribed book is owned by the author of this work. The handwriting in this inscription is the same as in parts of the Little Gaddesden Churchwardens' Account Book written up by Ellis.

if you'll please direct for ------ at Broughton near Banbury, Oxon, to be left to the Care of Eagle the Cropredy Carrier, at the George-on-the-Hill, who sets out on Thursday Morning; as soon as you let me know what they come to, the said Carrier shall pay it to any Person in London you shall appoint. I don't know of any readier conveyance, than sending them to London, our Carrier going the Oxford Road which, I suppose, is out of your Road, unless by a great Chance, you should have an opportunity to send to High-Wickham or any other Town on that Road near you, through which the Waggon passes down-wards on Fridays.[22]

Transactions by post and carrier could be very complicated, as this extract from a letter sent to Ellis by the agent of an Irish peer demonstrates:

My Lord of ___ desires you to write by the post, to Mr Murray, merchant in Chester, and to ask him, whether, upon your delivering to the Chester Carrier at Dunstable sundry Parcels of plants for my Lord's use, he will not lodge, in the Chester Carrier's hand, four guineas to pay for those parcels of plants at the time you deliver them to the carrier's waggon at Dunstable. Be pleased, under a cover directed to the Lord of ____, at _____, in Ireland, to send your answer to me. You will agree, either at London, or Dunstable, before-hand, with the Chester Waggoner. The Waggoner puts up at Blossom's-Inn, Laurence Lane, London; you may agree at any time with the Warehouse keeper there. My Lord had lately three Bags of Hops by the Waggoner: The person that sent them agreed, that eight shillings per hundred should be paid for the carriage. Now, Dunstable being thirty miles nearer Chester, it is supposed you may agree, that the Plants may be carried after the Rate of Six Shillings and six pence, or at the most seven shillings per hundred weight. Whatever agreement you make, it is desired, that by post you acquaint Mr. Murray, in Chester, what he is to pay when he receives the sets, to be shipped off by his care for Ireland. There are wanted to be sent by the Chester Carrier, in the first open weather in January[....]

One thousand sets of the land sort of sallow.
One thousand sets of witch-elm
Two thousand sets of the tree, which you call White-wood, in the 182d page of Chilturn and Vale Husbandry explained.

You are desired to pack these carefully, either in fresh matts, or in pease-haulm,[23] that they may take the less harm by carriage and shipping, between your House

---

22  Ellis, *New Experiments in Husbandry*, Preface.
23  Pease-haulm is the stems and stalks of peas.

and Ireland, it being probable that it may be a Month or six weeks before they will be planted at _____ after you have delivered them to the carrier.²⁴

Ellis is keen to advertise that he is willing to organise such long-distance transactions and that they are viable for the purchaser. Here he talks of seed barley:

I have sent it as far as Cumberland, by putting it on a ship at London for Newcastle, from whence it was carried (as I am informed) sixty miles by Land. But where such water carriage lies near the Place of sowing, or if land carriage directly from my house, or from where the seed grows, is not too expensive [...] My way is to charge the Neat Price I buy it at, and leave it to the buyer to allow me, for my trouble, what he thinks I deserve.²⁵

This latter remark gives the customer the feeling that this is not a commercial transaction, rather a favour from one farmer to another, with a little 'thank you' present to the supplier. A risky strategy if the customer was dissatisfied (or mean), but presumably Ellis judged his gentlemen customers a generous sort overall.

Copies of letters from and to customers are scattered through the *Modern Husbandman*, 'irrelevancies' which so irritated later commentators on his work. But he received many more than he published for he must have done a good deal of his business by mail order; in his study he showed Kalm 'a pile of divers letters addressed to him and copies of letters which he had written'. He tried to catch up with correspondence in the winter: 'I answer letters between Michaelmas [29 September] and Lady Day [25 March] provided postage is paid to my house.'²⁶

As Sherman explains, using correspondence with 'J L' as an example, Ellis's publishing of letters from readers and his replies were an important part of his advertising:

In response to a letter requesting various types of assistance, including provision of certain tools, Ellis emphasizes the particularized service that he provides: 'whoever sends me for this Horse-break, they should let me know not only the Use they intend to put it to ... but likewise the Nature of their Soil and Situation, that I

---

24  Ellis, *Modern Husbandman*, February, pp. 123–4.
25  Ellis, *Modern Husbandman*, September, p. 150.
26  Mead, *Pehr Kalm*, p. 39; Ellis, *Modern Husbandman*, May, p. 12; August, p. 6. Ellis always stressed that all letters to him should be 'postage paid'. In his time, postage was charged on the recipient unless the sender paid up front.

may order one to be made according to the same'. Ellis is offering a personalized service to one correspondent such that this does not seem like an advertisement although his readers would understand he is offering them the same service. This personalized approach to his readers was something often lacking in rival publications but Ellis concentrates mainly on what he considers to be factual inaccuracies in these books.[27]

## Criticising rival publications

In order to advertise his own forthcoming books or reassure his readers that his existing works are the best books currently available, Ellis criticises existing works on agriculture, contrasting the wrong or incomplete advice in them with his own published or planned works. He claims that John Worlidge did not give practical advice on growing peas and beans and criticises Jethro Tull's agricultural machinery for being too complicated. He condemns John Houghton for writing about cole-seed when he knew nothing about the plant, 'which I have here, in a more extensive manner discovered by an illiterate pen, in comparison of his, because I write from the field of experience, as having sown this seed in my own farm, and which I have not been without for years past'. Ellis saves his most savage criticism for Richard Bradley, perhaps because Bradley was entering the same market as Ellis, writing agricultural part-works and a book on country living. He quotes Bradley in order to draw an unfavourable comparison between Bradley's comments on barley in August and his own, explaining:

> I have here transcribed all that he has published of barley for the month of August, in his book entitled – The Gentleman and Farmer's Director, printed in 1732, Price 2s. 6d. wherein my reader may see how little purpose such short sketches are. Had he, indeed, wrote of Husbandry as well as he did of gardening, he would have come off more like a practitioner, than a mere scholar, in this copious science. I mention this, because I have been solicited to write a lesser number of sheets for one month, that the price of each book might be lessened accordingly; but, if I had acquiesced to such proposal, I must in course have marred my design, which is to explain the intricate art of husbandry, according to the present practice, in its numerous branches, for the benefit of the farmer, gentleman, and the nation in general.[28]

In a further dig at Bradley's supposed inexperience of practical agriculture, Ellis lampoons him for claiming Sainfoin would grow in clay soil. Implying that he spends all his time indoors, not out observing farms, he calls him

---

27 Sherman, 'Advertisements for Myself', pp. 74–5.
28 Ellis, *Modern Husbandman*, August, p. 30.

'a certain Chamber Georgic Philosopher'. Ellis also criticised Bradley's book on country living, contrasting it with the much superior book *he* was writing, which would deal comprehensively with country matters and be more relevant to farmers' wives and servants than Bradley's work. This he described as 'filled up with little else but cookery receipts, more fit for a nobleman's kitchen than a farmer's'.[29] Ellis told Pehr Kalm 'that he had never thought of writing on rural economy, but when he read Bradley's writings and saw how badly they were put together, he took to his pen to write something better'.[30]

Bradley's periodical *The Gentleman and Farmer's Director* is indeed a slight work. It covers farming month by month but, whereas Ellis's monthly parts of the *Modern Husbandman* run to well over 100 pages a month, Bradley's book covers a year in only 185 pages. It has many short remarks on monthly activities, some of them of little importance. For example, in December the reader is advised: 'Still continue to destroy ant-hills, by spreading them on the ground'; 'Still look after your drains, and suffer no water to stand upon your corn'; 'Still feed weak stocks of bees'. As 'Still' suggests, all this advice is contained in earlier chapters, in no more detail than quoted here. Bradley's chapter on November is thirteen pages long, nine of which are taken up by the husbandry of goats and the suggestion that antelopes should be farmed in England! Given its shortcomings, one is struck by how *mild* is Ellis's attack on Bradley's book.

In discussing pasture for sheep Ellis neatly criticises Bradley's ideas, puts forward his own recommendations and advertises what he has for sale, all in the same paragraph: had Bradley

> known the Virtues of the Lady-finger Grass, the Tyne Grass, and the Honeysuckle Grass, he would undoubtedly have recommended the Sowing of these most excellent Sorts for this Purpose, because, if Ground is laid down with only these three Sorts of Seeds and their Grasses improved by Mr. Livings' Manure, they will not only cause Ewes to have a Propensity to take Ram, but will assuredly produce the sweetest Butter, Cheese, and Flesh. If Gentlemen, therefore, were truly sensible of the Advantages attending the Sowing of these Grass-Seeds, they would not sow a Parcel of trumpery, promiscuous, weedy Hay-Seed, out of Hay-Lofts, but send to me for them, as I am their first Discoverer, and the two first Sorts are sold by none but myself in England. I, also, sell the Receipt to make Mr. Livings's Manure, which, for the great Profit, attending its Uses, when sown among Grain, Grass, Plants, or any Vegetables whatsoever, the Inventor of it endeavoured to obtain a

---

29  Ellis, *Modern Husbandman*, March, p. 85; December, p. 492.
30  Mead, *Pehr Kalm*, p. 41.

Reward for, to make it publicly known, from the Government, but not receiving it, it remains a Secret to this Day.[31]

Bradley began his writing career in 1716 and published his last book in 1733, so he and Ellis just overlapped. He produced approximately the same number of books as Ellis and those on husbandry and country living were aimed at the same market as Ellis's. But Bradley was not in the same social class as Ellis. He was a Fellow of the Royal Society and Professor of Botany at Cambridge. He travelled abroad and was conversant with Latin and Greek. As well as the practical books on husbandry and several on gardening, he published research into botany, a translation of Xenophon and a botanical dictionary. Ellis may have been resentful of Bradley's status but there is no doubt that Ellis's agricultural works were on the whole superior to Bradley's and a farmer's wife would have gained more useful knowledge from Ellis's book of country living than from Bradley's.[32]

As to his other criticisms, it is probably not too difficult to find some faults in a comprehensive work such as Worlidge's. His *Systema Agriculturae*, first published in 1668, was composed 'by assembling the knowledge already available, adding what he knew of contemporary farming and organizing the whole into what he was pleased to call a system of agriculture'.[33] It was sufficiently well thought of to go through five editions in Worlidge's lifetime. John Houghton established the first attempt at a weekly agricultural newspaper in 1692. It ran for ten years and, given the demands for weekly copy, no doubt he made mistakes from time to time. The fact that a second edition, in book form, was edited by Richard Bradley and issued in 1727 may have coloured Ellis's judgement. Finally, no one today would deny that Tull's diagrams are mind-numbingly complicated.[34] It may be of significance that Worlidge, Bradley and Houghton were all Fellows of the Royal Society. Ellis, on the other hand, was keen to emphasise that he was a working farmer, living among a community of such. He knew weeds and the like by their country names, not their botanical ones:

> I am not, nor never was master of any Book capable of informing me so far as to give a Botanical Account of these Vegetables, nor can I learn it by Conversation,

---

31 Ellis, *Compleat system of experienced improvements*, pp. 296–7. Nothing more is known about 'Mr Livings' or his manure. G.E. Fussell, 'The Farming Writers of Eighteenth-century England', *Agricultural History Review*, 21/1 (London, 1947), p. 7.
32 Bradley, *The Country Housewife*, pp. 11–25.
33 G.E. Fussell, *Old English Farming Books* (Collieston, 1978), pt I, p. 56.
34 Ibid., pp. 81–2.

for most of our Parishioners are downright Dunstable Farmers; that is, those who know nothing of the matter [...] I write in the main from the Field of Practice.³⁵

He was proud of his own situation as a working farmer rather than an academic or gentleman amateur. His indifference to botanical nomenclature may also have been another dig at Bradley, who published, in 1728, a two-volume *Dictionarium Botanicum* – a botanical dictionary for use in husbandry and gardening.³⁶

Ellis uses the technique of attacking another work again when he introduces his book on cider. Here he criticises the parts of Sir Jonas Moore's book *England's Interest, or the Gentleman and Farmer's Friend* relating to cider. Ellis claimed that Sir Jonas (another Fellow of the Royal Society) was in error when he suggested planting Golden Pippin trees in order to make cider: 'Its Juice is of too weak a Nature to keep long', and it had not the power to 'warm the Drinker, unless mix'd with a stronger Sort'. Despite Ellis's misgivings, one use of this old variety is still as a cider apple.³⁷ Ellis is on stronger ground when he challenges Sir Jonas's advice that to make cider taste better a mixture of sugar syrup and brandy should be added to each cask. Ellis fails to mention other books on cider, such as the well-received *Vinetum Britannicum* of John Worlidge or John Philips's didactic poem *Of Cyder*. Published a year earlier than Ellis's book was *A Treatise on Cyder-Making* by Hugh Stafford. This work, in contrast to Ellis's, makes no claim that the Devon cider of South Hams is stronger and superior to that of Herefordshire, despite the book being largely concerned with Devon.³⁸

Overall, Ellis's criticisms of existing works read more like advertising puffs for his own books than genuine critiques of rival publications. He seems on occasion to have invented or at least exaggerated controversies to show his works in a good light, and he sometimes had to dig up fairly ancient tomes to attack – Worlidge's book on agriculture was first published in 1669 and Moore's book appeared in 1703. He laid emphasis on the

---

35   Ellis, *Modern Husbandman*, March, p. 125.
36   Richard Bradley, *Dictionarium Botanicum, or a Botanical Dictionary for the use of the curious in Husbandry and Gardening* (London, 1728).
37   Ellis's objection to this apple as a cider apple seems to equate its sweetness with a lack of strength. In a recent BBC2 programme it was revealed that Bulmers of Hereford, Britain's biggest cider manufacturer, were experimenting with a sweeter variety of apple, so the debate goes on. Sir Jonas Moore, *England's Interest, or the Gentleman and Farmer's Friend* (London, 1703), pp. 27, 8; Ellis, *Compleat Cyderman*, pp. v–vii.
38   John Worlidge, *Vinetum Britannicum* (London, 1678); John Philips, *Of Cyder* (London, 1708); Hugh Stafford, *A Treatise on Cyder-Making* (London, 1753).

practical nature of his books – they were written in plain language, calling crops and weeds by their country, not botanical, names. He portrayed himself as a countryman, contrasting himself to the gentlemen who wrote the books he was criticising.

## *More goods and services for sale*

Taking a closer look at some of the commodities Ellis tried to sell, we find that some were frequently advertised, whereas others are mentioned only briefly in the printed material that has survived. Two of the latter are compost and fowls, both of which are offered for sale in only his two 'flyers' and one of his books.[39] He sold Poland, Dorking and Dunghill fowls. Poland fowls (nothing to do with Poland: the name comes from the poll or crest on top of the bird's head) are an ornamental bird, bred, like tame pheasants and Guinea hens, to strut about a country house garden. Dorking fowls had long been recognised as the best breed in England: attractive, largely white birds, they were good layers and suitable for the table, with a short, plump body. Dunghill fowls, on the other hand, were the most basic of chickens – cross-bred and left to fend for themselves, literally feeding off the dunghill in the farmyard. Why would a gentleman apply to Ellis for a dunghill fowl?[40] The answer was that, according to Ellis, these were top-quality Hertfordshire fowls:

> Ours, being all of a snow-white Colour, of a good Size, lay large thin-shelled Eggs, that cause them to be hatch'd the sooner; breed commonly three times in a Summer; which is a particular beneficial Quality to us Farmers, when we have Offal-corn in Plenty, for feeding and bringing-up great Numbers of such fine white-legg'd Chickens, that sell for the best Prices.[41]

The paucity of advertising of fowls by Ellis may mean that selling them was not a successful venture – transporting live birds by carrier and/or coastal shipping must have been a hazardous activity. In 1746 he put 'six tame Pheasants, six Hertfordshire white Dunghill-fowls, and other Things, on board a Ship in the River Thames', bound for a northern customer. One wonders in what condition the birds arrived at their destination. Ellis meant to drum up interest by writing more on pheasants and bustards, 'that I

---

39 Invention of composts was nothing new: Sir Hugh Plat in 1596 offered the formula for 'A new and extraordinary meanes for the inriching of arable grounds'. Plat, *Sundrie new and Artificiall Remediall Against Famine* (London, 1596).
40 See Appendix I.
41 Ellis, *Agriculture Improv'd*, p. 148.

may be instrumental towards increasing the breed of these majestic fowls, I intend, hereafter to give an account, how persons may breed them in private houses, as I have done the pheasant in farm-yards and apartments. I intend to write a large addition on this subject in some of my future writings.' He never did.[42]

Other commodities were advertised frequently and with overt enthusiasm. Ellis was, we have seen, very proud of the local varieties of fruit trees he had growing on his land and gives glowing accounts of their virtues before offering to sell scions or plants. He makes a particular virtue of the size of the best trees he owns. He could supply 'the Kerroon, May Duke, or other improved Cherries', good for cooking and for making wine.[43] He is also effusive in his praise of the Parsnip Apple: 'I will furnish grafts of this to any person that thinks fit to send me a proper order for their delivery to London, or elsewhere.'[44]

Ellis could supply a range of other trees – ornamental, hedge and timber. He was particularly keen on selling the 'White-wood' tree, which was 'of the species of those aquatick Trees, the Poplar, Ash, and Abel'; after several pages in praise of this tree he concludes: 'And if any Gentlemen have a mind to propagate this Tree, they may be furnished by me, with these sets, that I can so order from August to April, as that they will grow if sent to any Part of England by the Carrier.' He could also supply 'Oak, Beech, Ash, Elm, Sollars, Hornbeam, Thorn, or Holly Sets or Acorns, Mast, Keys of Ash, or Maple, Seeds of Hornbeam and several other sorts, provided I have timely Notice given me'.

He did have a nursery of trees on his farm, which he described as large, but I doubt whether Ellis could supply large parcels of trees – probably he had an arrangement with a London nursery that they would fulfil large orders and he would charge commission. We have noted above a transaction with an Oxfordshire gentleman involving trees sent by carrier.[45]

Ellis frequently advertised seeds of various kinds, whether grown by himself or procured elsewhere; judging from the size of some orders, his advertising was successful. Being very small, seeds were easier to send by post or carrier. Nevertheless, Ellis must have fulfilled large orders either by going to London and buying from seedsmen or again charging commission on an order fulfilled by a seedsman. A large seed order is reproduced in the

---

42  Ellis, *Modern Husbandman*, January, pp. 32–3; H.D. Richardson, *Domestic fowl: their natural history, breeding, rearing, and general management* (London, 1847).
43  Ellis, *Modern Husbandman*, February, pp. 114–16.
44  Ellis, *Modern Husbandman*, June, p. 37.
45  Ellis, *Chiltern and Vale Farming*, pp. 182–5.

*Modern Husbandman* for November, from 'a Gentleman [who] has begun improving his estate, by sets or plants, and seeds, sent him by the Author, after a new Method':

500 Acorns of the Evergreen Oak
500 of Beech-Mast
1000 Beechen Sets
2000 Bay-Tree Berries
12 Lignum Vitae Berries
2000 Horn Beech Seeds
2000 Cypress Seeds
100 Cedar-Tree Seeds
1 Pound of Juniper Berries
20 Almond Nuts
20 Service-Tree Seeds
1 Pound of French Furz Seeds
360 Of Arbele Plants[46]

Meadow grass seeds were grown by Ellis and also bought in from local farmers, as he explains in response to a letter from a Dublin gentleman. The letter requested 'one bushel of your meadow-grass seeds' just for a trial – if it is as good as Ellis claims, he will be 'dealing with you for a large quantity'. As with his advertising of fruit trees, Ellis first enthuses about these seeds. A mixture of 'Lady-finger, Honey-suckle, wild Thetch, and Cinque-foil seeds', these natural grass seeds, Ellis claims, are good for fattening cattle as well as feeding milch cows. Light and easily carried, they are economical to buy for gentlemen hundreds of miles from Gaddesden. Moreover, these seeds could only be obtained from Ellis: 'there is no such thing as coming by these fine Upland Meadow Hay-seeds at any of the London Seed-shops'. He explains that he and his neighbours sell their hay to the duke of Bridgewater to feed his deer but do not sell it until springtime, when it is easy to thrash out the seed before selling the hay. Ellis claimed, 'Lady-finger Grass I am the first Discoverer of, for making it known in this publick Manner'. Ladies' Finger, or kidney vetch, was a plant long known to English botanists and farmers and so it is not true that Ellis first found it, but he is claiming to have 'discovered' that it was a particularly good seed to sow in a meadow. He enthuses to a correspondent about this crop:

---

46 Ellis, *Modern Husbandman*, November, pp. 354–5. Arbele is the black poplar tree; service (*Sorbus torminalis*) is a small tree with edible fruits.

> It is a Seed so scarce to be got, that it is difficult to gather two Quarts of it among five Acres of Meadow-grass [...] If there be proper Care taken of its sowing and preserving, you may increase it to what Quantity you please; for it is a very hardy Grass, and will grow almost upon any Soil; by which you will become Master of, perhaps, the finest natural Grass in the whole World.[47]

Although it was a useful meadow plant, Ellis's enthusiasm for it was not at all general at the time. In the *Modern Husbandman* for January he writes that, if any gentleman or bailiff is interested, he will leave his grass crop 'until the seed is ripe [when] he shall have the liberty of having the seed picked and gathered by itself, free and clear of all other grass-seeds'.[48]

Ellis did offer many other seeds for sale that were not grown by himself, such as seed grain. He sold seed wheat, and also Sprat, Raith-ripe or Fulham barley, which, we have seen, was much prized for its quality and early ripening.[49] He also sold 'Tick Horse Beans For Splitting, Rouncival Field Pease, Winter Thetches, any sort of Turnep seed'. At the end of a piece emphasising that the largest specimens of seed are the best, he sums up his offerings, emphasising his readiness to provide them:

> This, therefore, is to advertise and give Notice, that I sow and sell the largest of Wheat-Seed, Barley, Oats, Pease, and Horse Bean Seed; which, by a particular management, I every year obtain, and am ready to furnish any person with it, to any part of Great Britain or Ireland, for ready Money; and I answer Letters, provided postage be paid to my House.[50]

Unsurprisingly, Ellis took the opportunity, especially in his monthly instalments, to advertise forthcoming books. He assured prospective

---

47 Ellis, *Agriculture Improv'd*, vol. I, p. 189.
48 Ellis, *Modern Husbandman*, January, p. 122; February, pp. 97–8; Ellis, *Country Housewife*, p. 395. Ellis is correct about upland meadow seeds: mixtures of such seeds were not sold by London seedsmen in his time (see the various seed catalogues reproduced in John Harvey, *Early Gardening Catalogues* [Chichester, 1972]). Ellis several times emphasises that the largest and heaviest seeds were the best sort to sow. This was not a new idea: in 1653 Samuel Hartlib published papers written by his correspondents stating that 'In the choice of seed-corn, prefer that wheat which is most weighty'. Robert Child in the same publication reported that in Kent seed barley was steeped to clean it and to skim off the 'light corn' which floated to the surface. Child was sceptical, however, that steeped corn yielded a better crop. [Samuel Hartlib], *A Discoverie for Division or Setting Out of Land* (London, 1653), pp. 13–14.
49 Mortimer, *Whole Art of Husbandry*, pp. 130–1; Ellis, *Modern Husbandman*, September, pp. 36–7.
50 Ellis, *Modern Husbandman*, June, pp. 37, 47–8.

readers that they were based on considerable research, as he had travelled extensively looking at various methods of husbandry. On several occasions he claims that his books are the first or best available to tackle a topic: his 'Treatise on Sheep and Lambs, that I published last Year, is the most useful Book that ever was wrote of the Kind'. It *was* the first English book devoted to sheep and would have been undeniably useful to shepherds.[51] The new techniques revealed in his book on brewing, 'a book far exceeding all others for its ample accounts of the several methods of brewing malt liquors etc.' would, he claimed, 'be of considerable service to the world'. The book was undeniably popular, running through several editions. A present-day expert on historic brewing techniques considers that it was, when it first appeared, the best book available on brewing.[52]

As well as advertising commodities, through his publications and correspondence Ellis ran a primitive form of employment agency, advertising young men of his acquaintance as bailiffs or ploughmen. There is no mention of fees for this service, but one would expect the successful candidates for employment to recompense Ellis for his trouble:

> Therefore if any Gentleman thinks it fit to send to me for this, or any other Man-Servant necessary in any of the branches of farming, I will use my best Endeavours to serve him, at any time of the year [...] and they may depend on it, they shall have the genuine character of him, as I have it from where he last lived.[53]

In an article on fodder crops he mentions a young man who is skilled in the use of the drill-plough, praising him for his many other farming and gardening skills before setting out a detailed advertisement to seek a position for this 21-year-old. He

> understands how to perform all manner of plowing, sowing of seeds, mowing and cutting down all manner of corn and grass, and trees; plant new, and plaish old hedges, in great perfection, clean, and sell corn, &c. and is truly honest and diligent, as will be certified, he writes me word, by his present master; he likewise writes, and can keep accounts.[54]

Reading of a successful placement, a gentleman writes to Ellis asking him to recommend a ploughman. Ellis has a candidate but advises that he should

---

51 Ellis, *Country Housewife*, p. 382.
52 Ellis, *Practical Farmer*, p. 32; Marc Meltonville, pers. comm.
53 Ellis, *Modern Husbandman*, November, pp. 265–6.
54 Ellis, *Modern Husbandman*, January, pp. 122–4.

employ both him and his wife, as she 'is also so good a house-wife, that she can perform several cures on horses, cows, and sheep'. At least one person successfully placed by Ellis – 'a young man well qualified in husbandry affairs, whom I sent into Devonshire to a gentleman of a landed estate there, as his servant or bailiff' – showed his gratitude by sending him recipes to include in *The Country Housewife*.[55]

Ellis also makes plain his readiness to act as a consultant: being 'ready to wait on any Gentleman in any Part of England or Wales, that thinks fit to consult his Advice in the Improvement of his Estate, according to the ancient, or the newest Methods of Husbandry'. This was one of the purposes of his travels. Early on in his career as a farmer he was consulted by a gentleman on the purchase of a farm; alas, we will never know the extent to which he gave practical advice to farmers he met or who wrote to him.

## *Ploughs, drills and horse-hoes*

Ellis had a particular interest in advertising ploughs, drills and horse-hoes and his enthusiasm for various types of horse-drawn plough and hoe or break was matched by his efforts to sell them. In the flyers (see the Appendix) Ellis advertises six different ploughs and horse-hoes and stresses that he can supply any other type requested. When writing about ploughs, Ellis gives details of their mechanism, how they function, the advantages – especially financial – to be gained from their use, and sometimes where and by whom they were invented. Naturally, he remarks on the cheapness of what he is offering compared with other available machinery and he inevitably highlights his willingness to provide them.

In discussing a great many ploughs in his writings he was, like others before him, conscious that many regional variations in these implements had developed over time.[56] He also recognised the growing interest in row cultivation and the challenge given to inventors seeking to mechanise their system of agriculture by ploughing and simultaneously planting seeds. He details the usefulness of a plough from his own county before, typically, offering it for sale:

> the Hertfordshire double plough [...] this excellent new-invented Plough [...] comes to little money when made. The wood, the iron socket, share, etc and making, amount to no more than one Guinea in all; which is so small a price, for so useful a plough, that, I think, none can well grudge to lay out this money for an instrument that will do all manner of work in gravelly, chalky, sandy, and in

---

55   Ellis, *Modern Husbandman*, January, p. 102; Ellis, *Country Housewife*, p. 311.
56   See reference above to Blith, *The English Improver Improved*.

dry, and wet loamy, or clayey grounds. In short, it is the most general plough of all others that I know of, for plowing in all grounds, except in Ridge Vale lands, in Fen lands, in Marsh lands, and too stony lands, which are soils that require, each of them, one particular sort of plough. Now this cheap, light swing-plough I furnish to any person for the price before-mentioned, paying me for my charges of sending it him.[57]

He was initially keen also to promote his own invention, the four-wheeled drill-plough: 'I am persuaded many would send to me for this plough, if they were sensible of the several advantages belonging to its uses.' He includes a plate of the plough as a frontispiece to *The Farmer's Instructor* (1747). This illustration informs readers that the plough 'was first invented in the year 1745 and is now in Use with Wm. Ellis at Little Gaddesden [...] where any person may view the same. It is so light that a man may draw it but generally drawn by a pony or little Horse.' The picture shows a carriage with four equal wheels, a circular coulter at the front producing a furrow, a small hopper dispensing seed set in front of a larger one presumably for manure and a small number of harrow tines at the back to cover over the seed. No connection between the hoppers and the wheels of this machine is visible, although Ellis, in describing the plough, claimed there was one. This would be necessary to successfully regulate the flow of seeds and manure. All in all, it looks to be a primitive type of drill-plough.[58]

Much of his focus is on these three- and four-wheeled drill-ploughs, which he clearly thought would greatly improve agricultural productivity. He had read Jethro Tull on the subject, which may have convinced him that such machines were the future of agriculture. Equally, he may have seen them just as a potentially lucrative business opportunity. He sought to highlight the advantages of this plough by calculating the savings a farmer would make by using it to sow peas:

| | |
|---|---|
| By the common Plough a Sower of Manure is generally employed a Day to sow it Broad-Cast on one Acre of Ground | – 0 1 0 |
| Plowman and Driver | – 0 1 9 |
| Two Boys a Day, according to Mr Trowell | – 0 1 6 |
| Keeping of two Horses a Day and their use | – 0 4 0 |
| | – 0 8 3 |

---

57 Ellis, *Modern Husbandman*, April, pp. 15–17. Arthur Young praised the double plough in 1804, although he condemned the old Hertfordshire plough as far too heavy and cumbersome. Young, *Hertfordshire*, pp. 37–8.
58 Ellis and Trowell, *Farmer's Instructor*, frontispiece.

By the four – wheeled Drill – Plough, one little Horse
draws it, and a man guides it, with a Boy driver sows an acre and
a half of Pease in Drills in one Day, with Manure, and covers all as
the Plough goes                                                                       – 0 3 9
                                                              Total saved 0 4 6

Further savings could be made by hoeing the peas with his two-wheeled hoe.[59]

The demonstration to Kalm may have been just bad luck, but the detailed description of the failure of the plough to work, which we have noted above, seems plausible: perhaps the four-wheeled drill-plough, with only a crude mechanism for regulating seed flow or co-ordinating the seed flow with the fertiliser, was inherently unreliable, leading Ellis to place more emphasis on trying to sell the three-wheeled drill-plough in his writings.[60] Ellis came across this latter plough, invented by a farmer named James Godden, on his travels. He explains 'the first knowledge I had of the three-wheeled drill plough, was at Franken near Bath, where Farmer Clements received it from his Landlord, who sent it above an hundred Miles to him.'[61] Ellis describes this implement in fine detail, outlining it as follows:

> This sort is a new, well invented, and most profitable machine, or plough, for making drills or furrows, with its light share, two broad boards, and its commodious fixed handles; for sowing horse and kidney beans, all sorts of peas, wheat, barley, thetches, tills, turneps, and artificial grass seeds.[62]

Unlike *his* machine, this plough had attachable hoppers for different types of seed and a spindle under the hopper to regulate the flow of seed. Although it looked quite complicated on paper, Ellis assured his readers that 'the three-Wheel Drill Plough is so plainly put together that it might be sold cheap.' In contrast, 'the very ingenious Mr. Tull has so mathematically contrived his Drill Plough […] as to render them chargeable to make.' Godden, in 1738, charged £4, without carriage, for the three-wheeled drill-plough and thirty shillings for horse breaks (hoes). Another newly invented plough, the Pulley Drill Plough, a lighter instrument suitable for Vale lands invented by Edward King, had a central 'Iron Cog Wheel of about ten inches in diameter […] to keep the share to an exact depth; and, as the wheel turns, it turns smaller

---

59  Ibid., pp. 49–50.
60  Ibid., pp. 43, 53.
61  Ellis, *Modern Husbandman*, June, p. 13.
62  Ibid., p. 1.

ones and pullies, that occasion the seed to drop regularly out'.[63]

Having successfully sowed crops in rows, the next challenge was to keep the crop clear of weeds, and weed eradication would be made easier and more effective, Ellis argued, if one of his machines was used to clear the space between the rows. Ellis recommends horse-hoes and thinks that over time they will do farmers 'hundreds of pounds worth of service' and completely replace hand hoeing. Ellis was enamoured of one particular horse-drawn hoe in 1746:

> This 8th day of August, 1746 I know of but one such contrived two-wheel Hoe; for the make of this is different from all other horse-breaks yet made, and is of great use, as to be of the greatest service for cleaning the inter-spaces or intervals between drilled rows, of wheat, rye, barley, oats, pease, beans, vetches, turneps, rapes, St, Foin, and Lucerne grasses etc.. In short, this Wheel-hoe is such a profitable machine, that I believe I may affirm it for truth, it is worth a hundred pounds for it, rather than be without it.[64]

Ellis boasts of international interest in his advertised ploughs and hoes, citing

> a letter from an eminent ingenious planter in one of the American colonies, who, by only reading my Monthly book for May, became so enamoured with my description of the three wheel drill plough, or horse-break, that he sent over an order [he was willing] to pay my price for them; and accordingly they were both made and delivered to him in January 1742.[65]

Ellis reminded his readers that English farmers were facing competition from abroad; vast tracts of land were being brought into cultivation in America and agricultural output was expanding in France and Ireland. English farmers needed to increase productivity by using drill-ploughs, and

> that I may be instrumental to promote my Country's good in this one main article, I hereby promise faithfully, to furnish any person with this excellent improving three-wheel drill plough, or pulley drill plough, or any other drill plough, horse-break, or other instrument, for improving husbandry, at the very intrinsic price it costs me, and leave what they think fit to allow me for my trouble, to their pleasure.[66]

---

63   Ibid., pp. 2, 4, 7–8; March, p. 41.
64   Ellis and Trowell, *Farmer's Instructor*, p. 24; Ellis, *Modern Husbandman*, March, p. 66.
65   Ellis, *Modern Husbandman*, January, p. 25.
66   Ellis, *Modern Husbandman*, December, p. 396.

A common theme running through his advertisements for drill-ploughs and horse-hoes is that of economy: the machines would save money because they replaced labourers and sowed less seed per acre; and, on the other hand, they resulted in better yields, which meant more profit for the farmer. They were a capital outlay that some farmers would have found difficult to fund, but Ellis seeks to persuade them that in the long run the machines will be very profitable. His claims of economy are doubtful: if the money saved by using the machines was obvious to farmers, take up would have been much larger.

Ellis had these ploughs and hoes made for him to order by ploughwrights. His Swedish visitor Pehr Kalm was disappointed not to be able to see these implements laid out for inspection, much like a present-day car showroom.

> I asked Mr. Ellis if he had at home all the kinds of ploughs of which he spoke in his writings and especially those he held in great esteem for their usefulness. He answered no, giving as an excuse that if he had them at home he would never be left in peace since they would either be taken away or stolen [...] I asked, if gentlemen wanted to order them, how could they get them made, and if there was anybody in this place who made them? He answered that no one here could make them, because they required a singularly clever head to do so. There was, however a man who lived 30 or 40 English miles away who would construct anything that gentlemen might order, but it was necessary to pay for the ploughs or other equipment in advance and, furthermore, to pay for transport from the maker to Mr. Ellis as well as from him to London or such place as they were needed.[67]

Kalm asked local farmers if this was true and they told him Ellis had the ironwork done by the smith who lived next to Ashridge park (and *he* lived next door to Ellis) and the ploughs were made by a ploughwright who lived close to where Kalm was staying. Ellis partially explains what he told Kalm when he writes 'The three-wheel drill-plough and horse-break is another person's contrivance, made and sold by a plough-maker and smith, who live in another part of the country.' Replying to a gentleman who proposed to send his bailiff to view the implements on offer, Ellis explains

> they are seldom made beforehand, it may be a month before I can have them ready [...] I shall do what I did not intend, that is, give you Notice of the Day and Place where your Bailiff is to meet me, and I will go with him to the two Plough Wrights, where the ploughs and horse-breaks are made.[68]

---

67  Mead, *Pehr Kalm*, p. 40.
68  Ellis, *Modern Husbandman*, March, p. 95; January, pp. 99–101.

Finally, in a long explanation of the way in which the implements are made, Ellis again implies the makers are some distance away:

> Now, if any gentleman shall think it fit to employ me to furnish him with one or both of these drill-ploughs and horse-break, I will take care, they will be done by the original makers, who live in different parts of the country, as they were first made by different inventors of them, strangers to each other [...] Also if any gentleman, after I have bespoke and given earnest (as is customary) for these instruments, is pleased, either to come himself, or send his bailiff, or other servant, to me, where I shall appoint him, I will ride with him, and shew him several fields in different parts of the country, that are, or have been sown with wheat, barley, oats, grass-seed, &c.[69]

So, both Ellis and his neighbours were right about the location of the manufacturers of his machines. Those invented by Godden were made by *his* subcontractors some distance away, whereas the drill-plough that Ellis invented, and possibly some others, were made by smiths and ploughwrights locally.

Ellis used the advertising technique of describing a previous customer's favourable reaction to seeing his implements in use. One customer's bailiff was, before visiting Ellis, very sceptical about the new machines:

> But when I had shown this person the several drill-ploughs and horse-breaks, and the several standing crops of wheat, barley, oats, and grass &c. sown and improved by them, he seemed struck with amazement, to see the ingenuity of their contrivances, and the probable services, their structures gave him to believe, would accrue by their field and garden-uses.[70]

Ellis is not backward in claiming that what he advertises would be to the greater public good. Summing up his trade in ploughs and horse-hoes, Ellis considers that, 'by the use of this three-wheel easy worked Drill Plough, and the several instruments I have discovered in my travels, and before published in my Monthly Books, this Nation may (by the blessing of Heaven) be made to become the greatest magazine for corn in Europe'.[71] He in turn seeks aid from his (he hopes) grateful nation. He solicits new inventions that he hopes will be freely given to him to exploit in order to

---

69   Ibid., February, p. 54.
70   Ibid., February, p. 54.
71   Ibid., October, p. 167.

help defray the expenses of an author, who could not do these works without travelling often: for I am necessitated to ride to distant parts, now and then, to get master of such and such a practice, that is carried on in a particular part of the country, and nowhere else. Again, I am sometimes forced to desist from such a proceeding, because the charge would be above my pocket; and, through my inability, many a brave secret lies hid from the publick.[72]

This chapter has covered most of the goods and services Ellis offered the public and the way he advertised them. He is revealed to have been much more than a farmer and writer and show him to have been an innovative salesman and entrepreneur. In 1745 he gave a particularly detailed account of what he could supply the country gentry with by mail order:

I therefore hereby give Notice to all Gentlemen, Ladies, and others, that, on a proper Order, I will furnish them with Ploughmen, or other Men and Boy Servants, usually employed in Husbandry Affairs; as also Grooms, Dairy and other Maid-servants; and buy for them Saddle, Coach and Cart-horses, as I live near Dunstable, Leighton, and Aylesbury, where the best of these Sorts of Horses are brought several times a Year to be sold; as also Bulls, Cows, Sheep; the large Leicestershire, or the small foreign Breed of Hogs; Setting Dogs, Gun-Dogs and Pointers, broke by the best Hands in our sporting Country; Mastiffs and Shepherds Dogs; tame Rabbets of several Sorts, and Guiney Pigs; young Squirrels and Dormice, that are very plenty with us; tame Pheasants of the common or white Sort, from Half-a crown apiece to seven Shillings and Six-pence, according to their Age; Guiney Hens, white Peacocks, Muscovy and others of the best English Sort of Ducks; the large Virginia Turkey, some of which have weighed forty Pounds, Feathers and Guts included; the true Hertfordshire Breed of white Dunghill Cocks and Hens, that lay large Eggs with thin Shells, and have commonly two or three Broods of Chickens in a Year; divers Sorts of Wheat-seed, proper for particular Soils and Climates; rath-ripe, sprat, and common Barley-seed; Oats of different kinds; Tick and common Horse beans various Sorts of Rouncivals, and smaller Peas, for Field or Garden Uses; Turnep and artificial Grass-seeds, and, the most excellent of all natural and artificial Grass-seeds, that called the Lady-finger and St. Timothy Grass-seeds; Fruit and Timber young Trees, and their Sets or Seed; Hedge-wood Sets or Seeds; and all manner of Implements of Husbandry: So that Persons may have the Three-wheel Drill-plough and Horse break, Two or One-wheel common Plough, the Swing and Foot-plough without Wheels, the Marsh or Bog-Plough, the best and lightest sort of Plough for cutting Water through; the profitable Chaff, cutting Engine; several

---

72  Ibid., March, p. 113. This 'excellent cleaning hand wire-sieve' he sold 'for half a guinea' in 1747. Ellis and Trowell, *Farmer's Instructor*, p. 39.

Sorts of Instruments for improving Hop-grounds; with most or all Sorts of Utensils usually employed in Corn or Grass Dairy Farms; Furze or Whin-seeds, from our Commons; Beech-mast or Seeds, or its Sets, at Eighteen pence an Hundred; and Keroon young Cherry trees, of which particular Sort (being the best of black Cherries) I have a large Nursery, and sell them at one Shilling apiece; and which no Person should be without, for its valuable Qualities, that has a convenient Place for their Growth.[73]

Many of his advertising techniques are still in use today: advertisements disguised as sources of information; enthusiastic and detailed description; emphasis on the advantages of use; references to satisfied customers and large orders successfully undertaken; and, perhaps of most importance, promising to save customers money in the long run.

---

73 Ellis, *Agriculture Improv'd*, pp. 148–9. Although the tame rabbits he advertises might have been bred for eating, the other small animals he lists were presumably destined to be children's pets and many of the tame fowls were offered for sale to gentlemen who wanted them to strut about their lawns and look decorative.

## Chapter 5
## Food, drink and medicine

Ellis's writings on food, cookery and medicine are almost all confined to *The Country Housewife's Family Companion*, which appeared in 1750. Ellis was no cook: all his cookery recipes came from others and he did not touch a pot or pan himself. Nevertheless, this is an important work for culinary historians for it gives an insight into the kitchens of ordinary farms and labourers' cottages of the time. In the words of a distinguished historian: 'for the food historian he is one of the most precious informants of his age, shedding much light on the cooking routines of working folk'.[1] This chapter will discuss these recipes and routines, especially those used to feed harvest workers in the summer months. It will also look at the medical recipes which Ellis collected, mostly from rural informants. He records the remedies used by ordinary Hertfordshire folk to combat the illnesses to which they were prone and tells us something of the structure of rural medicine at a time when qualified doctors were few and far between, especially outside London. Moreover, doctors were expensive and, on the evidence of Ellis, often no more effective than his neighbours in curing illness.

*Collecting culinary recipes*
He gained a good deal of culinary information close to home: his maid is frequently cited as a source for recipes and the poor girl must have been fed up with his questioning. Friends and neighbours provided most of his recipes; occasional help came from gentry households, but he relied most heavily on the wives of husbandmen and yeomen, who, he hoped, would also be the bulk of his readership.

Although he did not cook himself he must have stood in his neighbours' kitchens and closely observed what was going on – this description of pancake-making reads like an eyewitness report:

---

1  Joan Thirsk, *Food in Early Modern England* (London, 2007), p. 167.

when one side of the pancake is fried enough, our housewife, or her maid-servant, turns it in a clever manner, by giving it only a toss with the frying-pan, and when this is dexterously done, it is the best way of turning them. Thus she goes on frying pancake after pancake, and as she lays them one upon the other, in a platter or dish, she sprinkles some coarse sugar for their sauce; but takes what care she can that the family eats them hot, for the hotter they eat them, the less danger there is of rising in their stomachs, if the lard should be rankish.[2]

As in his writings on agriculture, many recipes are introduced as 'The Hertfordshire way', but Ellis also gathered recipes on his travels, asking for details of dishes he ate at inns. On 13 June 1749, 'baiting at the Cat-Inn at East-Grinstead', he watched the cook–maid make Sussex pond pudding and noted the recipe.[3] On another occasion he asked at a public house for a meal to be served quickly and was impressed by a dish of pan-fried pickled pork and poached eggs.[4] He obtained a good deal of information on the use of oatmeal from Cheshire and Lancashire visitors to Hertfordshire fairs and markets.[5] The Welsh recipes scattered throughout the book were probably given to him by passing drovers or migrant workers, although a London correspondent passed on the Welsh way of preparing hogs' puddings from his wife, 'being what she practised when she lived with her Aunt in Wales', and he did go on one tour of south Wales.[6] Letters containing recipes were sometimes inserted straight into the text of *The Country Housewife* – a 'worthy gentleman' wrote from London about baked pears in 1735 and a grateful young man, whom Ellis had recommended as bailiff to a Devon estate, wrote from Plympton with a number of local recipes. These were, like many of Ellis's recipes, hearty country fare beef-steak pie, pigeon squab pie and gooseberry vinegar.[7]

As was common among cookery writers at the time, Ellis took recipes from published sources. Many suspected 'borrowings' are unacknowledged but the characteristic opening word 'Take', which he does not use for recipes written in his own words, indicate a printed source. Not that Ellis was

---

2 Ellis, *Country Housewife*, p. 72.
3 'Baiting' means dining. Sussex Pond Pudding is a small suet pudding with a hollow centre stuffed with sugar and butter. Today a sliced lemon is usually added to this mixture. The liquid centre oozes from the pudding when a spoon is inserted, somewhat akin to a sweet Chicken Kiev.
4 Ellis, *Country Housewife*, p. 287.
5 Ibid., pp. 264–5.
6 Hog's Pudding is a sausage made of pork, suet, oatmeal and barley, typically flavoured with pepper, salt, basil, cumin and garlic. It is served fried in chunks, like white or black pudding.
7 Ellis, *Country Housewife*, pp. 300–2, 311.

bashful about plagiarism: he freely admits to copying from other books. His culinary reading was, however, quite narrow and almost entirely of very old cookery books. He took recipes from works published in the first half of the seventeenth century in the main: those of Gervase Markham, John Murrell, William Rabisha and Kenelm Digby. John Houghton, who wrote in the 1690s, was a source and the more recent *Country Housewife and Lady's Director* of Richard Bradley was also mentioned, although Ellis did not like this latter work. Either he looked at the old books because they had the traditional country recipes he sought or, more probably, these were the works he found in a local gentleman's library to which he had access.[8]

As to the recipes themselves, Ellis's *Country Housewife* is the best book of the period to consult for plain country fare, the everyday food of the families of labourers, husbandmen and yeomen. Although he had lived in London and must have made frequent journeys there on business, Ellis ignores all fashionable food. There are no ragouts or fricassees here, nothing *à la crème*, no bisques, not a salad, and butter the only sauce. Meat recipes are for plain roasted joints, roasted, baked and fried offal and cheaper cuts such as ox cheek. Many recipes are given for brawn and haslet. Meat could also be boiled, placed in pies or used to flavour puddings. Puddings, both savoury and sweet, abound. Ellis explained that 'PUDDING is so necessary a Part of an Englishman's FOOD, that it and Beef are accounted the Victuals they most love.'[9] Black, white and hogs' puddings were by-products of killing a pig and pigs were the most usual source of meat in Ellis's recipes – but these puddings were types of sausage, different from the puddings extolled by Ellis above. Pease soup, broth, gruels, frumenty, porridge, possets and similar wet and stodgy foods reflect a diet that in some ways had changed little in centuries.[10]

Some of the foods mentioned may be unfamiliar to a modern reader. Haslet is today a pork-meat loaf made from minced or chopped lean pork, breadcrumbs, onion, herbs and spices. In Ellis's time it was made of the spleen, lungs and neck of a pig roasted then minced and formed into a loaf. Served cut into slices, it was often eaten cold. Brawn is made from offcuts of cooked pork or cooked and chopped pig's head. It is encased in gelatine and often eaten cold in slices. Black, white and hogs' puddings share oat or

---

8   The books he made use of were probably Gervase Markham, *The English Housewife* (London, 1615); John Murrell, *Murrell's Two Books of Cookerie and Carving* (London, 1638); William Rabisha, *The Whole Body of Cookery Dissected* (London, 1661); Sir Kenelm Digby, *The Closet of the Eminently Learned Sir Kenelm Digby, Kt, Opened* (London, 1669); John Houghton, *Collection of Letters for The Improvement of Husbandry and Trade* (London, 1692); Bradley, *The Country Housewife*.

9   Ellis, *Country Housewife*, p. 78.

10  Ibid., pp. 78–84.

barley meal, pork fat, pork meat and various spices and herbs as ingredients, and are encased in sausage skins. Black puddings are made with pig's blood and white puddings without the blood, while hogs' puddings are spicier and often have more offal than white puddings. Frumenty is essentially a porridge made from barley or wheat grains usually boiled in milk. For added richness dried fruits, sugar and spices were added. A posset was a hot drink flavoured with nutmeg or cinnamon that was made by boiling milk and adding ale or wine to curdle it. Gruel was a watery porridge, often drunk rather than eaten. Made from any type of grain, it was considered the food of the poor.

Pudding, considered the basis of most English meals, came in many varieties, some baked but most boiled, and Ellis provides many recipes. His own serving maid's pudding made a frequent appearance on his dinner table:

> It is also my way to have a plain pudding made most days in the year; and for doing it, my maid-servant mixes a pint of new milk with a quart of flower, one egg, a little salt, and the powder of ginger. This, when she has flower'd her pudding-bag, she puts into it, and boils it in an hour and a half or two hours.[11]

This is a typical plain pudding, hovering in taste between sweet and savoury. His household also consumed with relish a sweet apple pudding, especially if there was a glut of apples.

> To make it, my servant-maid boils a pint of milk with a quarter of a pound of lard or dripping, then mixes it with as much flower as will make it into a dough or paste, rolls it, and when the paste is cool and stiff enough, she puts on it sliced or minced apples, which she incloses in the paste; then puts it into a cloth, ties it up, and boils it two hours and a half at least; our sauce is melted butter with sugar, or sugar and milk.[12]

The common thread running through the recipes is economy. 'Cheap' is the word most frequently encountered in the recipe headings. One such economical dish closely allied to apple pudding was apple pie; as well as being 'a main part of a prudent, frugal Farmer's Family-Food', Ellis genuinely liked it. He accounted apple pie 'some of the cheapest and most agreeable Food a Farmer's Family can make use of' and filled two pages with a poem in praise of pies. Apple pasties could be pocketed and eaten by farmers and their servants in the fields. Ellis had his maid make apple pasties every week

---

11   Ellis, *Country Housewife*, pp. 81–2.
12   Ibid.

or ten days to feed harvesters 'from August to all the Time when my hoarded apples last'.[13]

Frugal housewives were singled out for praise. Mindful that some of his readers were richer than others, some dishes have plain versions for the poor and variants with added cream, meat, fruit or sugar for the gentry. This is a recurring theme. The section on *'The use of Pease in Families'* is typical. Three recipes for 'pease-porridge' from farmers' wives are given: first a poor man's family recipe; then pease-soup made by a gentleman, 'my next neighbour' (which contained much meat and milk); finally, he supplies the 'Hertfordshire way' of making green pease-porridge, and tells us what types of pea he sows to use in his own pease-porridge and pease-pudding.[14]

Pancakes, which were 'one of the cheapest and most serviceable Dishes of a Farmer's Family in particular', were another dish with different ingredients given according to wealth. The poor could eat barley-meal pancakes, or Water Pancakes; a slightly more palatable alternative was 'Hertfordshire plain cheap Pancakes for Farmers Families etc.' 'Pancakes [...] for rich People', with butter, cream and eggs, were eaten strewn with sugar. Another luxury recipe was for 'Apple Pancakes for the Gentry'. Although his recipes are predominantly for the poor and 'middling sort' of country families, Ellis tries to include recipes suitable for his gentry neighbours, but even here he concentrates on 'country recipes' – the recipes from London tavern cooks or French chefs found in Bradley's book are absent.[15]

## Bread

Ellis is unusual in spending some time discussing bread and giving recipes for making it. Most cookery books of the time ignore bread, apart from French bread, either because, in London, most bread was bought in from bakers, or because it was considered such a basic skill that all cooks knew how to make it. This is disputed by professional bakers, who tell Ellis that many countrywomen mix all the ingredients as fast as possible, do not let the dough rise long enough and put their loaves straight into the oven without leaving them to 'ferment, swell, and rise'.[16] Ellis agrees that country housewives need advice; he is surprised, for instance, that he can find no book that gives directions for using 'grown wheat' – that is, wheat that has sprouted because it has been soaked by rain before harvest. He considers that

---

13  Ibid., pp. 84–7. The term 'pasty' was in common use for these triangular filled pastries all over England by 1750 and not solely in Cornwall.
14  Ibid., pp. 290–3.
15  Ibid., pp. 71–5, 126–9.
16  Ibid., p. 63.

11. Frontispiece of *Dictionarium Domesticum*, 1736, showing the domestic activities of a country housewife.

the lack of information on bread in cookery books for country housewives is because the authors are London-based, somewhat long-windedly explaining:

> if books of this nature are wrote in a London chamber; for then, in course, their authors must be deprived of that necessary country knowledge as is requisite for enabling them to write those full and genuine instructions, which are perfectly wanted to assist a country housewife, in carrying on a true oeconomy in managing her domestic affairs in the cheapest and most housewifely manner, for her family's greater advantage.[17]

He approaches the topic of bread methodically, starting both the first and second parts of *The Country Housewife* with his opinions on the best types of wheat to make into bread. Several pages are devoted to storing wheat as grain and flour. Dry conditions were essential, as was occasional stirring to prevent fermentation, mustiness or 'stinking'. The storage conditions should also try to keep out insects, worms, mites and any other creatures which might ruin the flour or grain. Ellis is considering storage from the point of view of the small farmer or labourer, who bought or ground his flour or grain a sack at a time and could not afford to lose this to disease or infestation. Ellis is suspicious of millers, thinking that some cheat customers by putting inferior flour with that which they return to them.[18]

Yeast was an expensive commodity for the poor but essential for bread-making. Ellis considers ways of storing it for future use: in cold water; in a pitcher with a bladder stretched over the top to seal it; or in stopped-up bottles. An alternative to preserving yeast from one baking to the next was to use leaven. This is a piece of dough from the latest batch of bread which is used as a starter for the next lot. Ellis recommended the dough (about the size of a fist) be preserved in salt. When used it should be dissolved in warm water and sieved to remove hard bits. The liquid should be mixed with some flour to make a thin paste which is then covered with the rest of the flour. This is left overnight. Next morning half as much yeast as normal should be added and the mixture kneaded into a stiff dough, formed into loaves with holes pricked in the tops to let out surplus air when cooking, and baked. This is sourdough, or will be after some time, for 'The staler the leaven the closer [that is denser] will be the bread, and the sooner sour.'[19]

Some of his neighbours sold their home-grown wheat at market and bought inferior grain for their own consumption. Being close to London,

---

17  Ibid., p. 51.
18  Ibid., pp. 41, 46–8, 248, 260–2.
19  Ibid., pp. 54–61.

Hertfordshire markets were sensitive to fluctuations in supply and demand and farmers could easily calculate whether eating their own corn was the best option – Ellis thought it usually was.[20] He describes the common Hertfordshire recipe for making wheaten bread and another recipe for half barley and half wheat bread, a cheaper option. This recipe involves grinding the two grains together, warming skimmed milk and adding yeast to it, then adding this to the flour. Using milk rather than water takes off any bitterness of the yeast and makes the bread 'hollower, sweeter, and whiter'. Ellis comments that the 'use of barley-meal in making bread was very much in practice amongst the poor people in Hertfordshire and elsewhere'. A labourer's wife tells him how to avoid barley bread becoming cracked and hard: knead the dough until it is tender and soft. A yeoman's wife who brought up a large family subsisting on barley bread also used milk to make her dough.[21] This latter bread went against the social hierarchy of bread: finest wheat bread for the richer and coarse wheat or barley bread for the poor. Ellis finds such social stratification in Suffolk's wheat flour. The finest is used by the farmer's wife for 'manchet to eat with tea'; the second grade is for 'the master's and mistress's table'; and a third for servants. A boulting hutch was used to sift out these various grades. Ellis, like some other commentators before him, thought that the bread with a fair proportion of bran in it eaten by Suffolk servants contributed to their robust health: 'it is remarkable, that most of the people of this country look with a fresher colour than those in any other county in England'. It is noticeable that the poor, although constrained to eat barley bread, took care to handle it in such a way as to make it palatable.[22]

Agricultural historians do not agree on the extent that wheaten bread was eaten in England in the eighteenth century. Sir William Ashley, in 1928, thought that 95 per cent of the population ate it by 1800, while George Fussell in 1929 thought the percentage was 90. Ted Collins in 1975 thought the percentage of wheat-eaters was lower than conventionally assumed and put the figure at 70 per cent overall, with more consumption in the south-east than elsewhere. In view of the instances of barley bread and mixed grain bread recorded by Ellis, Collins's lower estimate would seem most likely.[23]

---

20  Ibid., p. 42.
21  Ibid., pp. 62–4.
22  Ibid., pp. 67, 250.
23  For a full discussion of the composition of bread eaten in the countryside in the eighteenth century see Malcolm Thick, 'Breads of the English Husbandman and Woman, c.1750', *Petite Propos Culinaires*, 104 (2015), pp. 89–105.

## Oatmeal

Ellis is impressed by the actual, and potential, uses of oatmeal: 'Oats are so valuable a pulse, that their meal is made use of in many nations', especially in northern Europe, where many grain crops do not thrive. He believes there are six grades of meal from which oatcakes can be made, from the coarsest-ground to fine-ground mixed with wheatmeal, which 'maketh a dainty oatcake, such that no prince in the world but may have them served at his table'.[24] He points out that oatmeal is the main constituent of white and black puddings and that gruel and flummery are made from it, as is loblolly or burgoo. It is used to stuff a goose and is made into porridge. 'In short, the right management of oatmeal ought to be one of the chiefest parts of a housewife's study and care.'[25]

Ellis gets his own oatmeal from Leighton in Bedfordshire, because 'there it is exceedingly smaller ground'. This fine oatmeal keeps well because it packs down tight in a pot or bin, and it is quickly prepared. He gives recipes for boiled and baked oatmeal puddings from as far afield as Cheshire, as well as Hertfordshire ones. A typical baked Hertfordshire oatmeal pudding is made thus:

> We first boil a pint of grouts or oatmeal, which is commonly sold for five-pence the pottle; when boiled tender, we mix it with a quart of milk, half a pound of chopt beef suet (but hogslard or flair[26] is better) half a pound of plumbs, two eggs and some sugar, and bake it.

To make a boiled Hertfordshire oatmeal pudding the oats are soaked in milk then mixed with half a pound of suet and half a pound of plums. The mixture is boiled in a bag. The poor substitute water for milk. It eats moister than its baked equivalent: 'However, it is accounted by all a wholesome, palatable, good pudding.'[27]

## Potatoes

Apart from potatoes and dried peas, Ellis does not bother much with recipes for vegetables. Pease soup, porridge or pudding he regarded as cheap and filling, but he sees potatoes as a food of the future. Potatoes were already a

---

24 This author is very fond of oatcakes made with fine oatmeal, white plain flour, butter and salt.
25 Ellis, *Country Housewife*, pp. 269–70. Burgoo is today a mixed meat stew eaten often out of doors in the USA, especially in Kentucky. Loblolly is another type of stew, made with grains but not usually with oatmeal. Flummery, today a cream-based dessert, was, in Ellis's time, made from soaking oatmeal, then boiling the liquor drained from it until it became a jelly.
26 Flair is pig fat from around the kidneys or in the loin. It makes the best suet.
27 Ellis, *Country Housewife*, pp. 264–79.

staple in the north of England and Ellis remarks that 'At Manchester, a great Market in Lancashire, Potatoes stand in many Sacks as well as Oatmeal for publick Sale.'[28] Ellis sees much potential in potatoes to sustain the poor, who ate them mashed with milk or made into a hasty-pudding with added flour. He claims a diet with potatoes is a safeguard against scurvy, but, as a food for the poor, 'this noble root supplies, in a great measure, the scarcity of meat and bread, and becomes, in a large degree, part of many poor families subsistence', serving 'to save much Consumption of eggs, Meat, and Bread'.[29] His upbeat assessment of potatoes for the poor is in contrast to the opinion of Cobbett in the 1820s: 'It is a root of slovenliness, filth, misery, and slavery; its cultivation has increased in England with the increase of paupers.' Cobbett thought potatoes dragged English labourers down to the condition of the Irish.[30]

Despite his emphasis on potatoes as a food for the poor, Ellis acknowledged that richer people were eating potatoes because

> its nourishing and healthy qualities [...] of late, has tempted the great part of the wisest of our nobility, to feed on the potatoe as one of the best of supper victuals, during all their season; when they give an ingenious cook an opportunity of employing his skill, in a way of preparing them.[31]

He then describes the many ways in which country housewives cook potatoes, revealing that they were becoming increasingly common at Hertfordshire farmers' tables:

> where these earth apples can be conveniently had she often boils them with either a piece of bacon, pork, or salt beef, or by themselves, and when boiled she takes off their skins [...] thus boiled, she lays them in a dish under meat to be eaten without butter or any other sauce, except pepper and salt, or in a dripping pan under roast beef, mutton etc. for their being improved by the fat and gravy that drops down on them while the meat is roasting.[32]

There follows a long list of other ways to cook and serve potatoes: boiled, then cut up and fried with onions or garlic; stewed with meat and onions in

---

28  Ibid., p. 295.
29  Ellis, *Modern Husbandman*, February, pp. 74, 81. Potatoes are a good source of vitamin C and so would protect against scurvy.
30  William Cobbett, *Cottage Economy* (London, 1824), paras 77, 80, 84, 85.
31  Ellis, *Modern Husbandman*, February, p. 81.
32  Ellis, *Country Housewife*, pp. 293–4.

ale; baked with herrings or pilchards; mashed and seasoned with herbs and spices; boiled with milk and sugar; roasted in embers; mashed and made into a pudding with currants and suet; baked in a pie with meat; in a sweet pie with raisins, suet, butter sugar, marrow and maybe apples; boiled and eaten with salt fish; and in a pie with pig's offal.[33]

## *Preserving*

Cookery books in Ellis's time usually devoted many pages to preserving all sorts of food. *The Compleat Housewife* of 1753, for instance, had over 100 recipes in a section on preserving. Whole books were devoted to preserving all sorts of delicate fruits, in syrup, dried or as jams and preserves, providing the raw material for elaborate confectionery. Mary Eales's much reprinted book *The Compleat Confectioner* (1733) is a prime example. As he was addressing a country audience, Ellis does not bother much with delicate fruits for confectionary; he was concerned with the range of produce that might come from a farmer's wife's garden or yard. Nevertheless, preserving was an important skill for a farmer's wife to master, providing variety in the diet all year round. He brings out the diligence with which country housewives preserved a variety of foods that could make dishes for special occasions such as Christmas. Here we have a hint of occasional indulgence, breaking the oft-repeated theme of economy.[34]

Ellis describes a range of preserving methods, including five methods for preserving potatoes: drying them in a kiln and storing in a dry place; covering them in the ground with straw; keeping them in a cellar covered in straw; drying them in the sun; or digging a narrow trench in dry soil, lining it with straw and filling it with potatoes, adding straw, and capping with earth. Carrots, turnips and parsnips may be kept in a similar manner to potatoes, including storing them in a dry room between wheat straw. More fleshy vegetables, such as French or kidney beans, might be kept in large glazed pots between layers of salt. Cabbages and cauliflowers could be harvested and covered in straw, they might be left in the ground with their outer leaves tied over them, or they could be hung by their stalks in a dry place.[35]

Fruit might be kept in a variety of ways. Hard fruits such as apples and pears could be carefully picked over so that all those with any rot were discarded, then placed separately on floorboards with straw over them. Alternatively, apples and pears could be baked whole, after which the liquid was squeezed out of them and they were dried on sieves. Ellis advised

---

33  Ibid., pp. 293–5.
34  Smith, *The Compleat Housewife*; Mary Eales, *The Compleat Confectioner* (London, 1733).
35  Ellis, *Country Housewife*, pp. 295–8.

bottling soft fruits; some, such as cherries, were bottled raw without sugar or syrup in close-stopped jars; other,s such as gooseberries, were bottled and then cooked in their bottles. Delicate fruits such as nectarines, peaches and apricots kept well resting on a bed of wood ashes in a box, with another layer of ashes put over them.[36]

Ellis spends many pages in the *Country Housewife* describing various methods of pickling pork for future use and also devotes space to preserving bacon. He praises both these meats but particularly bacon as an ideal food for an ordinary farmer's family: 'Bacon is a serviceable, palatable, profitable, and clean meat, for a ready use in a country house.' It was easy to prepare, universally available and relatively cheap. It made a satisfying meal: 'Where there is bread and bacon, there is no want', he declared. Ellis describes many ways of curing and smoking bacon from his own locality and various places he has visited but he also sounds a cautionary note about some bacon produced in London. A 'London seller of bacon', not knowing who Ellis was, boasted about how quickly he could produce bacon. Hogs were killed in the early morning, salted for a maximum of a week, smoked for between twelve and twenty-four hours, and then sent to market. The meat would 'eat sweet and good' at first but would soon grow rank for lack of preservative.[37]

### *Dairy and calves*

The dairy was, from the earliest times, the domain of the farmer's wife, deriving its name from the Middle English 'dey', a serving maid, and 'erie', her place of work.[38] After an unsatisfactory attempt to cover the topic in part one (only eleven pages were devoted to it, almost all the text being concerned with the health of cows), Ellis does give a full description of dairying in the second part of the *Country Housewife*. But there is more here than dairying. He has much to say on improved grasses and fodder crops for cattle, including, characteristically, an advertisement for his own seed business. We learn about specialties in many other parts of the country: correspondents write about Devonshire clotted cream and a dairymaid reveals Somerset dairying methods; Welsh butter producers coloured their butter with marigold flowers to make it a pleasing yellow colour. In this book and in *The Modern Husbandman* cheese-making methods in Cambridgeshire, Somerset, Cheshire, Wales, Gloucestershire and Shropshire are described, thanks largely to talkative dairymaids. Ellis also mentions a mixed ewe's and cow's milk cheese made in the Vale of Glamorgan and he found another one close

---

36  Ibid., pp. 299–300.
37  Ibid., pp. 147, 150.
38  Robin Weir and Caroline Liddell, *Recipes from the Dairy* (London, 1998), p. 9.

to home made by a Hertfordshire gentleman 'for his family's use; and so delicate a sort it proved, that it was preferred to all others'. Cheese, durable and portable, was a major item of commerce for many areas. Butter too was a valuable commodity. Dairies near London sold it fresh, but those further afield salted it in pots or barrels for sale and country people did the same with butter for use at home. Ellis met a grazier from Towcester on the road who told him he sold butter to London the year round.[39]

The section on veal calf production was included as this part of a farm was supervised by the farmer's wife. It was a by-product of dairying which, Ellis claimed, might be sometimes more profitable than butter or cheese. He sold his calves at Leighton market to specialist calf-rearers who prepared them for the London markets (the pull of London's demand is evident here as in many aspects of Hertfordshire husbandry).[40] The descriptions of cramming calves for market and bleeding them to produce the white flesh demanded by London customers are not pleasant reading but they do further remind us that, by the mid-eighteenth century, many farmers near the capital tailored their production closely to the whims of consumers and thereby made a good living.[41]

## *Other farmyard produce*

Ellis gives advice on other 'farmyard' activities, such as pig-keeping, poultry and eggs, which had traditionally been tasks for the country housewife to perform, producing food for the family or, at most, pin money for wives and daughters. By the mid-eighteenth century, however, such was the demand from London for eggs, fowls, milk and cheese, as well as the butter and veal mentioned above, that these by-occupations had economic importance, especially in counties such as Hertfordshire, near to the capital. Ellis notes that Hertfordshire Dunghill Fowls and their eggs were highly esteemed in London 'insomuch that the very cryers of eggs about London Streets take particular care to make the Word Hertfordshire be well known'. The money to be made from poultry was recognised by Hertfordshire farmers, who let their wives have all the profit, but only to buy 'what we call common or trivial Necessaries in the House, as Sugar, Plumbs, Spices, Salt, Oatmeal &c. &c.'[42] These 'trivial' items form part of some of Ellis's recipes and were luxuries that lifted a diet which might otherwise become monotonous. Ellis

---

39   Ellis, *Modern Husbandman*, May, pp. 86–98; June, p. 132.
40   The price of veal increased significantly the closer one got to London at this time. Thirsk, *Agricultural History of England and Wales*, vol. V, pt 1, p. 233.
41   Ibid., pp. 193–4.
42   Ellis, *Country Housewife*, p. 211.

recognised that for some poultry-keeping had become big business, no longer the province of wives. Turkeys and geese were kept in large flocks in East Anglia, being driven to London for sale to poulterers.[43]

## Food for harvest workers

Much attention is given in *The Country Housewife* to food and drink for harvest workers. Although the theme of economy runs strongly through Ellis's book, here he emphasises that a balance had to be struck between frugality and generosity for the few weeks of summer harvest in order to keep the harvesters working hard. Other agricultural writers recognised the problem that the brief season of harvest (two, three or four weeks in the case of the grain harvest) was a period when the usual mastery of farmers over labourers was reversed – for these few weeks the farmer was at the mercy of the labourer. Farmers desperately wanted all the effort expended in growing the crops to be crowned with a swift and efficient harvest. The anonymous writer of the fourth edition of *The Complete Farmer* in 1807 explained:

> The method of engaging labourers for harvest-work is nearly the same in all the districts of the kingdom: part, or all, of the constant workmen upon the farm receive harvest-pay for a certain number of weeks: and the extra hands agree for their work by the acre, according to the condition of the crop, heavy or light, lodged or upright.[44]

William Ellis gave a similar picture of harvest wages in 1750s Hertfordshire:

> In this county we hire harvest-men long before harvest, by way of security, that we may not be at a loss for them when we most want them: and give each man thirty or thirty and six shillings for his month's service, besides victualling and lodging them in the house all that time, for then they are ready early and late to do our work.[45]

As important as the high wages paid was the quality and quantity of food provided by the farmer, and good food might, in the end, save money, for, as Daniel Hillman remarked in his 1710 edition of Thomas Tusser's book on agriculture, 'for all that time they do expect a full Dyet, and he that keeps a plentiful House, shall have more Servants at Command another year, than he

---

43 Ibid., p. 225.
44 Ellis, *Country Housewife*, p. 94; Anon, *Complete Farmer* (London, 1807), heading 'August'. 'Lodged' means flattened by wind and/or rain.
45 Not all were lodged in the farmhouse; many spent the night on straw in a barn – not too uncomfortable in August.

had that gives a Crown more in wages, and pinches, neither shall his Work be so well done'.[46]

It is the balance between feeding harvesters well and at the same time doing it without needless expense that runs through Ellis's advice to his readers – he devoted some thirty pages to this topic in the *Country Housewife*.[47] He describes how he victuals harvest workers and how others he knows of do this, and he gives advice to other employers of harvest workers. The emphasis is on keeping the men happy while spending as little as possible on their food and drink: 'Now on victualling these men there are varieties of ways practised by country housewives; and she that can do it cheapest, and most satisfactory, is the best housewife.'[48]

Ellis summarises his harvest workers' typical daily diet and work routine: 'In wheat harvest time, which commonly lasts about a fortnight, our men set out for the field by four of the clock in the morning, and return home about eight at night. In Lent grain harvest time later in the morning and sooner at night, as the days are shorter.' Note the sixteen-hour day in the main harvest season; it is no wonder that 'the men generally eat five times a day'. For breakfast, 'at their first setting out, they eat a little bread and cheese or apple-pye, with a draught of small beer, or half a pint of strong each man, in part of his quart for the day'. A second breakfast is taken in the field:

> At eight o'clock some send for breakfast, boiled milk crumbed with bread, others, milk-porridge with bread; others posset with bread, and bread and cheese besides, or instead of bread and cheese, apple-pasty; others send into the field, for breakfast, hashed or minced meat left over the day before; others send it cold (as left) but hashing or mincing is best, because if it is a little tainted, it is thus taken off by a mixture of shred onions and parsley, or with butter and vinegar, which relishes it, and makes it well suffice for a breakfast, and now they drink only small beer.

The men were very hungry by dinner time and it was important to have the food in the field in a timely manner:

> At dinner time, which should be always at one o'clock, the victuals should be in the field; for it was the saying of a notable housewife, that as the men expected it at

---

46 Daniel Hillman, *Tusser redivivus: being part of Mr. Thomas Tusser's Five hundred points of husbandry* (London, 1710), p. 4.
47 Ellis, *Country Housewife*, p. 94.
48 Ibid., pp. 84–8, 94–129.

that hour, if it was not brought accordingly, they would lag in their work, and lose time in expecting it. Broad beans and bacon or pork one day, beef and carrots, or turnips, or cabbage, or cucumbers, or potatoes, another day, is, with plumb-pudding in wheat-harvest-time, and plain pudding in Lent harvest, good dinner victuals.

The men worked for another couple of hours, until

> four o'clock in the afternoon [...] what we call cheesing-time, that is to say, a time when the men sit on the ground for half an hour to eat bread and cheese with some apple-pasty, and drink some strong beer; then to work again, and hold it till near eight of the clock at night, when all leave off and come home to supper, where is prepared for them, messes of new milk crum'd with bread, or posset sugar'd and crum'd with bread, or fat bacon or pickled pork boiled hot with broad beans but although fat bacon at night is in common use with some farmers, with roots or with beans, yet others refuse to make this supper victuals, because it is apt to make men sick. No matter, say some, we must give them that which cloys their stomachs soonest. But my way is this: I allow them most nights a supper on hot milk crum'd well with bread, apple-pasty and bread and cheese if they will eat it. – Others sometimes give harvest-men wigs sop'd in ale for supper, or a seed loaf or cake cut in pieces, done after the same manner.[49]

As well as a summary of the food consumed by harvesters in a normal day, Ellis goes into more detail on some foods, gives variations in the diets of labourers hired by his neighbours, and digresses into various methods of preserving meat in summer. Meat was the central part of the harvester's diet but buying it from butchers was expensive (and Ellis had a profound mistrust of butchers). A way to lessen the expense was to provide meat from one's own farm, especially if the animals were coming to the end of their useful lives, such as 'broken-mouthed sheep (that is to say, such who by age have lost most of their teeth before)'. These were put 'into good grass' and fattened for slaughter at harvest time. Farmers with larger labour forces might slaughter an old cow, sharing some of the meat with neighbours who reciprocated when they slaughtered such a beast.[50] One thing had to be bought from butchers: a good store of suet for puddings. Introducing the 'Hertfordshire way of Making plumb-pudding in Harvest Time', Ellis remarks that 'Pudding is so natural to our harvest men, that without it they think they cannot make an agreeable dinner.'[51]

---

49  Ibid., pp. 121–2. Wigs are small, light buns, sometimes flavoured with caraway.
50  Ibid., p. 94.
51  Ibid., p. 78.

Pork was much used at harvest time,

> for its being a most pleasant and serviceable meat, especially for the diet of harvestmen now and then, because a porker, newly killed, admits of many ways of dressing it, is cheaper done, is less cloying, and keeps [salted] sweet and sound longer than any other meat whatsoever.

Many pages are devoted to ways of preserving pork, mostly culled from Ellis's neighbours. He recommends making pork pies from odd cuts of pork for harvest consumption.[52]

Vegetables helped the meat go further:

> In our Chiltern country of Hertfordshire, several of our prudent housewives forsee the great conveniency of having broad beans, pease, carrots, turnips, potatoes, cabbages, onions, parsley and other kitchen ware, ready for use against a want of them in harvest-time; for that some of these not only prove a sauce, but also help meat to go the further.[53]

He is especially keen on broad beans,

> for it is this most cheap and serviceable vegetable which allays thirst, and so relishes fat bacon, or salt pork, that the men often eat it with a good stomach, to the saving of much expense in the consumption of beef and other meat; it is easy of carriage to the field, and will keep hot some time, and prove a very wholesome nourishing vegetables [...] carrots, turnips, cabbage and potatoes, are also good kitchen provision to be eaten with salt or fresh meat.[54]

Savoury herbs and onions, especially Welsh onions, were useful to disguise tainted meat when boiled with it and peas were 'cooling and pleasant to the taste'. As well as being informative on harvest food, Ellis portrays rural Hertfordshire as a place where ordinary folk generally sat down to meals not dominated by meat but with many vegetables as well.[55] Ellis also devotes a page to cheese consumption during the harvest: 'so great a stress is then laid on this eatable'. As already noted, workers ate bread and cheese every afternoon at four o'clock.[56]

---

52 Ibid., pp. 98–120.
53 Ibid., p. 97.
54 Ibid., p. 98.
55 Ibid., pp. 97–8.
56 Ibid., pp. 123–4.

As well as savoury dishes, Ellis has some recommendations for sweet foods to give to harvest workers. His fondness for apple pies and pasties has already been noted:

> Apple pyes and pasties are a main part of a prudent, frugal farmers family-food, because the meal and apples that make them are commonly the produce of his land, and are ready at all times to be made use of in pyes or pasties [...] a covered or turn-over pasty for the field.[57]

An additional reason for including apple-based food was that Ellis had a nursery of young Parsnip Apples, the cooking apple peculiar to his home village, which he advertised for sale.

Cake was another sweet food Ellis recommended for harvesters. He gives recipes for wigs – small sweet buns – and several for filling cakes such as seed cake, plum cake and spice loaf. Seed cake 'serves for beaver [drinking time] victuals upon a change [...] it is sent into the field about four of the afternoon with some cheese, for the harvest men to eat this cake dry with.' He also recommends spice-loaf and Hertfordshire Plumb Cake for harvest time, and he gives detailed directions for making dishes to satisfy harvest workers.

The recipe for Harvest Posset the Hertfordshire way:

> The maid servant boils new milk, and when it is done she puts about a pint in each man's dish, and immediately adds a quarter of a pint of stale strong beer, some coarse sugar and crumbled bread, which turns the milk into a posset, and gives the men a palatable supper.

The recipe for 'A Hertfordshire Plumb-cake for Harvest' was:

> a quart of flower, a quartern of currants, or half a pound of Smyrna raisins [...] a quartern of sugar, four spoonfuls of yeast, some warm milk made better by the addition of a little cream, grated nutmeg, and some carraway-seeds.[58]

> To make a Hertfordshire Seed-Cake for Harvest-men. This cake is made [...] by stirring flower, yeast, milk mix'd with some cream, sugar, and carraway-seeds, which, after being kneaded and fermented, is baked in a round, deep, earthen or tin pan, on a hearth, or at the oven's mouth, and serves for beaver victuals upon a change.

---

57  Ibid., pp. 84–5.
58  Ibid., pp. 126–9.

Wigs, small sweet buns that were light and airy, were a particular favourite of Ellis's harvest workers. A recipe from 1760 for these was:

> Take a pound and a half of flour, and half a pint of milk made warm, mix these together, cover it up, and let it be by the fire half an hour, then take half a pound of sugar and half a pound of butter, then work these into a paste and make it into wigs, with as little flour as possible. Let the oven by pretty quick, and they will rise very much. Mind to mix a quarter of a pint of good ale yeast in the milk.[59]

Ellis concludes that the most important principle when victualling harvesters is to provide them with lots of appetising food:

> In short, it is our notion in Hertfordshire, that that gentleman, yeoman, or farmer, manages best, who victuals his harvest-men with beef, bacon, or pickled pork, beans, pease, puddings, pyes, pastie, cheese, milk, with other culinary preparations, and all with well brew'd strong and small beer and ale; for such a one ranks the best chance of hiring the best hands, that will go on briskly with their work, and do a good deal of it in a day.[60]

This wholesome and enjoyable food was, nevertheless, to be provided in the most economical way, but Ellis's emphasis on economy never goes as far as parsimony. Many recipes in the *Country Housewife* come from his own household and a dinner of a cut off the joint, a baked pudding, fresh vegetables in season and preserved ones at other times, followed by apple pie and cheese or baked pears, sounds appetising fare. And many of his relatively poor neighbours may have been eating almost as well – Craig Muldrew sums up Ellis's writing on food thus: 'All in all, Ellis provides us with the best single account of how labouring families ate and how their food was prepared and he certainly shows that labourers ate a more varied diet than common stereotypes about bread and cheese and pottage would have us believe'.[61]

## *Medicine*
Food was recognised as a crucial component of a healthy lifestyle in the eighteenth century, but many diseases required medicine to cure them or at least treat the symptoms. Only in the *Country Housewife* does Ellis write about medical matters. He had no medical training that we know of but

---

59   Hannah Glasse, *The Art of Cookery made Plain and Easy* (London, 1760) p. 277.
60   Ibid., p. 95.
61   Craig Muldrew, *Food, Energy and the Creation of Industriousness* (London, 2011), p. 45.

as head of a rural household he had to have some knowledge of medicine to keep himself and family well, especially as his second wife, who in normal circumstances would have been in charge of medical matters in the household, may have been no longer able to carry out this responsibility. He draws on this knowledge to provide many of the prescriptions in the book, sometimes telling us of specific ills he has cured. The medical sections of the book provide an insight into the social history of medicine in eighteenth-century Hertfordshire and remind us that life was hard at a time when so many ailments were likely to lead to death.

In his usual disordered fashion, Ellis imposed no system on the sections in the book on medicine. In the first part a passage headed 'Of Cheap, Approved, and Experienced MEDICINES and REMEDIES for Divers DISEASES incident to Human Bodies' gives out after seventeen pages with some sensational tales of poisoning. The more modest heading 'Diseases and Medicines' in Part Two opens a more substantial section of over fifty pages. One has the impression that here, as with other parts of the book, Ellis knew he had to cover this topic but he made a start with little research and had to come back to it: the first medical section is largely composed of letters to Ellis from various gentlemen with advice and prescriptions. In the end, however, he covered much ground, giving advice on the most troublesome diseases of his time, notably ague, consumption, diabetes, scurvy, smallpox, gout, dropsy, jaundice, King's Evil, measles, palsy, rheumatism, digestive disorders, swellings and skin diseases. Sprains, cuts and wounds, the hazards of hard labour and crude tools, are dealt with, as well as ailments of damp, cold, dirty living with a poor diet: lice, worms and other parasites, sore eyes, sore throats, coughs, indigestion, cramp, chilblains, chaps, toothache and general aches and pains.[62]

Ellis obtained his cures from many sources. He looked for some of his medicines in books. However, he made only about twenty references to books and those he identified were contemporary, unlike the old cookery books he used. He may have consulted the medical section of the library he used for printed sources. If this was that of his neighbour, the duke of Bridgewater, given the duke's interest in medicine, it may have been more up to date on medicine than cookery. Several times he referred to 'Dr Quincy', consulting his *Pharmacopoeia officinalis* of 1749.[63] He also used Thomas Dover's *The ancient physicians legacy* of 1733[64] and publications of the

---

62 Ellis, *Country Housewife*, pp. 192–210, 315–79.

63 John Quincey, *Pharmacopoeia officinalis & extemporanea: or, a compleat English dispensatory* (London, 1722).

64 Thomas Dover, *The ancient physician's legacy to his country, being what he has collected in forty-nine years practice* (London, 1733).

celebrated Low Countries physician Herman Boerhaave.[65] As might be expected, the prescriptions from these sources usually meant a trip to the apothecary for mercury, sulphur, turpentine, 'bark' (quinine) and the like.

Most of Ellis's medical advice came from his friends and acquaintances. Margaret Pelling has shown that medicine was of concern to all classes in early modern England and that, especially in towns, recipes for cures circulated freely, often across class boundaries. There were many more men and women engaged full- or part-time in medicine than there were university-educated doctors or formally apprenticed apothecaries, a situation reflected in Ellis's book. He did have advice from one fully qualified surgeon, his son William. William wrote to his father about the virtues of wood sage, quoting John Ray, who advocated the plant as a substitute for hops in beer as well as a cure for urinary infections.[66]

About forty of his cures were provided by the gentry, with whom Ellis would be in regular contact in the course of his business. Examples include a supposed cure for consumption provided by a Derbyshire gentleman, or the 'Gentleman Traveller' who regulated his system with Flower of Brimstone. Most medical advice from the gentry was obtained locally: a neighbouring gentleman had a cure for gout (an affliction of the affluent), while a lucky man treated for the Gravel (kidney stones) 'by a Lord in Hertfordshire with a seven-year old Bottle of Perry, voided almost a Handfull of small stones'.[67]

The diseases on which the gentry advised – colic, gout, indigestion and loss of appetite, piles and pimples – reflected no doubt the problems that particularly concerned them, but they were by no means indifferent to the illnesses of the poor. Ellis extolled 'The Character of a Lord's great and unparallel'd Charity'. This local magnate, possibly the late duke of Bridgewater, 'although he was not bred a Physician, extends his Charity in a very uncommon Manner; for he not only visits the Sick in the most contagious Illness, but supplies them with Medicines at his own Cost'.[68]

Some remedies originated from local medical professionals. Qualified men such as Dr Woodhouse, or Mr Goodwyn, a 'Country Apothecary', both of Berkhamsted, performed cures about which Ellis heard. Such lofty professionals were, as Margaret Pelling found, often willing to help the poor for little or nothing.[69] Ellis told of a 'poor Widow and Chair-woman'

---

65 Possibly H. Boerhaave, *Treatise on the Powers of Medicines* (London, 1740).
66 Margaret Pelling, *The Common Lot* (London, 1998), especially the Introduction; William Ellis, *The New Art of Brewing and Improving Malt Liquors* (London, 1761), pp. 30–1.
67 Ellis, *Country Housewife*, pp. 201, 325, 350, 354–5.
68 Lucas, *Kalm's account*, p. 221. John, 2nd duke of Bridgewater, died a young bachelor in February 1748.
69 Pelling, *Common Lot*, p. 1.

living near him who 'applying herself to a Physician, he out of charity bid her stamp the Leaves of Plantane and Nettles together, and take a Tea-cup of their Juice' to stop her spitting blood. One wonders if this was a country remedy suitable to her means, whereas a higher-class patient would have been provided with something compounded by an apothecary. In another instance a girl in Little Gaddesden whose arm would not stop bleeding from a wound 'cried mightily as she stood at the Door of her Mother's House' until 'a Hempstead Surgeon, coming accidently by' advised applying hog's dung to the wound. Presumably the dung formed a crust and staunched the bleeding. Ellis is ambivalent about doctors, giving them credit for successful cures but finding other cases where their treatment did not work, or when the patient despaired of a cure and effective treatment was eventually provided by a friend or acquaintance. He mentions several cures achieved by a medicine given to him by a gentleman – 'a disinterested, worthy person, owner of a considerable landed estate': this medicine cured Mr Hanowell of the King's Evil (scrofula) when five pounds' worth of medicine from 'a famous London practitioner in physic' failed to do so. The medicine prescribed by both these men would have been ineffective but this condition frequently went into remission, giving the impression that any medical procedures carried out at the time had cured the disease. Writing of jaundice he observes 'My next neighbour the widow Howard, who lives on her landed estate, and has more experience in medicines than thousands of others, says old women cure this distemper better than doctors.'[70]

Medical advice included in the book came from a range of non-professionals. Many of the prescriptions in the book originated from 'country housewives', by which Ellis meant women skilled in medicine. They had cures for both minor and serious illnesses, predominantly using herbs, vegetables and other homely ingredients: butter, treacle, honey, beer or pepper. While some may have been no more than neighbours handing on the wisdom they themselves had been taught, some were called 'Doctresses' by Ellis and clearly were highly regarded locally.[71] Ellis recognises the longstanding role of gentlewomen as 'family doctors' for the rural community, advocating that all should keep a stock of salves to treat injuries, as well as cordials, oils 'and a hundred others of such Kind of Necessaries' to treat illnesses. They should distil cordials at home.[72]

---

70  Ellis, *Country Housewife*, pp. 192, 321.
71  Suggested remedies for coughs and asthma are mostly composed of 'homely ingredients': Ellis, *Country Housewife*, pp. 318–21, 339.
72  Ibid., pp.vii–viii.

Both men and women sold herbal tonics by the bottle for a range of diseases. One enterprising yeoman's wife, Mrs Sibley of Water-End, produced a herbal tonic that she sold at 18d a quart and Ellis was a sales agent for a friend – 'a most ingenious Chymist' – who produced a healing balsam at one shilling a sealed bottle. Ellis may have obtained one of his favourite prescriptions, a fearsome concoction of water and mercury, from this same friend. Ellis heard of an Exciseman of Ivinghoe 'who [...] acted as a Surgeon' and also had a cure for 'the itch' (scabies), an affliction common to beggars, some of whom were surprisingly skilled at medicine. Ellis talked to a number of them about remedies for the diseases to which they were prone – lice, skin diseases such as the itch, and rheumatism – and,

> upon asking them of their method of curing the several diseases they are incident to more than others, they tell me that, for clearing their bodies of lice, they boil copperas in water with hogslard, and by rubbing it over their bodies, no lice have power to bite them; on the contrary, it will make them forsake the cloathes they wear and not damage their skin.

A case of 'Scald-Head' that defeated a local physician was cured by a passing beggar woman, as was a young man crippled with rheumatism.[73] The repeated instances of medical advice offered by passing beggars leads one to speculate that they may have made a living from it. Ellis seems to relish telling of instances where expensive London doctors have failed to cure one of his neighbours whereas a local amateur, or a passing beggar, has produced a homely remedy that has worked.[74]

The medicines suggested by Ellis are, as one would expect, predominantly either herbal or composed of ingredients available in a farm kitchen. Camomile, elder, rue, lavender, nettles, chickweed and sweet cicely from garden and hedgerow; mutton fat, honey, butter, vinegar, milk, eggs, ashes, hog's dung and the like; as well as groceries obtainable locally, such as tobacco, sugar, strong spirits, figs, prunes or pepper. Relatively few country remedies needed recourse to an apothecary for drugs or chemicals and there is often a touching (and misplaced) faith in the power of homely ingredients to tackle serious illnesses such as consumption or diabetes. Ellis mentions very few instances of magic or sympathetic medicine. Clearly regarded as nonsense today, they were given little credence in Ellis's time too, and it is surprising that he includes any. One magical recipe reported by Ellis was

---

73 Scald-head – one of several diseases characterised by hair loss and a dry, flaky scalp, usually the result of a fungal infection.
74 Ellis, *Country Housewife*, pp. 335–6, 338, 340, 364–5.

donated by a beggar-woman who came to the door of a 12-year-old girl in Little Gaddesden. The girl had 'the evil' in her feet and could hardly walk – perhaps her feet were swollen, like the neck is when scrofula is the ailment. The beggar advised cutting two legs off a toad and wearing the mutilated animal in a silk bag round her neck: as the toad died so the girl's affliction was cured and never returned. Such a 'cure' might be explained by the recognition by the beggar that the girl had an affliction that would probably get better given time.[75]

The first page of his section on cures for coughs and asthma sums up the eclectic nature of his sources of cures. Ellis was assured by 'my landlord, the late Mr. Colemare, rector of Little-Gaddesden, that *his* cure was "infallible"'. Colmare advised: 'boil two ounces of Spanish liquorice with three cloves of garlic, in a quart of spring water, till it comes to a pint; take a spoonful of it now and then as the fit happens.' One Daniel Watkins 'declared to me, that he was cured of an asthma by swallowing young frogs'. Mr Justice Duncomb, of Barley-End in Buckinghamshire, used bran boiled in water sweetened with sugar for a cough, while a farmer's wife used pepper and ale. The landlord of the Bear Inn, Southampton, told Ellis to put garlic and prunes in rum: 'nothing exceeds it'. Sir Hans Sloane's cure for asthma involved a raw egg and the duke of Bridgewater's farrier advocated balsam of sulphur. A clergyman, a judge, farmers' wives, publicans and tradesmen all had remedies that they swore by.[76] In the absence of qualified doctors in the countryside, these cures filled the gap. But they were more than just a few instances of 'folk medicine' – manuscript recipe books surviving from this period contain hundreds of remedies for all types of complaint, both trivial and serious. In the absence of affordable and effective medicine from professionals, an alternative system had developed and many people could, if asked, produce remedies for a wide range of complaints. And it should not be assumed that these country cures were of less efficacy than those dispensed by professional doctors; many were herbal remedies based on the experience of many generations. These medicines were not based on the hopelessly inadequate Galenic system taught at universities; many at least treated the symptoms of illness if they did not help to bring about a cure. Who has not, when a child, rubbed a dock leaf on a nettle sting and obtained much relief from the pain? Many medicines today are based on extracts from herbs that were discovered by the study of folk medicine.[77]

---

75  Ibid., p. 366.
76  Ibid., pp. 318–21.
77  Pelling, *Common Lot*, pp. 1–16.

## Beer and cider

We have sketched Ellis's early adult life as a brewer after, and probably for some time before, the death of his uncle Richard. One of his earliest (and most popular) books drew on his experience in his inherited Westminster brewery. The book covers all aspects of brewing, including the wide variety of regional beers that Ellis came across in his travels. In a few pages at the start of the book he describes 'The London Way of Brewing', based on 'a great Brew-house that I was concerned with'. This business 'used a considerable quantity of malt in one week in brewing stout-beer, common butt-beer, ale, small-beer; for which purpose they have river and well waters'. He gives brief descriptions of how each type of beer was brewed in this brewery and the amounts charged for each. Throughout the book Ellis is concerned with the quality of the ingredients, especially in the case of the big London breweries. For instance, he is appalled that London brewers do not filter the Thames water they use and many do not properly clean their vessels. Historians of brewing have used Ellis's book extensively and generally have found his ideas sound: 'Ellis's works on brewing are valued, not just for their contemporary technical content, but as a commentary on changes in the brewing industry over a quarter of a century', was the verdict of one historian.[78]

Ellis, in his travels, sampled a great many beers and often complained about the quality of his drink: 'For when I travelled the Road in 1737, at several Towns I could have no other than foxed Ales, and thick unwholesome stale beer.'[79] He had a much more pleasant stay in Plymouth, where he was introduced to the Devonshire White Ale, a beer for both 'Pleasure and Health'. He devoted several pages of his book on beer to describing the qualities of this brew, which was made from pale malt by alewives who were skilled at their task. The brew was fermented in earthenware 'steens'[80] and fermentation was started by adding a secret composition, 'a *Nostrum* known by few'. It was a diuretic: 'it is soon discharged out of the stomach', 'to give room for new supplies of this pleasant Tipple'. In the pompous opinion of an experienced physician, it was

> well fitted to pass the several secretions of the human body; but not only by its consisting of such rarefied adhesive particles from the saccharine juice of the

---

78   Ellis, *London and Country Brewer*, pp. 22–5. Alan Pryor, 'The Industrialisation of the London Brewing Trade: Part I', *Brewery History*, 161 (2015), p. 54.

79   'Foxed' ales were usually the result of dirty utensils and hot weather; in Ellis's words, they caused 'the beer and ale so tainted to acquire a fulsome sickish taste, that will, if it received in a great degree, become ropy like treacle, and in some short time turn sour'. Ellis, *London and Country Brewer*, p. 44.

80   Steen, a large earthenware pot.

vegetable, but its being drank in a particularly agreeable, brisk, and smooth state, in taste not unlike our first nutriment, which certainly renders it easy of concoction in the stomach, and being moderately taken, it may justly claim a place in the first class of diuretic restoratives.[81]

12. Brewing on a small scale using eighteenth-century techniques.

Ellis's verdict was more succinct: 'In short, this famous liquor is of such a salubrious nature as renders it a most agreeable drink both to the sedentary and active person.'[82]

With his usual journalistic methods, Ellis obtained much of the information in his beer book from people that he met. Innkeepers and brewers gave him recipes for beers peculiar to their town: 'A receipt for brewing drink after the Shropshire method'; 'The receipt for brewing Dorchester-beer'; a pale-ale recipe from Barnstaple; the Bridgewater, Bristol, Rochester and York ways of brewing. Individuals provided their own recipes, for, outside the larger

---

81  Ellis, *London and Country Brewer*, pp. 197–8.
82  Ibid., pp. 184, 195–8.

towns, many families still brewed their own beer: 'A country victualler's way of brewing'; 'An eminent physician's way of brewing'; 'Sir Tho. Seabright's method of brewing a pipe of pale strong beer'; 'Brewing a hogshead and a half of pale-ale from fresh malt, by a private person'. He had recipes from Philadelphia and South Carolina in the United States, donated in the latter case by a sailor in the navy.[83]

Much of the book is taken up with recipes for brewing beer, followed by comments by Ellis on the method. A typical example is the recipe for Dorchester Beer:

> Boil the water and let it stand, till you can see your face in it; then put your malt in by degrees, and stir it; let it stand two hours; then leak on your complement [i.e. drain off the liquor]: boil the wort and hops thirty minutes; cool it as soon as possible, stirring it that the bottoms may be mingled; then set it in the guile-tun, till it gathers a head, which must be skimmed off; then put in the yeast, and work it till the head fall; then tun it, keeping the cask filling up so long as it will work.[84]

In the section following this recipe, Ellis dissects it, approving of some parts but mostly criticising the method. This criticism fills seven pages.

Beer has simple ingredients: water, malt, yeast and hops. But the proportions used of these ingredients varied from recipe to recipe, and the method of brewing was capable of many subtle variations: time taken for the various operations, temperatures, type of vessels used, storage and so on. It is these variations that yield the many types of beer that exist today, and there were similar differences in Ellis's time.

A modern historian of brewing, James Sumner, has noted that this work was 'more extensive than any previous brewery publication' and that Ellis 'describes operations claimed to be particular to several commonly retailed styles' of London beer.[85] In the 1738 edition Ellis included an account of porter-brewing, which is the earliest printed account of London porter. His knowledge, however, was of the London trade twenty years earlier, and technology had moved on since he had ceased to be a London brewer. Sumner is not sure how much of the London trade Ellis really knew. He also notes that the second and subsequent parts of the book are disorganised and 'dissolve into miscellaneous compilation'.[86]

---

83  Ibid., pp. 119, 136–7, 150.
84  Ibid., p. 119.
85  James Sumner, *Brewing Science, Technology and Print, 1700–1880* (Pittsburgh, PA, 2013), pp. 26–8.
86  Ibid., pp. 26–8.

Ellis also wrote a book on cider, much of which is taken up with the care and management of fruit trees. The part dealing with cider-making leans heavily on reports of the methods used in the South Hams area of Devon. Ellis, in his preface, justifies the book on the grounds that

> several Authors have wrote on the Herefordshire Cyder Apples, but most of the Southams Sort, and their delicate Properties, have not been so much as mentioned by them. Nor could I have been Master of this superior Knowledge, had I not travelled in Devonshire, and settled such a Correspondence with a most accurate Planter and Cyderist there, who from Time to Time communicated to me the different Natures of their Soils, their best Methods of raising and planting their Apple-Trees, dressing them afterwards, gathering and hoarding their Fruit, grinding and pressing them in their several Sorts of Mills and Presses, making their Cyders, fermenting and racking them, and preserving them in Casks rightly prepared, for keeping them long in a sound, pleasant Condition.

In other words, Ellis tells us little about his own cider-making activities. I presume that, unlike brewing, he had little personal experience of it. His arguments for encouraging cider production are conventional: 'Thousands of Acres of barren Lands may-be improved by it in the highest Degree' and 'great Numbers of the Poor [would be] imployed'. Cider, he was sure, was 'much wholesomer, than most Foreign Wines', so the cost of imports would decrease and domestic Excise duty on it would help the Treasury.[87]

All in all, Ellis wrote much on food and drink. His book on beer obviously drew on his years as a London brewer – he was an expert. The cider book was much more based on the experience of others. The *Country Housewife* drew heavily on recipes from Ellis's Hertfordshire neighbours, but he also proclaimed on the title page that the book was based on 'near thirty Years Experience' as a farmer at Little Gaddesden, and in the preface he explained that in the book

> The Art [...] of saving the Penny, and making Money go the farthest, I have here endeavoured to make known, by publishing great Numbers of serviceable Matters, as they have been really practised in the most provident Country Families, and some of them in my own.

So, he was spreading 'best practice' and accumulated wisdom. He also saw a gap in the market not filled by the more gentrified book on country living of Richard Bradley.[88]

---

87  Ellis, *Compleat Cyderman*, Preface, pp. iii, iv.
88  Ellis, *Country Housewife*, title page, Preface, p. i.

## Chapter 6
# Ellis the man

What sort of man was Ellis? In this chapter we will note what he says about himself in his writings, weigh up what the Swedish visitor Pehr Kalm thought of him and pick out opinions and attitudes, social and religious, revealed in his books and periodicals, as well as noting his work in the administration of the local community. We will also consider whether some of his actions accorded with his own morality.

He seems to have lived quietly in Little Gaddesden, getting on with his neighbours, albeit he was occasionally exasperated by their conservative farming methods and they were suspicious of many of his suggested innovations. His relationship with his family was, as far as is known, cordial. He had a large family of children which he raised probably without help from his second wife after her spell in Bedlam. At least two of his sons were apprenticed to potentially lucrative trades and he took care to place another in good farming positions.[1] He believed in hard work, making a virtue of setting his sons on farm work at an early age, and at least one of his sons enjoyed such hard toil. There is a question mark, however, over his treatment of his second wife, who he had committed to Bedlam for several months in 1733. Conditions in this charitable asylum were spartan; those who could afford it sent mentally ill relatives to private asylums. Was Ellis not caring in sending his wife to Bedlam, or could he not afford to have her treated privately? At least one villager thought Ellis was hard-up at the time and his writing activities had scarcely started. It is highly likely that he was aware that she had also been admitted to Bedlam in 1715, two years before her marriage to him. Was theirs a love match or did money come into

---

1   His son William was apprenticed to a London barber-surgeon. He was made a Freeman of the Barbers' Company in May 1736 and a Liveryman in 1741, indicating a steady rise in his profession. C.P. Willoughby, Transcript of the Court Minutes of the Barbers' Company, January 1731–December, 1743. I am grateful to Victoria West, archivist of the Worshipful Company of Barbers, for this information. Another son, Henry, was a clockmaker.

it? Matilda was 34 when they married, quite late an age for first marriage at the time, and she brought a sum of money with her. Was the money an inducement from her family to Ellis to marry Matilda? If so, he may have considered the money his to spend on experiments, despite her distress at his expenditure. Her disquiet was enough to bring on the renewed mental illness from which she seemingly did not recover. It may be surmised that Ellis was an unscrupulous adventurer who married Matilda for her money. On the other hand, in his will Ellis mentions a jointure owned by Matilda of £400 which he had invested in land and, under his will, would pay to Matilda's eldest son. Investing his wife's money in land is hardly a reckless experiment.

On another occasion, when Ellis had to administer large sums of money and negotiate with relatives – his executorship of his uncle Richard's estate – he seems to have acted with the right amount of tact and firmness. He had to administer the will and took decisive action to start legal moves against his aunt when she refused to hand over cash and securities in her possession. On the other hand, he soon reached a settlement with her that gave her a substantial lump sum and freed him to sell the brewery. Presumably he used the money to further his farming activities in Little Gaddesden. The only cloud of doubt in this affair was the allegation in the legal papers, noted above, that Richard had travelled out of London shortly before his death in good health, after which William turned up, announced his uncle's death and produced a will that his aunt had not seen before. These vague allegations of misdeeds were not, however, pursued and look like negotiating tactics.

Ellis must have had a certain charm, an easy-going manner and some patience. He depended on information from farmers, brewers and many other sorts and conditions of people for copy to fill his books and he would talk to anyone he thought had useful knowledge. He explained his technique to Kalm:

> when he noticed that such a person was interested in an exchange of views, Mr. Ellis always had something choice and agreeable to tell about farming which pleased. In order to repay the other man would then tell something to Mr. Ellis and so on, until Mr. Ellis managed to find out all that he knew. Often, Mr. Ellis pretended that it was not his purpose to learn anything so that he could obtain a better insight into what he really wanted. For this purpose, the other man must not take him for what he really was.[2]

Ellis demonstrated this technique of swapping information when obtaining recipes to keep cows in good health from a Somerset dairy farmer, particularly:

---

2  Mead, *Pehr Kalm*, p. 42.

A most excellent first Drink to be given a Cow after Calving, to keep her in Health [...] which I learned of an eminent Farmer in Somersetshire, where they run chiefly on Dairying; who being a perfect Stranger to me, and, as I was informed, Master of several rare Receipts, which he practised with Success, I could not tell a better Way to come by some of them, than to talk of some Improvements in Farming, which he liked so well, as to be free with me, and accordingly we exchanged some; and among the rest he communicated this superlative one to me, which I have since several Times tried, and never found it fail my Purpose.[3]

Ellis particularly valued the knowledge held by ordinary workmen: 'I have had many rich secrets communicated to me by the mean working man; I may say, more from him, than from many of the greatest learning, because the former discourses of facts, when the other does it from his theory uncertain philosophy.'[4]

Although Kalm and Ellis did not get on particularly well and sometimes Ellis refused to talk to Kalm, overall he did devote quite a lot of time to discussions with him and to showing him some of his implements. According to Kalm: 'He took great pleasure in discussing with me all sorts of things both in farm management and in agriculture.'[5] It sounds as if Ellis was using his technique of swapping information on Kalm and he must have used it on his fellow villagers, as evidenced by the wide variety of people from his village whom he credits with giving him information to include in his books. Many recipes and practices are 'Hertfordshire' ones, indicating that he gathered them locally. This was especially so when he gleaned medical and food recipes. He talked to the duke of Bridgewater's gardener, butcher and farrier. Scroop Edgerton, the duke, a near neighbour at Ashridge Park, was given a laudatory obituary by Ellis when he died, the detail of which seems to indicate that he had personal contact with him.[6] It is likely that Ellis used the library at Ashridge to carry out research for his books.

Ellis spoke to people of all classes in his village and elsewhere. An example is the juxtaposition on the same page of a recipe from 'Madam Howard' for a diet drink and the fruits of Ellis's talk with beggars.[7] He used his interviewing skills on his travels round southern England – one can imagine him talking earnestly to yeomen and gentlemen during the day at their farms and in the evening sitting in an inn tap room extracting information from husbandmen,

---

3   Ellis, *Modern Husbandman*, May, pp. 105–6.
4   Mead, *Pehr Kalm*, p. 42; Ellis, *Modern Husbandman*, September, p. 99.
5   Mead, *Pehr Kalm*, p. 43.
6   Ellis, *Country Housewife*, pp. 198, 245–7, 298–9.
7   Ibid., pp. 364–5.

labourers, travellers and the innkeeper. He used the information he gained about local beers in his book on brewing and on occasion picked up a recipe from the inn's cook.

In terms of his religious beliefs, Ellis was a member of the Church of England and was what today we would call a Puritan. Contemporaries would have used the term 'Godly'. In the preamble of his will he places his 'soul into the hands of Almighty God hoping through the merits of Jesus Christ to be saved' – a Puritan phraseology. He is not, as were some Puritans, certain of Election (the guarantee of eternal life through faith), but he has hopes of salvation. He believed in strict observance of an austere and religious Sunday. He was not alone in this; Kalm noted 'To dance, play upon instrument, or to sing songs on a Sunday is regarded as a very great sin or scandal and, especially in the towns, anybody who engages in such activities, soon finds himself in trouble.'[8] Indeed, Ellis complained that,

> by an ill Custom, in some Parts of our Country of Hertfordshire, we can hardly keep our Servants at Home on a Sabbath-Day, because of the bad Example of others, who go shooting of Birds, or play at Bandy-wicket, Pitch and Chuck, Hooper's-Hide, Pat-Ball, &c.[9] besides which, our poor labouring People generally frequent Alehouses on the Sabbath-Day, in Neglect of going to Church [...] there is not a Day in the Week which God is so much offended on, as on Sundays, and Saints Days, by Drunkenness, Blasphemy, Impiety, and other Wickedness; by Men's' passing the Day in Taverns, in Alehouses, and at other Placed of Debauchery; by young Peoples playing, gaming, dancing, walking abroad, and by sinful Conversations.[10]

In commentating on a dispute between farmers and the parson of a nearby parish, Ellis thought the farmers should think themselves fortunate to have a resident minister rather than share with another parish, for in that situation,

---

8    Hertfordshire Archives and Local Studies, 39 HW 37; Mead, *Pehr Kalm*, p. 121.

9    At the risk of another Ellis-like digression, it might be useful to say more about these rural games. Bandy-wicket was played by two teams, each player using a 'bandy' – a long stick with a curved end like a hockey stick used to try to hit a ball into a goal. It was a cricket-like variant popular in East Anglia in the eighteenth century. The aim of Pitch and Chuck was to pitch or throw a penny or metal disc into a hole in the ground. The game leant itself to illicit gambling. In Pat-ball two players struck an inflated leather ball with hands or arms to and fro, like modern volleyball. Hooper's-Hide was the antecedent of Blind Man's Buff. Tony Collins et al. (eds), *Encyclopedia of Traditional British Rural Sports* (London, 2005).

10   Ellis, *Compleat system of experienced improvements*, pp. 197–204.

13. Little Gaddesden church, where Ellis was in some years elected churchwarden and for many years wrote up the Churchwardens' Account Book.

I heard one Farmer say, their women seldom went to church, because in the morning they staid at home to dress dinner, and in the afternoon of a Sunday the church doors were shut up, by reason the minister officiated in two parishes in the same day. In short, it is a deplorable case to see farmers' children and servants in particular, by this means, tempted to seek out opportunities of spending their time on a Sunday, in playing, and running into those commissions of evil, that may, perhaps by custom, lead them into ruin, for want of opportunity of employing the same time better at church.[11]

Ellis advocates the use of fierce dogs to protect farmyards on cold, dark nights, when lack of work prompts 'loose fellows to pillage and rob farmers, to supply their wants, and, too often, their extravagances, chiefly against the Holy-Days of Christmas, partly out of the ignorant false notion, that such days are set aside for rioting and luxury'.[12] Ellis was worried about rural theft in general, perpetrated by 'the crowds of strolling vagrants, that infest

---

11 Ellis, *Modern Husbandman*, November, p. 399.
12 Ellis, *Modern Husbandman*, December, p. 470.

the shires of Hertford, Bucks, Bedford, Middlesex, and others, who travel about almost all the year, to the great damage of farmers'.[13] He wanted the already harsh laws against thieves strengthened, explaining:

> In our Village of Gaddesden, because it lies three Miles distant from the nearest Market-town where a Justice of Peace lives, some of the Inhabitants are every now-and-then insulted to a very high Degree by Vagrants. I have seen one of these that begged, having but one Hand, throw a Stone with the other against a creditable Woman, because she would not relieve him; and had it hit her in some Part, was big enough to kill her: Another, with a sham plaister'd Arm, clapt his Foot between the Door and the Threshold to prevent shutting it, when he saw there was an opportunity to get some thing, by his Swearing, and insulting Impudence (a reigning sort of Villainy), as knowing, at the worst, it will be only the Stocks, or other light Punishment [...] Others of them keep Dogs that will nimbly seize our Poultry for their Masters to carry off [...] But it is to be hoped the Legislature, this next Session, will, when they amend the Black Act, level a severe Law against all those Vagrants who shall in any wise insult or damage Farmers.[14]

The Black Act of 1723 (9 Geo. I, c. 22) was already a harsh measure when Ellis proposed it be amended. Entitled 'An Act for the more effectual punishing wicked and evil disposed Persons going armed in Disguise, and doing Injuries and Violences to the Persons and Properties of His Majesty's Subjects, and for the more speedy bringing the Offenders to Justice', it was enacted in response to a series of raids by poachers near Waltham in Hampshire, men who blacked their faces as a disguise. The Act, which was several times amended, included more infringements punishable by death than any other single act of the eighteenth century. It was a template for later pieces of capital legislation.[15]

Ellis devotes several short chapters to describing the modus operandi of certain types of vagrant. Sham mad-men and mad-women vagrants aroused his ire. These, and those who did not pretend madness but had been discharged from Bedlam and licensed to beg, known as 'Tom o' Bedlams', may have been an uncomfortable reminder to Ellis that his own second wife had been confined to Bedlam twice and discharged, apparently, as incurable. He was scared of roving gangs of Gypsies. They were 'these miscreants' who, together with 'their loose women, for, no doubt, all of them are so, as they

---

13 Ibid., September, p. 71.
14 Ellis, *Agriculture Improv'd*, p. 21.
15 Leon Radzinowicz, 'The Waltham Black Act: A Study of the Legislative Attitude Towards Crime in the Eighteenth Century', *The Cambridge Law Journal*, 9/1 (1945), pp. 56–81.

lie and herd together in a promiscuous manner' travelled 'in Terrorem, to the country people'.[16]

He advises keeping servants in-house, not letting them 'stay long, or lie out at nights, to go to common dancing or drinking bouts' and, somewhat incongruously, he devotes much of his introduction to the *Country Housewife* to providing instances of thefts from housewives by servants and neighbours. He also condemns rural shopkeepers for overcharging, selling inferior goods and using false weights.[17]

Some long and rambling passages in Ellis's book on sheep further emphasise his religious and moral outlook on life. He tells of a prosperous farmer who resented the poor gleaners who invaded his fields as soon as the harvest was ended. In the harvest of 1743, when the gleaners started to pick up ears of corn, the farmer made his shepherd turn his sheep flock into the field, anticipating that the sheep would eat up the loose ears of wheat before the gleaners could gather them. The sheep choked on the wheat 'for, as these are a rough Food, furnished with a strong tough Straw and Chaff, the Sheep could not eat them so clean [...] no less than seventeen were choaked and killed on the Spot'. Ellis thought it likely 'that this fatal Misfortune came to pass, by Way of a just Judgment on this covetous Farmer'. He then confuses the issue by giving instances of gleaners who *did* steal grain at harvest time, returning at night to pilfer from the stooks.[18]

Ellis's morality meant that he was harshly critical of swearing. He describes 'The Case of a Wicked Farmer, living near Leyburne in Buckinghamshire, who on Cursing and Damning his Sheep, Twenty of them, the Night following, were drowned' (they were washed away by a flood).

> He was notoriously remarkable for the frequent Oaths and Curses that he usually belched out in his common Discourse; a Wickedness the most unprofitable of all others, and most highly offensive to Almighty God, who has denounced his severe Judgments against the Commission of it: *For because of Swearing the Land mourns.*

The swearing farmer's business failed, and he became a day labourer. The reason for the prevalence of swearing at Laybourne, Ellis says,

---

16 Ellis, *Modern Husbandman*, September, p. 101. *In terrorum* is Latin literally for 'in fear'. It is most commonly used in clauses in wills stating that if a legatee challenges the will automatic disinheritance will result. Here, Ellis is making a pun.

17 Ellis, *Country Housewife*, pp. 33–7.

18 Ellis, *Compleat system of experienced improvements*, p. 195. A stook is three or four sheaves propped against each other to dry.

is because as Laybourne lies but about two Miles distant from Leighton Great Market, where many of the London Cow dealers and Drovers weekly resort, they, by their bad Examples, teach others to do the like; so that such horrid Oaths and Curses are uttered by great Numbers of young and old Persons, in these Parts, as may justly grate the Ears of virtuous People.

Ellis goes on to attribute the cattle plague and sickness in humans in his area to this vice.

These instances of puritanism may lead one to think of Ellis as a somewhat dour character, but this seems not to have been the case. We see a flash of humour when Kalm remarks 'that through him and his writings Little Gaddesden had acquired an immortal name and that no-one knew of Little Gaddesden before his time' and Ellis replies, 'no prophet is accepted in his own country'.[19]

His neighbours may have been confused by his farming methods, his time spent writing, his gentry visitors and his frequent absences from his farm, but most seem to have regarded him as a harmless eccentric and many may have appreciated his sense of public duty. He participated fully in the local government of the parish and seems to have been a trusted and able administrator. He was elected a churchwarden of Little Gaddesden in 1720, 1721 and 1726, one of two wardens elected annually at Easter each year. The position was unpaid and involved a wide range of duties. The wardens kept order at church services; were meant to present to higher ecclesiastical authorities parishioners acting immorally; were responsible for the upkeep of the fabric and furnishings of the church; and had to raise money for their expenditure by levying rates. To judge from the handwriting, Ellis wrote up the income and expenditure of the wardens in the parish account book for many years, including when he was not a warden – this activity may have been connected with the making of rates for various years, for which he was paid one or two shillings each time. He was also paid for other small administrative jobs, such as writing letters.[20]

He set a rate in another local unpaid office he undertook, that of Overseer of the Poor. This could be an onerous task, chasing the fathers of bastards for money to support the child, distinguishing between deserving and undeserving poor, paying alms to those deserving support and sending paupers who could

---

19 Mead, *Pehr Kalm*, p. 42.

20 W.E. Tait, *The Parish Chest* (Stroud, 2012), pp. 84–108. Little Gaddesden parish records, Churchwardens' Accounts. The distinctive hand in these records is the same as in the dedication 'from the Author' in a copy of the *London and Country Brewer* (see above, p. 81, n. 21). The coincidence of these manuscripts identifies Ellis as the writer of the dedication and also confirms that the hand in the parish records is Ellis's.

not establish their right to receive money from the parish back to the parish from whence they came. The level of poor rates was a source of constant complaint by the richer people in parishes, which did not make the overseer's job any easier.[21] He was an overseer in 1727 and 1744 but, again, he made a rate for many other years and seems to have regularly written up the overseers' account book. He was also paid for specific jobs done in connection with poor law administration. For instance, in 1732 he was paid 2s 6d for 'his journey to Mary Brazier' and in December 1734 a payment of seven shillings was made to him for 'rideing to Lilley about Sarah Higley'. Ellis seems to have acted as accountant to the Little Gaddesden parish administration for many years. That he was a firm but fair administrator is demonstrated by an entry in the Gaddesden churchwardens' book:

Memorandum this 20th day of December 1721. I William Ellis, one of the Churchwardens for the parish of Little Gaddesden in the year aforsd. did sometime before Christmas observe that at the end of the communion service in the Common Prayer book it was ordered that the Offertory money given after the Sacrament should be distributed to the poor by the minister and churchwardens after the service was ended. And being informed that the former Officers during [blank] years that Mr. Eddowes had been Rector never see the said monies given away I thereupon demanded of Mister Eddowes the distribution of what monies might be given at the Christmas sacrament in mine and other Church wardens presence, which he accordingly did to some poor people who I ordered to attend church for that purpose. And so I intend by God's permission to see the like done while I am in that Office according to my sworn duty. And I do by this warn all succeeding Churchwardens that they do not omit so material a part of their Duty.[22]

In entering this memorandum in the book, probably shortly after he became a churchwarden, Ellis showed some courage because, after all, he was depriving the rector of some of his income and the rector was Ellis's landlord. Note the tone of the memorandum – Ellis *demanded* that the rector distribute the money, he *ordered* the poor people to attend church and *warned* succeeding churchwardens that they must carry on the custom. Moreover, this entry in the book is prominently placed and, in contrast to entries in Ellis's 'ordinary hand', is in a bold and immaculate copperplate

---

21 Tait, *The Parish Chest*, pp. 188–241.
22 Little Gaddesden Parish Records, Overseers' Account Book; Churchwardens' Account Book. Ellis was also, in 1748, surveyor of roads for the parish. Ellis, *Compleat system of experienced improvements*, p. 269.

**Memorandum** this 20th day of December 1721. I Wm Ellis one of the Churchwardens for the Parish of Little Gaddesden in the year aforesd. Did sometime before Christmas observe that at the end of the Comunion Service in the Common Prayer Book It was ordered That the Offertory money given at the Sacrament should be distributed to the poor by the Minister and Churchwardens after the service was ended. And being inform'd that the former Officers dureing    years that Mr Eddows had been Rector; never see the said moneys given away I thereupon demanded of Mr Eddows the distribution of what moneys mought be given at the Christmas Sacrament in mine & the other Churchwardens presence, which he accordingly did to some poor people who I ordered to attend at Church for that purpose. And so intend by Gods permission to see the like done while I am in that Office according to my sworn duty. And I do by this warn all succeeding Churchwardens that they do not omit so material a part of their Duty.

14. William Ellis's entry in the Little Gaddesden Churchwardens' Account Book in December 1721 declaring that certain collection money should be distributed to the poor.

style. It shows Ellis to be forcefully on the side of fairness and social justice.[23] Comments to Kalm by his neighbours show him in the same light:

> One quality they had to accede to Mr. Ellis, that he never let any hired man stand waiting after payment, which is a common feature here, but he let them have their money every evening. And if they went home in the evening, without coming and taking their money, they would speedily be given it by him the next day. If they worked several hours longer in the morning or afternoon than they were required to work, they received additional payment. Others, who did anything for him, immediately received their payment as soon as they had done what was required of them.[24]

As it was the custom in Little Gaddesden not to hire labourers on an annual basis but just to employ them by the day, prompt payment was vital to their wellbeing. Ellis was well aware that dependence on casual labouring caused poverty in his home parish and elsewhere, especially in the dead of winter, when work was scarce. Of December he remarks:

> The shortest days, the longest nights, and generally the coldest weather, accompany this month; and therefore it becomes the most expensive and most necessitous season in the whole year to thousands of the poorer sorts of people and their families, who are hereby incapacitated to get their daily bread by their usual labour and industry.[25]

He approved of charity to help the poor in times of difficulty, devoting a chapter in the *Modern Husbandman* to local charities and individual acts of charity, and tells us of one charitable act he has done: in the winter of 1740 he visited a tradesman of his acquaintance in a workhouse in the London suburbs. Finding the man ill, he arranged for an apothecary to attend him, but he died. Ellis was appalled that the inmates had 'but two ounces of beef besides broth and bread allowed to a man a day for dinner'.[26]

---

23   21 December was the Feast of St Thomas and it was customary on that day for the poor to beg for alms. 'In past times in rural England children, the poor, and the elderly might go "Thomasing" on that day. The most typical participants in this old customary practice, however, were poor, elderly women. Also known as "mumping," "doleing," "corning," or "gooding," the custom permitted these folk to go door to door asking for small handouts in order to enjoy good things to eat at Christmas time.' <https://encyclopedia2.thefreedictionary.com/St.+Thomas%27s+Day>, accessed 15 November 2020.

24   Mead, *Pehr Kalm*, p. 41. On the other hand, on Ladyday 1745 Ellis paid nine years *back-rent* for land called 'Town Acre', the rent from which went towards relieving the poor of the parish.

25   Ellis, *Modern Husbandman*, December, p. 487.

26   Ellis, *Modern Husbandman*, December, pp. 487–92; September, p. 79.

Another manifestation of Ellis's humanity was his attitude towards enclosure. In agricultural terms he was all in favour of this radical change in the way the land was exploited, but he was appalled by the effect of many enclosures on the poor, who lost their rights to use the common lands for grazing, fuel and other benefits. He complained of

> the great disadvantages that have arisen from the unlawful and unjust inclosing of lands from the poor, who had a proportionable title with the greatest farmer, and yet have been entirely excluded from their just right for ever, by the Lord of the Manor's privately bribing a few of the chief inhabitants to obtain their consent.[27]

In Little Gaddesden his reputation was high, but his status elsewhere is more unclear. Not many yeomen wrote books or talked on easy terms to Fellows of the Royal Society, let alone became the most prolific writer on agriculture for a generation and attracted the attention of learned Europeans. One has the feeling that he was a different person in the capital, and a different one again in his books. Furthermore, as a dealer in a wide range of agricultural goods and machines, he had yet another persona. It is these different aspects of his life that make him such an interesting character. He describes himself in his will as a 'yeoman' – an accurate description for a farmer who owned at least some of the land he farmed and whose farm was large enough to produce a regular surplus of produce for sale at market after his family's subsistence had been satisfied. At a manorial court hearing after his death however, he was accorded the title of gentleman. This ambiguity of status is explained by his unusual circumstance – he farmed and owned land but he was also a writer who corresponded and talked on easy terms with the elite of his day.[28] In 1745, for example, a countess wrote to him asking advice on improving an estate she had in the north of England and several letters were exchanged between them. Ellis supplied her with various agricultural goods – ploughs, seeds, fowls – recommended a ploughman and discussed agriculture with her at her town house in St James's over 'a dish of tea'. No doubt he was a much more refined character when meeting this countess than he was interviewing drinkers at an inn on one of his tours.[29]

The countess was delighted with his efforts on her behalf and in all the letters he published from gentlemen who wrote to him there is little criticism of his writings or his dealings with customers. These tell us that many customers were satisfied, but we would not expect him to publish critical

---

27 Ibid., September, pp. 113–14.
28 Stanbridge, *William Ellis*, Appendix C, pp. 166–9.
29 Ellis, *Agriculture Improv'd*, pp. 141–57.

letters. Ellis did in fact publish one letter of criticism – from an anonymous Lancashire gentleman, lamenting that there are no pictures of the farm implements described. He also asks Ellis to explain the various dialect words he uses via a glossary, otherwise he is likely to be accused of just demonstrating his expertise rather than informing the farming public. Ellis replies that cost considerations rule out illustrations and that:

> In case any envious or ill-natured Persons say, I write to shew my excellent Qualifications in the Art I profess, my Answer is, they have no room, in my humble Opinion, for any such Censures, because the many Blunders, incongruous Words, unconnected Sentences, and, perhaps, Tautologies, &c. plainly shew, I am no logician, nor rhetorician, and therefore have no pretention to Scholarship. But this, indeed, I insist on, that I had rather write plain, and be well understood, than either with Logic or Rhetoric, dispute and garnish over a Matter, which has no Foundation in my Knowledge; for useful Knowledge is certainly more to be gained by Practice and Conversation, than by Study and Contemplation.[30]

Were no book purchasers annoyed that he reprinted material from earlier books in later ones? They may have forgiven the appearance of the same frontispiece appearing, word for word, in *Chiltern and Vale Farming* and the *Practice of Farming*, but would they not have been miffed to find that more than half of the *Practice of Farming* was in fact a reprint of *The Timber Tree Improved*, and the rest was taken from *Chiltern and Vale Farming Explained* and *The Modern Husbandman*? The eight-volume edition of *The Modern Husbandman* was bulked out with reprints of *Agriculture Improv'd, or, The practice of husbandry displayed* and *The Timber Tree Improved*. Moreover, much of the second part of the latter work was essentially a paraphrase of Evelyn's *Sylva*. The apparent lack of criticism of this self-plagiarism may indicate that the book-buying public were inured to it – everybody did it, either recycling their own material or borrowing from earlier published works. One correspondent of Ellis's *was* irritated by rehashed material in books on agriculture published before Ellis started writing, condemning books 'which have proved no better than arrant Impositions, upon Perusal, of Transcripts from old musty Authors', but his complaint was not common. The editor of the collected works of Ellis published in 1772 thought Ellis was put under much pressure to produce text for his monthly journals, which might excuse some self-plagiarism, but Ellis did not himself complain of such pressure. The advent of Google Books makes it possible to comprehend the extent of eighteenth-century plagiarism – it can be startling to see the number

---

30   Ellis, *Modern Husbandman*, January, pp. 93–9.

of hits generated by the entry of a sentence from an eighteenth-century work into its advanced search facility.[31]

To sum him up: Ellis was a complex character. He was undoubtedly hard working, bringing up his sons to be hard workers too. He looked after his children and sought to place them in good positions or occupations. His second wife may not have fared as well in his hands; there is the suspicion that he married her for the dowry she brought with her and we have no knowledge of how well he looked after her in her long mental illness after her discharge from hospital. He had an intense dislike of Gypsies and vagrants in general, yet he talked to beggars, obtaining medical recipes from them. He was very sympathetic to the poor, administering the local poor law regulations and ensuring church funds earmarked for the poor were properly distributed. He paid his casual workers promptly and fully. His claim that he hoped to be 'instrumental to promote my Country's good' in selling agricultural machines may well be accepted at face value, as his conduct in local affairs leaves one with the impression that he would have been a genuine patriot. He recycled a good deal of his earlier books into his later ones but was not criticised for this. He was a Puritan and favoured an austere lifestyle but at the same time he was an engaging journalist willing to speak to all and sundry if they had anything to say he could use in his books. One has the feeling that, if he struck up a conversation with you one night before a good fire in a public bar, you would have a pleasant evening talking of a wide range of things.

---

31 Cookery books were particularly likely to contain recipes taken almost word for word from earlier publications. For instance, the recipe 'To Dress Carp' in *Domestic Economy* of 1794 is repeated in *The Art of Cookery made Plain and Easy*, 1796; *The English Art of Cookery*, 1788; *The Lady's Complete Guide*, 1791; and the *New Art of Cookery*, 1798.

## Chapter 7
# Other matters

We have examined the major themes in Ellis's working life – agriculture; food, drink and medicine; trading in many types of goods; and, of course, his writings – but there are other interesting aspects of his life to consider. Ellis devoted a chapter in the *Modern Husbandman* to improvements in road and farm vehicles, showing he had some skill in mathematics and physics. The readership of his books and the impact the books had on his readers needs examination – did these books and periodicals merely instruct and amuse the gentry or did his ideas reach the ordinary farmers who, in many cases, he was trying to reach? Did these farmers resist his new ideas? He was a shrewd observer of agricultural change but did he realise the amount of general economic change occurring in England in his adult lifetime? And what of his own economic circumstances – can we estimate the contribution writing and trading made to his income? Lastly, we will note the changing posthumous reputation of Ellis's writings: some historians have dismissed them as trivial; others have regarded them as of prime importance.

### *The improvement of vehicles*[1]
Quite suddenly, Ellis breaks away from strictly farming matters and devotes a chapter in the *Modern Husbandman* to 'The improvement of Wheel Carriages. How Waggons, etc, may be made and managed to a much greater Advantage than heretofore has been done'.[2] He has, apparently, been 'diverting myself with drawing up reasons to shew that coaches, waggons, and other four wheel vehicles whose fore wheels are less than the hinder ones, go easier when the weight, contrary to common

---

1 I am very grateful for the help Dr Graham Sumner and Phillip Owens gave me in interpreting and commenting on Ellis's observations on four-wheeled vehicles.
2 Ellis, *Modern Husbandman*, January, pp. 111–19; J. Geraint Jenkins, *The English Farm Wagon* (Newton Abbot, 1972), pp. 8, 10, 11, 13, 101.

practise, is laid on the hinder wheels'. As sometime surveyor of highways for his parish, Ellis would have concerned himself with the state of his local road surfaces and in his extensive travels he would have noted the many regional variations in farm transport that had developed over centuries. Many of these variations may, as was the case with ploughs, have been sensible accommodations to local conditions, but Ellis wanted to draw up some basic rules to ensure the efficiency of carts, wagons and the like. His interest in such vehicles must be observed against a background of increasing traffic on the roads near him taking heavy loads to London markets, and the increased demand for bigger farm vehicles for such operations as harvesting on the larger farms created by enclosure. In the chapter Ellis discusses weight distribution in carriages and carts, wheel sizes (especially of rear wheels), the most efficient way to harness horses to vehicles and the best length for vehicles. He displays a knowledge of mathematics and physics not demonstrated in other writings. There is no evidence, however, that his views on this topic were noticed.

## *'Book agriculture'*

James Fisher has investigated the conflict between landlords, tenants and agricultural writers towards the end of the eighteenth century caused by the increasing numbers of agricultural textbooks published at that time.[3] The conflict can also be discerned in the years when Ellis was writing and this chapter will examine how Fisher's conclusions fit with Ellis's works. Fisher points out a potential conflict between husbandmen, who farmed using their accumulated knowledge handed down from past generations together with the collective wisdom of their peers, and the knowledge absorbed by their landlords, who read the textbooks. In his words, 'the growing use of agricultural books disrupted established ways of storing and transferring knowledge, raising fundamental questions about the source of knowledge and expertise in agriculture'.[4] Textbooks were read by landlords who did not want to be less skilled at farming than their tenants, for that laid them open to being misled by them or at least ridiculed for their ignorance. 'As an ideal, therefore, the manager of a farm or estate should know as much as his servants in order to maintain complete authority.'[5] On the other hand, husbandmen resented being told how to farm by landlords, either by exhortation or by covenants in their leases. They pointed to the poor

---

3  James Fisher, 'The Master Should Know More: Book-Farming and the Conflict over Agricultural Knowledge', *Cultural and Social History*, 15/3 (2018), pp. 315–31.
4  Ibid., p. 315.
5  Ibid., p. 319.

quality of advice in many textbooks, some of which was just copied from earlier works. Writers retorted that husbandmen would not read anyway and learned only through example. Tenants in turn responded that they were dubious about experiments carried out by gentlemen with land in hand who they thought of as 'idle visionaries'.[6] Richard Bradley in the 1720s thought that working farmers would not innovate and is quite damning about farmers' abilities:

> For altho'our English Husbandmen are allowed by all nations to have a superior genius in agriculture, preferable to those in other countries, yet it is rare to find one of them who ever attempts any new Discovery, or even can give any other reason for what they do, than that their fathers did the same before them [...] Country people generally pick out such of their children to employ in husbandry, as they judge are not worthy of good education; and whom they suppose have so little genius, that they are only fit to drudge in hard labour.[7]

But husbandmen *were* working farmers who over generations had accumulated local knowledge that many were now unwilling to share with their landlords. Ellis tells of

> a gentleman of a considerable estate, [who] told me, he was going to take one of his farms into his hands of three hundred a year, and that he did not doubt that, what with observing his neighbours' management, and regaling them now and then into a free conversation, he should go on as well as they, but this notion has proved fatal to many [...] for to say the truth, the common farmer is as subtle a man in his way as any mechanic whatsoever, and will be so far from leading any gentleman into the true method of farming that most of them very justly hold it as contrary to their interest.[8]

One wonders what the tenants of a gentleman customer of Ellis's truly thought of their landlord who purchased thirty-four bushels of three sorts of seed wheat from Ellis and distributed it among them 'to provoke them to vie, who will obtain the best crop'.[9]

We must set Ellis's various publications against this background of book-agricultural conflict. His books undoubtedly were book-agriculture. All contained varying amounts of material from published textbooks.

---

6  Ibid., p. 323.
7  Bradley, *General Treatise*, pp. 1–2.
8  Ellis, *The Practice of Farming*, Preface.
9  Ellis, *Modern Husbandman*, June, p. 37.

Ellis consulted published works on agriculture, gardening, brewing and cookery in writing his books. Some were near contemporary, such as 'Dr Hales' Philosophical experiments', Batty Langley or 'Mr Lawrence'. Others were older: Richard Bradley's *Country Housewife*, and works by Evelyn, Worlidge, Houghton, Grew and Mortimer, while some dated from the seventeenth century – books by Rabisha, Speed, Markham, Sir Kenelm Digby, Murrell and Lawson, and what he coyly calls 'Ancient Authors'. Although he used published works, he did, we have seen in the case of agriculture, food and drink, and brewing, place much emphasis on practical experience and experiment.[10]

Take as an example Chapter One of *The Modern Husbandman* for July, which is on the subject of ploughing. It starts with three and a half pages detailing ploughing regimes in the Chilterns and the Vales of his native country. There is a short piece on a farmer ruined by incorrect ploughing, followed by reports and criticism of practices in Middlesex and several pages on ploughing in other counties in the south of England. After two examples of local farmers 'broken' by incorrect ploughing, Ellis highlights the good practice of a neighbour. Finally, he discusses the merits of several types of plough, all recently invented. Since this chapter records current farming methods in the Chiltern and Vale country and other areas of southern England, surely the local husbandmen would not object to this? They might, however, resent the criticism of some of their number who were not skilled at ploughing or did this agricultural operation at the wrong time or under the wrong conditions. They might also find the discussion of ploughs 'high flown'; for most of them, expenditure on a new plough would strain their finances. I suspect that the neighbour whose good practice was highlighted was a gentleman with a farm in hand rather than a husbandman. Ellis's monthly editions abound with chapters like this, mixtures of reportage and discussion. Like Bradley, quoted above, Ellis was, on occasion, frustrated by the attitudes of some of his fellow farmers: 'But of such force is the chain of antiquity and custom, that biases farmers, more than any other set of men in England, oftentimes to follow and practise those methods less advantageous, than what their neighbours do.'[11] Some 'who are averse to new Discoveries' dismiss innovation too readily; they 'slight an essay on the first sight, because it is not within the compass of that narrow understandings'. He expects that

---

10   Ellis, *Country Housewife*, pp. 245–7. Ellis seldom supplies more than the name of the author of a book he has consulted.
11   Ellis, *The Modern Husbandman*, July, September, p. 148.

the many [...] new things that I am going to publish in Agriculture &c will be followed and practised in time by those very Cavilists, for the sake of their interest only; for I don't expect dint of reason will ever get so much the ascendant with these sort of people as to reduce their obstinacy to practice on any other footing.[12]

Nevertheless, he was optimistic: 'however, I am in hopes the eyes of their understanding will be open'd in time, and if reason won't convince them, the examples of their more discerning neighbours will.'[13] Alleging that many orchards have been planted incorrectly, Ellis defends the value of textbooks: '[h]ow necessary then are these Books, that may convict Persons of such fatal Mistakes, and shew them at the same time a way of planting, that will be truly successful, and give them fruit in a little Time, as well as many Years afterwards'. Ellis was, therefore, using his books to try to instruct farmers but, by quoting many examples of farmers' successes and failures, he was using their own practice to do this.[14]

Most agriculture books did not attempt to educate the husbandman; they were written for gentlemen in the hope that their example would tempt husbandmen to follow their lead. The editor of Edward Lisle's *Observations in Husbandry* (1757) thought the book contained 'valuable hints to those who have the judgement to make use of them [...] to encourage them in making trials'. And Ellis, although he reported the ways of husbandmen, in practice was writing books on agriculture that would be read by the gentry and yeomen of England because only these classes had the money to buy books and the education to enable them to read.[15]

Books such as Laurence's *A New System of Agriculture* (1727), the works of Mortimer, Worlidge and Hale, or those of Richard Bradley (frequently criticised by Ellis) are didactic and methodical, sparing in their use of examples, setting out what they consider to be the correct way of doing things. In contrast, Ellis devotes a considerable amount of space in his books to reports, positive and negative, of his own farming activities, his neighbours', and those he has observed in his travels. So, Ellis's books are, in theory, more evenly divided between instructing gentlemen and reporting husbandmen's activities. After all, he was an unusual example – someone who had benefited from book learning via his study of books, probably in a gentleman's library, but had also gained much basic knowledge of farming from his neighbours when he began farming,

---

12 Ellis, *Practical Farmer*, pt II, pp. 195–6.
13 Ibid., p. 180.
14 Ibid., pp. 195–6.
15 Lisle, *Observations*, p. viii.

apparently with no prior knowledge. Despite the even-handedness, in practice his books were probably as little read by husbandmen as any other agricultural textbook and they were as likely to be sceptical of his books as any other textbook.[16]

## Awareness of economic change

The mid-eighteenth century was a period of economic change: it saw the pace of industrialisation quicken, and with it the increase in agricultural productivity that was an essential concomitant if industrialisation and rapid population growth were to be sustained. How much of these changes did Ellis recognise and understand? He was a keen observer of the rural economy outside his farm gate, from the local to the national. The duke of Bridgewater's country estate, Ashridge House, was practically *at* Ellis's front gate and he saw its influence on local agriculture and society. The duke's establishment gave employment to the village – Ellis reported that he had two 'man cooks', sixty 'menial servants' and thirty day-labourers on his estate, as well as specialist tradesmen, such as a butcher, a farrier and a head gardener. The duke's animals created a demand for fodder: he owned 150 horses of all types and 1000 deer roamed his park. Ellis tells us that he and his neighbours sold their hay to the duke of Bridgewater to feed his deer in springtime. There was a renewed interest at this time among the aristocracy in keeping game for sport and pleasure, and no doubt the duke's deer were also a source of lean fresh meat. The gentry, recognising that the diminution of commons by enclosure gave them less land to hunt or shoot over, created more private parks set aside for deer and other game.[17] Bridgewater's park at Ashridge was described by Ellis as 'the best planted park in England'. Trees in the park beautified it, gave shelter to his game and were long-term capital improvements, as was the duke's diversion of the Gaddesden River to improve drainage of his meadows. Most of the 150 horses at Ashridge would have been draught animals for work on the farm or carriage horses, but some may have been racehorses – another pursuit becoming increasingly popular among those who could afford it. So, Ellis recognised that the Ashridge estate loomed large in the local economy of Little Gaddesden.[18] The village reminds one of the ideal 'model' villages at the gates of a country house envisioned by Timothy Nourse in 1700:

---

16 Laurence, *New System*; Mortimer, *Whole Art of Husbandry*; Worlidge, *Systema Agriculturae*; Thomas Hale, *A Compleat Body of Husbandry* (London, 1756). Several of the Ellis's books owned by the author of this book have bookplates indicating gentry ownership.
17 Ellis, *Modern Husbandman*, February, pp. 97–8.
18 Ellis, *Country Housewife*, pp. 245–7.

At the entrance of the Park therefore I would have a little Town or Village, consisting of about thirty or forty houses, built or rang'd in one streight Street, leading to the Park-Gate; the building to be low, uniform, and suitable for such as may inhabit them, as Carpenters, Masons, Plaisteres, a Glasier and Plummer, Smiths, as Lock-Smith, Gun-Smith, and for Tools and Implements of husbandry, a Wheelwright, Sadler, Taylor, Shooe-Maker, Mercer or Chandler, a Butcher; in a word, for all sorts of artificers and labourers, which any nobleman's house can stand in need of.[19]

On a wider scale, Ellis was conscious of the influence of London, by far the biggest urban area in England, on the economy of his county. He tacitly realised that the major part of his business depended on the capital: the books and periodicals in which he advertised his goods and services were published there; the depots of the carriers and shipping he used were at several large inns in London, so that goods often had to be sent to London before being carried out again to rural customers; the seedsmen who supplied the agricultural seeds he sold were all based in shops in London; and the rudimentary banking system that customers used to pay him was centred on London. Fruiterers who purchased some of his, and his neighbours', fruit on the trees before they were ripe were London-based, and London cow and calf dealers came to nearby Leighton Great Market, buying up cattle and corrupting the young with their profanities.

Ellis constantly emphasised the proximity of London. Phrases such as 'Now we that live in Hertfordshire, at twenty or thirty miles distance from London' appear over and over again in his books and some of the produce of Gaddesden and round about was specifically produced for the London market: honeysuckle was grown in the parish and 'these parts furnish great quantities of its seed to London, where they sell it under the name of Cow Grass'.[20] Farmers' wives tended poultry and sent eggs to be cried in the streets of London and raised calves for the London veal market; Hertfordshire turnips for human consumption sold for most money in London because they were the earliest – 'the first turneps at market make the rarity, and that the greater price; for it is both a great pleasure and conveniency to eat these turneps in June, July, and August.'[21]

We have already discussed the heavy use of various types of waste imported from London to improve the soil of Hertfordshire farms. The Chiltern lands were

---

19  Timothy Nourse, *Campania Foelix* (London, 1700), p. 331.
20  Ellis, *Modern Husbandman*, January, p. 77; December, p. 409.
21  Ellis, *Modern Husbandman*, April, p. 19.

most of them naturally poor soils of themselves, but of late greatly improved by the industry of its farmers, who living within a day's journey of London, many of them have been encouraged to employ their teams at vacant times to carry meal, bran, chaff, corn, wood and other vendible's thither, in order to load back again with soot, ashes, hoofs, horn-shavings, rags, &c. for dressing their land, that by the help of these and good ploughings, many have the benefit of grain, grass, turnips, &c. yearly, without the loss of one summer for the fallow season; which of late has become so profitable, that our Chiltern farms let for more than the Vale grounds.[22]

The farmers of Chalfont, in Hertfordshire, profited from proximity to London:

Here their soil is a gravelly loam, for the most part, that lies enclosed, at about twenty-three miles distant from London, which encourages most of these farmers to suckle house lambs; and the more, because the carrying of their own and neighbours, to make up a profitable load of them to Smithfield, gives them an opportunity by the same return to bring down soot, or horn shavings, or trotters, or hair, or glovers shavings, or hoofs, or sprats, or rabbit dung, made by those who keep the same sort in hutches, which many do in London and the adjacent parts, to considerable profit. I say, these farmers, by these means, sow a great deal of artificial grasses for their sucking ewes.[23]

Ellis and his fellow farmers thought it profitable 'to buy London coal-soot, even at one shilling a bushel charge, when at home, to lay on our meadow ground'. Arthur Young echoed Ellis's words on fertiliser brought from London, writing in 1804, 'It is the general opinion of the district that the soil cannot be kept in that degree of fertility necessary to support the rental and other expenses of it, without bringing large quantities of manure from the capital.'[24]

On his frequent visits to London Ellis went through Middlesex, north and west of the capital, and observed the increasingly strong pull of the London market in the growing intensity of agriculture there: the sandy loams of Kensington, Chelsea and Fulham were 'so much dunged, that it

---

22   Ellis, *Practical Farmer*, pp. 220–1.
23   Ellis, *Modern Husbandman*, November, p. 295; January, p. 73.
24   Young, *Hertfordshire*, p. 24.

is always under almost at hot bed-heat'.[25] Expanding on these remarks, he reports that in these areas

> they are here enabled to get three or four crops of grain, or culinary vegetables, off of an acre of their sandy, loamy ground, in one year; because they can lodge greater quantities of dung in this soil, than they can in clayey bottoms; for here they can plow and dig it in deeper, and rot it sooner, than in such stiff earths; insomuch, that some of their ground is almost in a continual ferment and chaleur, as their pea and bean gatherers often painfully experience, in long and dry hot seasons of the year [...] this ground lies near the hot air of London, and the soil is naturally dry and warm of itself, that defends the pea crops very much from the spoils of frosts, wets, and north-east winds [...] as they sow their peas for gathering them in the green pod, they sow them at several times a year, that one crop may succeed another; and thereby they are enabled to furnish the great city with their delicious green food, from May or June, at a cheap rate, till Michaelmas. And when a crop of early pease is got off, they sow pease again for a latter crop, or turneps, or wheat. &c. Thus, these Middlesex farmers get a crop or two more in a year, than we can do, who live at thirty miles distance from the Metropolis.[26]

It is interesting that he recognised that London and its suburbs were hotter the year round than other parts of England.

Ellis was aware that the whole country had seen agricultural output increase significantly during the time he had been farming. Looking back in 1749 he wrote:

There hardly needs Argument to prove, that new Discoveries in Husbandry have increased the Riches of this Nation, more within these forty years last past, than in Centuries before; the Improvement of many Thousands of barren Lands witnesses it: What Quantities of them have been gained from the Sea? What Numbers of Acres have been amended by subterranean Cuts, to drain off Waters? And what innumerable Parcels of poor, sterile Earths, have been fertilized by new-invented Drill-Plows, Horsebreaks, Manures, and other Managements? Whereby there have been obtained, with the Blessing of Heaven, such plentiful Crops of Grain,

---

25 A hot bed was a garden bed with a few inches of fine soil on top of a layer of fresh rotting manure. This dung gave off heat as it decomposed and crops matured fast in this rich, heated soil. Ellis likens the soil of some areas of Middlesex near to London to hot beds because they had so much manure dug into them that they are perpetually heated. Light sandy or loamy soils absorbed manure more quickly and, when heavily dunged, were more productive than cold clay soils. For a fuller discussion of this high input–high output agriculture near London see Thick, *The Neat House Gardens*.

26 Ellis, *Modern Husbandman*, December, pp. 402–4.

and artificial Grasses, &c. that our Forefathers were Strangers to the Enjoyment of: By which we have been enabled, not only to supply our own Nation with Fulness of Provisions, but also to support foreign ones, by the Sale of our Grain and other Commodities.[27]

His choice of factors that had led to the increase in agricultural output and the order in which he placed them would probably not be disputed by today's agricultural historians, one of whom wrote, 'the reclamation of land for some form of systematic cultivation was one of the major developments of the period'.[28] Finally, at an international level, he foresaw the potential of North America as a producer of agricultural produce for export to Europe, 'cutting down wood, sowing vast tracts of land with wheat, and importing it and selling it in Europe'.[29]

But Ellis was aware that, if, near London, the pull of market forces was strong enough to drive agricultural productivity forward, these forces were more diffuse further from big markets and ran up against the inertia of farmers set in their ways, either because they did not want to change their methods or because, living a hand-to-mouth existence on small farms, they could not afford to experiment – a disastrous year might be enough to ruin them. Ellis had hopes that gentlemen would experiment and demonstrate to husbandmen any successes they achieved; he gives many instances when gentlemen, on their home farms or farms they had taken in hand, tried new crops, new ways of growing crops, or the use of drill-ploughs and the like. He pointed out that, ultimately, they would gain by the increased rents they could extract from successful tenants who adopted new methods. In a particularly clear statement of the role of gentlemen (as regards, in this example, using drills to grow turnips) he writes:

> This is husbandry indeed, which may be carried on in a thousand and ten thousand places, where they practice no such thing; nor can be expected to be done, unless gentlemen of brighter parts, and heavier purses than farmers have, lead the way, and convince them by the only rule of persuasion, ocular demonstration, and experience; and indeed, for it is the interest of most gentlemen, who are possessed of landed estates, so to do; because by this they will have their rents better paid, as well as the tenant secured from breaking.[30]

---

27  Ellis, *Compleat system of experienced improvements*, Preface, f. a2.
28  Thirsk, *Agrarian History of England and Wales*, vol. V, pt 1, p. 121.
29  Ellis, *Compleat system of experienced improvements*, Preface; Ellis, *Modern Husbandman*, January, p. 25.
30  Ellis, *Modern Husbandry*, April, pp. 22–3.

In giving prominence to the role of gentlemen in demonstrating new types of husbandry Ellis was unwittingly giving ammunition to the agricultural historians who have laid emphasis on the part the gentry played in the so-called Agricultural Revolution.[31] Ellis's farming career, c.1717–58, may (or may not) have coincided with the English Agricultural Revolution. The nature and timing of this crucial part of agricultural history has vexed agricultural historians for over a century: it has been set at various times between the sixteenth and nineteenth centuries. There is some consensus about what it was – a sustained increase in agricultural output and productivity that enabled farming to feed, more or less, a large increase in population and also to release workers from the land to urban occupations – factories, mines, transport and the like. How exactly this was carried out – the relative importance of new crops and technology, the lure of the market, the drive and initiative of landlords, the reorganisation of agriculture (enclosure), an increasingly capitalist agriculture with larger farms, more investment and market orientation – has long been the subject of debate. Opinions on the timing of the Revolution to a large extent depend on which of these factors is deemed the most important. Mark Overton has placed the Revolution in the century after 1750, demonstrating this with statistics that show that crop yields only began to rise significantly after the mid-eighteenth century. The major factor in increased output and yields, he concludes, was the shift to a more capitalist organisation of farming. Do Ellis's remarks on local and national agriculture shed light on the nature and timing of the Agricultural Revolution?[32]

We have seen from his remarks on turnips, clover and other 'improvement' crops that *he* was convinced of their importance. His comment that clover 'is now become the most general artificial grass sown in England' seems to indicate that he thought its use was widespread.[33] He also saw many acres of turnips in his travels around East Anglia, but it is significant that they are listed as one of the crops farmers on enclosed land were free to grow and he is clearly frustrated by the limitations on individual land use in open fields. He was also frustrated by the lack of initiative shown by many of his neighbours – small farmers whose children and grandchildren were, like many more in England, destined to be reduced to the status of agricultural labourers working for market-orientated farmers cultivating larger, enclosed, farms in the century after his death.

---

31   Such as Charles 'Turnip' Townshend, Robert Bakewell and so on: heroes of the Agricultural Revolution in my schooldays, who, after being relegated to minor roles, are today being rehabilitated by some historians.
32   Mark Overton, *Agricultural Revolution in England* (Cambridge, 1996).
33   Ellis, *Modern Husbandman*, March, p. 68.

Increasing willingness among the most go-ahead farmers to respond to the market was noted by Ellis. Market influence sometimes induced small producers to respond before the bigger farmers – we have seen Ellis's comment that his neighbour, a wood-turner, made a significant living from selling poultry, eggs and rabbits at market, no doubt destined to be cried round the streets of London. Ellis understood the relationship between proximity to the market and intensity of agriculture: the von Thunen effect.[34] This he observed every time he went to London. In his own locality the pull of the London market was selective – dairy products, veal, poultry, eggs and new season's turnips were most evidently produced for London's consumption. Travelling through Middlesex he observed the farmer–gardeners who ploughed part or all of their land, producing barley and wheat of such perfection that farmers from other counties came to buy it to sow in their fields. On some of their land the farmer–gardeners carefully drilled in beans for human consumption and, in the case of Fulham, rotated field and garden crops, all to be sold fresh in London markets. Finally, he saw the Kensington gardeners who cropped their grounds almost continually by adding massive amounts of dung to their soils, producing fruits and vegetables wholly for the London market. Overall, Ellis was convinced that agriculture had become more efficient during his working life. He singled out folding as a particular example of agricultural advance on the light Chiltern soils. He was, however, conscious that much more could be done to improve farming in England.

So, Ellis's remarks could support the argument for a significant improvement in English agriculture in the eighteenth century both before and after 1750. Arthur Young in 1804 thought that Hertfordshire agriculture had essentially stood still since the time Ellis was writing. It had, he thought, advanced significantly earlier in the century (when Ellis was farming). Young was, apart from the practice of folding, in agreement with Ellis as to what these advances had been: turnips – 'This most useful plant was cultivated very early in Hertfordshire, as a general article of husbandry; and I believe, before they were commonly introduced in Norfolk'; clover – 'This noble plant, the introduction of which has wrought a greater improvement in English agriculture than that of any other, has been cultivated in this county, probably as long, or longer, than in any part of the kingdom'; and tares – 'I found tares very generally cultivated for soiling the teams; a husbandry that cannot be too much commended. It appears by the writings of Ellis, that this branch of agriculture was common in Hertfordshire above 60 years since, before it was at all practised in many other counties.'[35]

---

34 For more on von Thunen's theory see Thick, *The Neat House Gardens*, pp. 55–6.
35 Young, *Hertfordshire*, pp. 102, 115, 125. By 'soiling the teams' he meant causing the horses to produce dung.

We may conclude that Ellis, as well as being a good observer of the present, was also aware of the changes that were going on over time in his own locality and in the agriculture of the country in general.

## Income

Ellis seems never to have been particularly wealthy and at times was reported to be badly off. He left no accounts and no inventory of his household goods survives, but this chapter will attempt to pull together what evidence there is concerning his wealth and income. One of Ellis's neighbours thought he obtained 'considerable money' from his sales of agricultural machinery, seeds, plants and books. It is impossible, from the information he provides in his books, to give more than an impression of his income from these sources or decide which was the most lucrative. It was, however, possible to make a reasonable income as an author in the eighteenth century. Legislation on copyright early in the century had strengthened the position of authors when negotiating with publishers, but set against that was the sharp decline in patronage – no longer could an author dedicate a work to a wealthy patron and expect a substantial reward. The royalty system had not yet started, so each publication required an agreement between author and publisher to purchase the copyright for a sum of money. Obviously, there were occasions when the unexpected success of a work meant a windfall profit for the publisher at the expense of the author, but some non-fiction works, especially histories, in Ellis's time made large sums, some over £1000, for their authors. No accounts of Ellis's authorship rewards exist but it is plausible to presume that, once established as a writer, his bargaining power would have been enhanced. His books were, for some years, the dominant sources of new agricultural advice, giving him some 'monopoly' power.[36]

No reasons are given in his books for his decision to publish but he did enter his writing career with caution. Although later prefaces are confident or even assertive, that of his first publication, *The Practical Farmer* of 1732, is short and humble. In one and a half pages he acknowledges that existing books on agriculture have successfully encouraged improved farming, and that in writing this book

> I have humbly thrown my Mite into the Public Treasury: and, for the Sake of my good intention for the common wheal, I hope the generous will excuse the deficiencies that may have accompany'd my rustic pen; which hereafter I shall silence or employ in further enlargements of this kind.[37]

---

36 Harry Ransom, 'The Rewards of Authorship in the Eighteenth Century', *Studies in English*, 18 (1938), pp. 47–66.
37 Ellis, *Practical Farmer*, f. A2v.

He obviously did not lay down his pen. Three early works, published in 1733, 1736 and 1738, were printed 'for the Author'. This meant he took on the burden of publishing himself – persuading booksellers to stock the books and selling them on his travels. Self-publishing could be profitable if the book were well received, but the author shouldered all the risks and costs. One of his self-published ventures was *New Experiments in Husbandry, for the Month of April*. This book contains only two months' observations, April and May, and may well be what remained of a failed venture by Ellis to produce a periodical in twelve monthly parts, perhaps part of 'my monthly books that I have for these six or seven years past been endeavouring after'.[38] This may also be the same venture advertised as forthcoming monthly books on agriculture at one shilling an issue, with a discount for those who subscribed to six in advance. That he was struggling to make a success of this venture is clear from the preface of the part he *did* publish: he hopes 'some generous Persons will voluntarily assist him, with Subscriptions or other Ways, towards printing the Month of May (which is now ready) and the rest of his Books'. It may be that he found it harder than he anticipated to self-publish, for all his later ventures have publishers. The publisher who produced more of his books than any other was Thomas Astley, who published Ellis's first book in 1732 and his last in 1759.[39]

One problem he encountered when self-publishing was pirated editions. In *New Experiments in Husbandry, for the Month of April* he complains:

> I must also observe, the great Hardship I myself am under, being inform'd that my Books are reprinted at Dublin, and sold even as far as Gloucester, and the Northern Parts of Britain, where they sell them cheaper than I can afford, by reason of the low Prices that Paper and Printing are at there.[40]

Ireland was not covered by the Copyright Act of 1709 so publishers did not have to pay authors for the right to publish and other book production costs were lower in Dublin than in London. An Act of 1739 should have stopped the import of books printed abroad when the first editions of them had been published in England, but it was difficult to enforce. At least working with a publisher transferred the risks of publication away from the author.[41]

---

38  Ibid., p. 40. This remark, published in 1732, implies that he had been writing on agriculture since at least 1725.
39  Ibid., p. 214; Sarah Werner, *Studying Early Printed Books* (London, 2019), pp. 23–5.
40  Ellis, *New Experiments in Husbandry, for the Month of April*, p. 121.
41  Ibid.

Relationships between author and publisher could at times be tetchy. A correspondent complained to Ellis that it was now February and the monthly part of the *Modern Husbandman* for November had yet to be published. Ellis blamed the printer, explaining, 'I am forced to stay delivering one copy, till the former is printed off.' Ellis was clearly on top of his hard schedule of delivering perhaps 40,000 words a month for this periodical and there is no evidence that he was forced to include much irrelevant matter each month to make up his word target. This was a story made up by the anonymous editor of *Husbandry Methodized*, who attributed the numerous passages of 'absurd, trivial, or tedious material [...] to his connections with his booksellers who insisted on certain quantities of monthly Matter'. Indeed, Ellis wanted to write more:

> I have been solicited to write a lesser number of sheets for one month, that the price of each book might be lessened accordingly; but, if I had acquiesced to such proposal, I must in course have marred my design, which is to explain the intricate art of husbandry, according to the present practice, in its numerous branches, for the benefit of the farmer, gentleman, and the nation in general.

On another occasion he repeated that he could write more but it would involve increasing the price from thirteen pence to two shillings.[42]

Ellis was at times as frustrated by the lack of illustrations in his books: publishers viewed engravings, 'cuts' as he termed them, as expensive to commission and print. Ellis wrote that a horse-hoe would be depicted 'in my monthly supplement to the Modern Husbandman, eighteen pence', but no illustration was published. In 1749 he advertised a part-work that did not materialise, *New Discoveries and Improvements in Husbandry*. 'Each Book' was, he wrote, 'to contain five Cuts of new Instruments of Husbandry' – most likely the publishers baulked at five engravings per issue. He also announced in the same year a much more ambitious project, an illustrated catalogue 'with near forty [...] instruments' – this, too, did not materialise.[43]

---

42 Ellis, *Modern Husbandman*, February, p. 92; [Ellis], *Ellis's Husbandry*, p. viii. The way books were printed until the mid-twentieth century meant that a part print run was not possible. A book's whole print run had to be printed before any sales could be made. Consequently, much capital would be tied up in the production of a large book. A monthly periodical, with separate pagination of each issue, needed less capital and the prospect of a more immediate return.

43 Ellis and Trowell, *Farmer's Instructor*, pp. 144–5; Ellis, *Compleat system of experienced improvements*, p. 60.

His books were his main vehicle for advertising the ploughs, horse-hoes, seeds, trees, fowls and other miscellaneous goods he sold. From the copies of letters sent to him by prospective customers and his replies we can gain a few scraps of information of his income from these goods. He advertised a range of seeds of trees and fodder crops and some of the orders resulting from these offers could be substantial – in September 1742 Ellis sent over 10,000 tree seeds as well as 360 Arbele plants and a pound of 'French Furz' to a gentleman. For this he received three guineas in full settlement of his bill but, as Ellis invariably asked for a guinea deposit on new orders, the total bill may have been four guineas.[44] In another transaction involving seeds, Ellis explained to his customer that the price of agricultural seeds was rising: clover seed that had been 3½d or 4d per pound had now risen to 5d; trefoil in hull (i.e. not de-husked) was 3s 6d a bushel, and ray grass 4s a bushel. Ellis's special selection of meadow-grass seeds was 7d a pound. All but this last item Ellis obtained from the small number of London seedsmen who dominated the English market. On big orders from these firms Ellis probably was charged wholesale rates but we do not know how much he marked up his prices when he sold to customers. His special meadow-grass seed he obtained mainly from his own grasslands and local farmers but he frequently had to travel to find supplies, which is no doubt reflected in the price.[45]

In only one instance do we have in his writings full details of a transaction involving the sale of a machine. In 1743 Ellis supplied a Banking Plough to a gentleman who paid 13s on account. The total bill was itemised as follows:

| | |
|---|---|
| Wheeler and smith's work | £1 6s 3½d |
| Carriage for 5 miles | 3s |
| Ellis's time and trouble | £1 1s 0d[46] |

As well as supervising the construction of the plough, Ellis had ridden several miles in an abortive attempt to locate some meadow seeds and he accompanied the plough five miles to deliver it. As mentioned, a deposit of one guinea was usually asked for and, although on occasion he asked for a consideration, which he left at the customer's discretion, it is a reasonable assumption that a guinea per plough profit may have been his usual terms. We do not know how many transactions were carried out in a year, but

---

44  Ellis, *Modern Husbandman*, November, pp. 354–5.

45  Ibid., p. 368; Malcolm Thick, 'Garden Seeds in England before the Late Eighteenth Century – II, The Trade in Seeds to 1760', *Agricultural History Review*, 38/2 (1990), pp. 105–16.

46  Ellis, *Modern Husbandman*, January, p. 41.

there are three in consecutive months printed in the *Modern Husbandman*, and Kalm saw a pile of unanswered correspondence in his study when he visited Ellis. Moreover, Ellis boasted that in 1749 he delivered five ploughs and other such instruments to London in one batch for delivery by carrier.[47] If he did make a guinea on each substantial transaction, this compares well with his estimates of profits from farming. In 1732 he estimated his profit per acre from major arable crops as follows:

| | |
|---|---|
| Beans (an exceptional year) | £1 6s 6d |
| Oats | £1 0s 0d |
| Barley, a *loss* of | £0 3s 6d |
| Wheat, a *loss* of | £0 10s 9d[48] |

If, theoretically, he grew an equal acreage of these principal crops, his average profit per acre would have been 8s 4d, meaning that he would have to carry out all the operations of cultivation for a year on 2½ acres to obtain a profit equal to that from one plough sale. One plough sale at one guinea profit is equivalent to £1,838 at today's prices, so that one sale a month would equate to just over £22,000 annual profit today.[49]

These estimates for the writing and publishing, as well as the sales of ploughs, seeds and so on, are highly conjectural, but they do seem to bear out his neighbours' impression that a significant part of Ellis's income came from activities other than farming. Another indication that, at some point in his career, he was doing well is that he *may* have had his portrait made by the foremost portraitist in pastel of his day, John Russell. The picture was sold at auction in 1931, when it was described as 'a gentleman in brown coat, white waistcoat and cravat, holding a scroll inscribed "Improvement of wheel carriages"'. From the catalogue description of the clothing of the upper body only, this portrait was a head and shoulders rather than a full-length depiction. Nevertheless, at the height of his popularity Russell charged thirty guineas for such a picture. The clothes, a plain brown coat and white waistcoat, are what we would expect a working yeoman farmer to wear and accord with Ellis's estimation of his social status. The words on the scroll must be an allusion to the chapter in the *Modern Husbandman* in which Ellis sets out an elaborate theory on such improvements. But Russell was born in 1745 and Ellis died in 1759, well before Russell started his career as a fashionable portraitist.

---

47  See p. 83.
48  Ellis, *The Practice of Farming*, pp. 170, 171, 176, 193.
49  Floud, *Economic History of the English Garden*, p. xii (facing).

Either the picture is not of Ellis, or it is a posthumous portrait copied from another lost original. Given the 'wheel carriages' detail, it is likely to be a copy of an earlier picture of Ellis.[50]

## Later reputation

> FARMER Ellis was a very odd character, a kind of rough diamond, of intrinsic worth indeed, but that worth was concealed under a rude, unpromising form and appearance. He had a good practical knowledge of his business, the result of much attention and long experience; and he was, by the singularity of his fortune, induced to communicate that knowledge to the public, in a great number of ill-written volumes, filled with a strange mixture of just observations and old wifery, useful precepts, and silly stories; with a long train of receipts in cookery and physic, and endless cautions against gypsies, vagrant-thieves, and bad servants: the whole forming a rude, indigested heap, in which everything that was valuable was buried, and in danger of being totally lost in the rubbish.[51]

This is the unpromising start of a review of *Husbandry Methodized*, the abridged edition of Ellis's works issued some years after his death in 1772. It echoes some of the comments in the editorial introduction to that two-volume work and also sets the tone for many later comments on Ellis and his work.[52]

The introduction, which was anonymous, reviewed Ellis's writings and his reputation. Despite the quotation above it was, on the whole, a favourable review, as one would expect if the object of the new edition was to make money. The editor pointed out that Ellis's books had made 'his name familiar throughout Europe; for his works have been quoted and commended by numerous foreign writers on the subject of husbandry' (unfortunately, the author gives no references for this remark). Ellis spent many years as a hands-on farmer, 'so that his works, as he borrowed nothing from others, were really original, and contained genuine knowledge than far more shining performances abounded with'.[53]

The editor summarises the good material in Ellis's books:

---

50 Neil Jeffares, 'RUSSELL, John', *Dictionary of Pastellists before 1800*, <http://www.pastellists.com/Articles/Russell.pdf#search=%22John%20RUSSELL%22>, accessed 5 December 2021; Ellis, *Modern Husbandman*, January, pp. 111–19.
51 *The Monthly Review, or Literary Journal*, 48 (1773), pp. 129–32.
52 Ibid.
53 [Ellis], *Ellis's Husbandry*, pp. iii–iv.

he speaks clear, sound, good sense, and so much to the purpose that I will venture to assert no writer has in this path exceeded him: but the public have paid so little attention to his works from the quantity of rubbish they contain, that Ellis's real merit is little known. It is not at present recollected, that all the spirited practices of excellent common husbandry, which have of late years made so much noise, are clearly ascertained by him, their merit stated, and their conduct explained. The best turnip and clover husbandry are in particular set forth, as practically as they can be at this day: the whole conduct of manures, though not philosophically handled, yet are stated with practical precision; and the common management in them fully explained. A full knowledge of the use of soiling cattle with tares, clover, &c.—saving the drainings of the farm yard—forming composts—the variations of soils which require corresponding variations of manure and tillage (an article of great importance, and fully treated by no other writer) and the whole management of sheep—are among many other instances of Ellis's thorough knowledge in common husbandry.[54]

The editorial, however, commented on the shortcomings in Ellis's works and it is these comments that have formed the basis for many later reviews of Ellis's place in the history of English agriculture. The editor asked, 'how a man possessing a good understanding, long practice, and attentive observation, should produce so many faults as Ellis? And in truth his faults are so numerous, that they have prejudiced many good judges against his works.' The editor does not, however, go on to enumerate these faults. He attributes the problem to the insistence of his publisher that he churn out a large number of words each month for the monthly publication *The Modern Husbandman* and as a consequence 'he gave into all those random ridiculous details which have so disgraced his page'. This theory appears to have been originated by the anonymous editor. It was, as we have seen, contradicted by Ellis, who insisted at one point that he could have written much *more* on some topics but was restrained by the *publisher's* need to keep the price of the monthly parts down.[55]

The editor of *Ellis's Husbandry, Abridged and Methodized* excluded passages referring to new types of plough and horse-hoe because they were clearly advertisements. He also ignored various seed steeps, other recipes and nostrums, and much on drill husbandry because, according to the editor, Ellis did not do much of this on his own farm. He also excluded 'all his gypsies, wenches, thieves, rogues, &c [...] and his old woman's tales which filled a page but diminished from its value'. In doing so he ignored all medical and culinary recipes.[56]

---

54  Ibid., pp. x–xii.
55  Ibid., pp. iv–vi.
56  Ibid., pp. ix–xi.

Some seventy years later George W. Johnson, writing in 1852, concludes sadly that Ellis did not make a good living from farming and spent large sums on agricultural experiments.[57] After a full review of his various publications, in 1854 John Donaldson sums Ellis up with faint praise thus:

> Ellis was not the author of any originality on the subject of agriculture, nor did he write any conception that merited that appellation. But he was a large promoter of the art both by precept and example, and consequently occupies a niche of no low standing in the temple of agricultural fame.[58]

The *Victoria County History for Hertfordshire (VCH)* of 1908 damns Ellis in a couple of sentences: 'William Ellis, a writer on agricultural subjects, held a farm at Little Gaddesden for about fifty years. His works have now become useless owing to the advance of science; his best is The Modern Husbandman.'[59] No doubt the same could be said of all books on agriculture more than a century old. The *VCH* took its information on Ellis from the *Dictionary of National Biography*, which gives a brief, factual summary of his life, based largely on the editorial in *Husbandry Methodized* and containing several errors.[60] His reputation was partially rescued by George Fussell in the mid-twentieth century, who commented that he wrote the first book on sheep in English, that his books contain a great deal of information on life in eighteenth-century Hertfordshire and that 'his record of what was done in other counties may also be trusted'. But Fussell also comments that Ellis 'filled out his books with a farrago of incidental matters'. H.W. Gardiner's survey of Hertfordshire agriculture in 1967 is favourably disposed to Ellis, using quotations from his books as chapter headings and agreeing with Ellis on various aspects of soil management.[61] Ellis's reliability as a reporter of Hertfordshire husbandry is confirmed by a reliance on his writings in the description of the metropolitan counties in the *Agrarian History of England and Wales*, volume V, published in 1984. A decade later, however, Mark Overton

---

57 George W. Johnson, *Cottage Gardener*, vol. 8 (1852), p. 13.
58 John Donaldson, *Agricultural Biography* (London, 1854), pp. 50–3.
59 William Page (ed.), *A History of the County of Hertford: Volume II* (London, 1908), pp. 208–14; British History Online, <http://www.british-history.ac.uk/vch/herts/vol2/pp208-214>, accessed 28 September 2020.
60 *Dictionary of National Biography*, <https://www.oxforddnb.com/view/10.1093/ref:odnb/9780198614128.001.0001/odnb-9780198614128-e-8718?rskey=u6tMMz&result=5>, accessed 28 May 2020.
61 Fussell, 'Farming writers'; Gardiner, *Hertfordshire*, pp. 122–3, 128, 138.

dismisses Ellis as a slovenly farmer and incompetent journalist via two quotations from Kalm.[62]

Ellis's one book on food, *The Country Housewife*, has received the favourable reviews it deserves in recent years; Joan Thirsk thought that

> [h]e obviously had respect for the resourcefulness of women in the kitchen, and took a highly practical interest in details of their cooking. Indeed, for the food historian he is one of the most precious informants of his age, shedding much light on the cooking routines of working folk, including the families of farm labourers.[63]

But A.W. Oxford, a bibliographer of cookery books, writing in 1913, failed to grasp the nature of 'homely' country cures and found the book contained 'medical recipes, many of them of the usual filthy nature'.[64]

Ellis and his fellow villagers were accorded a short but entertaining biography by the local historian Vicars Bell in the 1940s that also helped to restore his reputation. One other book about Ellis has been identified: Paul Stanbridge's *William Ellis, The Forgotten Improver*. This is a typescript volume of over 180 pages, undated and to be found in the Museum of English Rural Life in Reading. This copy is the only one known. It may have been an extended essay or thesis for an academic qualification.[65]

Ellis's writings have been used as source books for several different types of history. Most obviously, agricultural historians have pored over his descriptions of farming in the Chilterns and Vale and he was the source of much information on rural diets in the 1750s. But he has had more unexpected uses. In 1880 James Britten used Ellis as a source of dialect words, mostly from Hertfordshire. Using mainly the multi-volume *Modern Husbandman*, Britten assembled no less than fifty-four pages of such words, from 'abel' – the tree *Populus Albai* – to 'youghth', a disease of sheep. Along the way he noted such evocative words as 'sullidge' (slush or sediment); 'stunnified' (stunned); 'strangullian' (a disease of horses); 'shackle-hammed' (bow-legged); and 'nickanockass' (a senseless person).[66]

The arrival of Pehr Kalm in Little Gaddesden is testament to the interest in Ellis's works in Europe, most of which would have been read in English there. Presumably his books were sold at the Frankfurt book fair. Some of

---

62 Thirsk, *Agrarian History of England and Wales*, vol. V, pt 1, pp. 247–65; Overton, *Agricultural Revolution*, p. 129.
63 Thirsk, *Food in Early Modern England*, p. 167.
64 Arnold Whitaker Oxford, *English Cookery Books to the Year 1850* (London, 1913), p. 80.
65 Bell, *Mr. Ellis*; Stanbridge, *William Ellis*.
66 James Britten, *Old Country and Farming Words* (London, 1880), Glossary I.

his writing was also available in German and French. A German publication, the title of which can be translated as 'the general magazine of nature, art and science', published in 1753, contained several sections of the *Modern Husbandman*. The *Farmers Instructor* was published in German in 1750 and a German version of the *Timber Tree Improved* was published in Leipzig in 1752. There were also German editions of *Ellis's Husbandry Abridged and Methodized*, published in 1772 and 1774, soon after the English edition. A French magazine, *Annales typographiques ou notice du progrès des connoissances humaines*, published brief reviews of the *Complete Planter and Cyderist* in 1757, and Ellis's book on farriery in 1760.[67] Copies of the German translations were deposited in several German university libraries.[68] Contemporary opinions that Ellis's works had a Europe-wide reputation during his lifetime therefore appear to be correct. Some of his books were available in translation, whereas I can trace no translations of other husbandry books of his time such as those of Richard Bradley, John Mortimer or John Laurence. Kalm was sent to England to see Ellis and specifically to investigate his new agricultural machines, setting out in 1747 before any of his books appeared on the Continent in translation. His English language books must therefore have been read in Sweden before then. German translations and books by Ellis in German university libraries may even indicate that his standing in the German-speaking parts of Europe was higher than in his own country. Kalm's visit no doubt made Ellis aware of his Continental reputation but he may have been already aware of it, hence his wry remark to Kalm quoted above, that 'no prophet is accepted in his own country'.[69]

---

67 *Allgemeines Magazin der Natur, Kunst und Wissenschaften* (Leipzig, 1753); *Annales typographiques ou notice du progrès des connoissances humaines* (1757, 1760), William Ellis, *Land Wirthschaft* (1774); Wilhelm Ellis, *Von Erbauung des Zimmerholzes, Oder, die vorzüglichste Art, verschiedene Ländereyen mit gutem Zimmerholze zu versehen: wie auch denenjenigen Obstbäumen, deren Holz den Eigenthümern den meisten Vortheil bringet; nach den neuesten Erfindungen, durch den Pflug, die Harke, und durch andere Mittel, die am meisten Beyfal gefunden* (Leipzig, 1752); Wilhelm Ellis, *Anleitung für einen Landmann oder neue Abhandlung von dem Ackerbaue, der Gärtnerey, und andern merkwürdigen Dingen, welche die Landwirthschafft betreffen ... zuerst ans Licht gestellet von Herrn Samuel Trowell, hernach aber ... vollständig gemacht von Wilhelm Ellis, Pachter zu Littlegaddesden, in Herfordshire* (Leipzig, 1750).

68 For instance, the German translation of the *Farmers Instructor* is to be found in Staatsbibliothek Bamberg; Technische Universität Berlin, Zentralbibliothek; Bibliothek und Archiv im Haus der bayerischen Landwirtschaft Herrsching.

69 Verified by a search of Google Books for German translations 1690–1760.

*Chapter 8*
# Conclusion

It *is* possible to reconcile, on the one hand, Kalm's disappointed description of Ellis, his farming and the machines he sold together with his neighbours' low assessment of his farming and general neglect of his land with, on the other hand, the impression from his books that he was an innovator, a writer who attracted readers from all over the British Isles and abroad, and a successful yeoman farmer. Ellis did spend a good deal of time *not* on his land – he travelled extensively, went to London frequently and wrote many books. Moreover, his wife was mentally ill, not helped by the large number of children she tried to look after, and probably needed looking after herself rather than doing a good deal on the farm and in the farmhouse as most farmers' wives would do. Add to these factors the experiments Ellis carried out on the farm, including trying out new drill-ploughs and horse-hoes, and it is no wonder that some of his land was neglected. He did not have the resources to farm successfully and undertake all his other activities. Ellis was, in his books and farming experiments, acting like one of the improving landlords he supplied with seeds and machinery. *They* were gentlemen, with rents coming in from their tenants, who could afford to indulge in new farming methods on a home farm or one they had taken in hand and, more importantly, they could afford for these innovations to fail – Ellis could not. No wonder he drove his second wife to distraction by spending her money on his novel methods. Had Ellis been a gentleman with a landed estate, might he not have been remembered as an innovator, another Bakewell or Townsend, each accorded a chapter in Lord Ernle's classic history of English agriculture, rather than 'a Hertfordshire farmer whose writings enjoyed a short-lived popularity', who occupied scarcely two pages of Ernle's book? The visit of Pehr Kalm has done the reputation of Ellis much disservice: without it we would have no knowledge of his neglect of parts of his farm or the shortcomings of the machines he sought to sell. Kalm has given Ellis 'feet of clay'.[1]

---

1   Lord Ernle, *English Farming Past and Present*, 6th edn (London, 1961), pp. 191–2.

In not making a success of his own farm Ellis was following in the footsteps of a number of earlier agricultural writers. In the second half of the sixteenth century Thomas Tusser's *Five Hundred Points of Good Husbandry* was a popular book but Tusser's attempts at running a farm were not successful. In the next century Adolphus Speed wrote a book advocating innovations in agriculture but at the time he was an impoverished gentleman living in London who had to be rescued from debt by Samuel Hartlib.[2] The next great agricultural traveller and journalist after Ellis, Arthur Young, farmed unsuccessfully in Essex. Moreover, some of these men, like Ellis, were not bred from generations of farmers who succeeded to their father's farms. Tusser, brought up as a chorister, tried many occupations before farming and Young served an apprenticeship as a wine merchant. One of the sources of suspicion felt towards Ellis by his fellow farmers at Little Gaddesden was no doubt the fact that he arrived there, probably in his late twenties, as a London brewer with no farming knowledge and, after a few years, began a steady stream of books in which he criticised those farmers around him for not adopting improvements he advocated while he himself neglected some of his land.[3]

Ellis claimed to have written nineteen books, a figure bibliographers have not been able to reconcile with the publications known to be by him that are extant today. Whatever the total, they formed, for a time in the mid-eighteenth century, the majority of new works on agriculture available in England. Add to that an extremely popular textbook on brewing and another on country living and we have a body of literature that makes him an important figure in eighteenth-century English agrarian and social history. Ellis never doubted that his writings on agriculture, brewing and country life were important and, if followed, would lead to significant agricultural improvements. He also recognised that the conservatism of ordinary farmers was a significant obstacle to progress. He sums up the position thus:

> There are some, I am very sensible, that are apt to cavil with, or condemn a thing meerly for its being new, or that the same has been wrote on before, as if a Subject could not be further improved; but whoever will without prejudice consider the practical and rational part of the following Chapters, may assuredly find their Expectation answered, if their several Rules are closely followed, by which the King's revenue will be surely augmented, and Great Britain, Ireland, and

---

2  University of Sheffield, Hartlib Papers, HP 46/5/1A; HP 46/5/3A; HP 46/5/5A.

3  *Dictionary of National Biography*, 'Young, Arthur (1741–1820)', <https://www.oxforddnb.com/view/10.1093/ref:odnb/9780198614128.001.0001/odnb-9780198614128-e-30256?rskey=iagalG&result=4>; Fussell, *Old English Farming Books*, Pt 1, pp. 8–9; Pt 2, p. 77.

his majesty's plantations in America, in all probability, vastly increased in plenty of Grain, Grass, Wood and Cattle, which rules are here freely exposed, not in chimerical notions, but in solid truths, not in relations of things taken upon trust, and furnish'd up by a politer pen than my own, but in experimental facts deliver'd in their true native rustic dress.[4]

The aim of this book has been to present William Ellis in his 'true native rustic dress'.

---

4  Ellis, *Practice of Farming*, Preface, f. bi.

# *Appendix*
# Two examples of advertising flyers issued by Ellis

Ellis inserted this advertisement in the front of the book on the management of sheep, *A Compleat System of Experienced Improvements*. It looks like the text of a flyer.

*Advertisement*
WILLIAM ELLIS, the Author hereof, gives Notice to all Gentlemen and others, that he is ready to furnish to any Person, on a proper Order, I. The light, and most excellent four-wheel, Drill-Plow, that carries on it two Hoppers, one of a Peck Size, the other of a Bushel Size; the first for sowing Wheat or Barley, Pease, or Turnip, or Rape, or Lucerne Seed; and the latter for sowing a Manure on the Seed; as soon as it is in the Drill; both which are covered, either by a very little Harrow, with six Teeth, or with a very little Instrument called a Gatherer, according as the Seed is that is sown, fix'd to the Tail of the Drill-Plow, and drawn along with it, all by only one Horse, as it is now in Use by this Author; and thus it sows, and finishes the sowing of two Acres of Land in one Day. 2. He also furnishes a four-wheel, light, Drill-Plow, that sows two Drills at once; and a Horsebreak that cleans two Intervals of Ground at once. 3. He sells the light, little Foot-Plow, the Sale of which, in common, was formerly protected by a Patent. 4. The Turnwrest Plow, which is a necessary one to prepare Ground for using the four-wheel Drill-Plow. 5. The Drain-Plow. 6. The Anthill-Plow, or any other Plow. 7. He sells the famous Dame Wheat-Seed, which carries a smooth, large Ear, like the Lammas Sort, is a very great Yielder; first sown by this Author in 1746, but now he has it growing in several of his inclosed Fields, as it excellently well agrees with all Manner of loamy Soils, either in Vale or Chiltern Countries. 8. He also sells the matchless Lady-Finger Grass seeds, and two other Sorts of natural Grass-Seeds, for converting Plow'd Land into the very best of Meadow or Pasture. 9. He likewise sells Receipts to make two different sorts of Composts or Manures, that infallibly improve all Sorts

of Field or Garden-Crops, in the highest Degree of Perfection, and which certainly prevents the Slug, the Snail, the Worm, the Turnip-Fly, and the Butterfly or Caterpillar, damaging any Sort of Vegetable, in Field or Garden, for a small Expence. 10. He sells a Receipt to kill Rushes or Twitch-Grass, and that will cause a fine Grass to come up the same Year in their Room. 11. Another for keeping all Manner of Field Fowls from hurting new-sown Corn, if it lies in a Field ten Miles off a House, by a cheap and durable Machine. 12. How to improve old, decayed, Meadow, or Pasture Ground, and kill Moss in one Season, by Receipts never yet printed. 13. He sells a Receipt to kill the black or Norway Rat, or to make them forsake a House or Barn. 14. He sells the black Kerroon Cherry Tree, the Orange Pear-Tree, and the Parsnip-Apple; three Sorts, that no Gentleman or Farmer should be without, for Reasons assigned in his Modern Husbandman; and these for one Shilling a-piece, at his House. 15. He helps Gentlemen to any Sort of Servants. 16. He is ready to wait on any Gentleman in any Part of England or Wales, that thinks fit to consult his Advice in the Improvement of his Estate, according to the ancient, or the newest Methods of Husbandry; and answers all Letters, provided Postage is paid to his House, that stands at thirty Miles Distance from London.[1]

A year later he published the flyer below.

ADVERTISEMENT.
*THIS is to give Notice to all Gentlemen and others, that I furnish them, on a proper Order, with the new invented, light, four-wheel, plain Drill-plough, either the single or the double Sort, that carries two fixed Hoppers on it, a Seed Hopper, and a Manure Hopper, being an Improvement made on all other Drill-ploughs whatsoever; for by its Uses, with the Assistance of a new invented Horsebreak, that is drawn on two Wheels by only one Horse, and a very fertilizing compound Manure, poor Land (by the Blessing of Heaven) may be made to produce rich Crops of Grain, Turnips, Rapes, or artificial Grasses. The double Drill-plough sows two Drills at once, drawing along by only one Horse, and the Break, being made to hoe and clean two Intervals of Drill Ground at once drawing along, it will thus do more Work in one Day than twenty Men can. I likewise sell the two-wheel Hertfordshire double Plough, the two-wheel single fallow Plough, the two-wheel bob-tail Plough, the Turnrise Plough, – which is a proper one to lay all the Ground even where it lies not too wet, by preparing it for the four-wheel Drill-plough.*

---

1  Ellis, *Compleat system of experienced improvements*.

*Also the Drain-foot Plough – for cutting Water-furrows, which it does so well, as to throw out Earth a Spit deep, and a Foot square, at once drawing along with a Team of Horses, and thus does more of this Work, in one Day, than twenty or thirty Men can: The Mole-bank-plough, that I sell but for one Guinea at my House if single, or two if double, will likewise do more of this Work in one Day than forty Men can: The late Patent little light Plough, that goes without Wheels, is an excellent Sort for working in soft Earth, and turning a Furrow the best of any Plough: And chaff-cutting Engines. I sell the famous Orange Bell Pear-Tree, not to be had in any of the Nurseries near London, as I could find, upon Inquiry: The Parsnip Apple-Tree, whose Fruit, with that of the Orange Pear-Tree, is always ripe in Harvest; being a most serviceable, pleasant Apple, for eating raw or in Pies and Pasties, and for. Making Cyder; White Damsin and White Elder Trees, The excellent black Kerroon Cherry -Tree, Tame Pheasants, Guinea Hens, and Poland Dunghill Fowls: The Lady-Finger and three other Sorts of the very best of natural Grass-Seeds; the first comes up the second Year, but the three last come up the first Year, the Seed of which produces the sweetest of Milk, Butter, Cheese, and Flesh, free of many dangerous noxious Seeds of Weeds that are generally sown when Hay-Seeds are taken out of Hay-Lofts. I sell Receits for compounding various Sorts of Manures for the Garden or field; also those for preventing assuredly the Damage of Flies on Turnips or Rapes in the Field, or Lice and Caterpillars on Cabbages, or on Wall Fruit Trees: Likewise Receits for preventing Rats of any Kind harbouring the Thatch of Barns or Granaries, Ceilings of Dwelling-Houses, or in the Ground, or in Malt or Mill-Houses, by several Ways, without giving them anything to eat; or I kill them and Polecats, Weasels, &so. Several Ways, by laying something for them to eat, which is no way poisonous or dangerous; with many other Receits never yet published. I have further to observe, that on the 12$^{th}$ of June, 1749, I brought to London, in order to be sent further, three four-wheel Drill-ploughs, one fallow Plough, a sowing Plough, a chaff-cutting Engine, and several other Instruments in Husbandry: the whole Number for those foresighted Gentlemen, whose Industry deserves high Praise, because they endeavour to introduce the greatest of Riches into their Country even the Foundation of all Trade and Commerce, viz. the latest Improvements in the Art of Agriculture. If therefore I say these Instruments of Husbandry viz. the four-wheel Drill-plough, with its two little Harrows of six Teeth each, and its two little iron Gatherers, that gather up the Mould, and leave it over the drilled Corn; the Horse-Break likewise, with its two larger iron Gatherers, that surprisingly deep gathers up the Mould of two Interval Grounds, as the Break is drawn along, and leaves it against the Stalks of Corn, without bruising them; were to be bought by some Persons, who occupy much Land,* *proper for their Uses, for hundreds of Pounds, I question whether they would buy them too dear. To which I add, that by the Work of this Plough and Break, and a proper Manure that is to be sow'd out of the Manure Hopper on the drilled Seed; no Worm, Slug, Snail, Fly, or Grub, can live near the drilled Corn. And I wish our English Gentlemen were as forward as Foreigners, in thus promoting the Interest of their landed Estates. And for proof of what I here write of the Drill-plough and Horsebreak, etc. their Operations may be seen at my Farm in Little-Gaddesden aforesaid.*

*N. B. As the four-wheel Drill-plough sows Corn, the Horsebreak almost finishes hoeing the interval Ground. Also that these Instruments will save great Expenses in large Gardens, and in manuring of Land: For that Quantity of Manure, usually employed to dress five Acres of Land the common old Way, will dress fifty Acres in the new Drill Way. This is the Break that exceeds all other Horse-breaks whatsoever, or any Hoe-plough of any Sort; for after it has hoed the interval Ground between the Drills of Corn twice in a Summer, and thereby killed all manner of Weeds, the Hoes are taken off, and the Gatherers are put on for two Men to hold and guide, because it cleans three interval Lands, as it is drawn along by only one Horse, at once, and throws up Mould to the drilled Corn, as aforesaid. And thus a Field may be sown every Year with Grain, Turnips, Cole, or artificial Grass, fifty Years together, without any Occasion to let it lie in the usual Way to fallow it at all, and this with the least Expence possible: For by these excellent Instruments the Land is kept in the finest Tilth, free of Weeds, and manured in the sweetest and richest Manner; so that the poorest, chalky, hurlucky, sandy, and other shallow, lean Earths, may be fertilized to a very great Degree, and thereby made to bear large Crops of these Vegetables, to the greatest Advantage of the Owner; to the Parson, by the Increase of his Tythes; to the labouring Men, and to the Nation in general. – I also recommend my Treatise on Sheep and Lambs, that I published last Year, as the most useful Book that ever was wrote of the Kind (for preserving them from the Rot, Red-water, Wood-evil, and all other Maladies, and for feeding them fat in a short Time, with the least Charge, and in the sweetest Manner) which is to be sold by R. Baldwin, Jun. at the Rose in Paternoster-Row, London.*[2]

---

2   Ellis, *Country Housewife*, pp. 303–6.

# An annotated bibliography of the works of William Ellis

Many of Ellis's books were general agricultural textbooks – they aimed to cover all aspects of English farming. Some, like his books on timber trees, brewing and sheep, were more specialised. His periodicals, reprinted as books, had a more diverse content. By his time the first textbook of English agriculture, Fitzherbert's *Husbandry* of 1523, was some two centuries old. Such English general textbooks were not plentiful at first. Fitzherbert's book was followed by Thomas Tusser's book on English farming in doggerel verse, *Five Hundred Points of Good Husbandry*, first published in 1557 with a much-expanded edition in 1573. Both these works were often reprinted in the sixteenth century and were the only textbooks specifically on English agriculture printed in that century. Gentlemen seeking further advice had to refer to translations from the Dutch, German or French, which were originally written for farmers in those countries, or, if classically schooled, they might try ancient authors such as Virgil or Cato, works advising farmers in Mediterranean regions. There were small pieces of originality towards the end of the century, such as Reginald Scot's *Perfite Platforme of a Hoppe Garden* of 1578 or Sir Hugh Plat's pamphlets on soils and drill-sowing, but the 1600s began with another translation (from the French), the *Maison Rustique*, a comprehensive textbook on all aspects of farming and country life. The third edition of this work, augmented by Gervase Markham, appeared in 1616, three years after Markham's own textbook, *The English Husbandman*. Markham produced more works on English agriculture, some of which were published in a compendium of six works in 1623: this was reprinted many times thereafter. In the aftermath of the Civil War an enthusiasm for change and technological advance led to the publication of a flurry of pamphlets and short books on agricultural improvement, many of them published by Samuel Hartlib from papers sent to him. Hartlib was at the centre of a group of men interested in science, including agriculture. After the Restoration the Royal Society also interested itself in agricultural matters and John Worlidge and John Mortimer, Fellows of the Society, published general agricultural textbooks in 1669 and 1707 respectively. John Laurence produced *A New System of Agriculture* in 1716. Stephen Switzer and Richard Bradley published general textbooks on agriculture in the second and third decades of the eighteenth century and Jethro Tull published his controversial book on row cultivation and mechanical hoeing in 1733, bringing the list of writers of general agricultural textbooks up to the time of Ellis. He saw that a market existed for practical textbooks written in a simple style. One of his correspondents in 1732 was sure his books were needed, for

> The World has been so pester'd of late Years with Books upon these Subjects, which have proved no better than arrant Impositions, upon Perusal, of Transcripts from old musty Authors, common beaten Tracts, or impracticable Schemes never reduced to Practice, by Speculation and unexperienced People, that it is no Wonder People now grow more wary in laying out their Money in Books of this Kind.[1]

Compiling this summary of Ellis's publications has been made difficult because of his constant self-plagiarism; over and over again one finds that material in one work turns up, word for word, in another. The initial idea of this bibliography was to find the earliest book by Ellis in which text appeared, noting when it was reissued as part of a later publication but disentangling the books and publication dates proved beyond this author. It is hoped that the material in the various titles and editions has at least been covered once.[2] *The Modern Husbandman*, which appeared in book form as a three-, four- or eight-volume work at various dates, is particularly difficult to classify. These books were compilations of the monthly periodicals on farming that Ellis beavered away at to the detriment of his farm for many years. The material in them was also used by Ellis in some of his other books. The bibliography of *The Modern Husbandman* is very confusing. The British Library has many of the monthly parts of this work, dated between 1741 and 1744, published in London or Dublin. The Bodleian in Oxford has a similar selection from the early 1740s. Fussell mentions that both the Rothamsted catalogue and McDonald claim *The Modern Husbandman* was first issued in 1731, and McDonald also lists a 1732 edition. It is probable that McDonald, who made other mistakes in his agricultural bibliography,

---

1 Ellis, *New Experiments in Husbandry*, Preface. Despite a lack of bibliographical rigour, the best surveys of English works on agriculture are Fussell, *Old English Farming Books* and Fussell, 'Farming writers'.

2 The most successful attempt to compile a bibliography of Ellis's works is found in Fussell, *Old English Farming Books*, pt 2, pp. 1–27.

is wrong about the 1731 and 1732 editions. Rothamsted may have listed the 1731 edition on the authority of McDonald (this edition was not in Rothamsted's library) whereas the monthly parts did not actually appear until the early 1740s. This confusion over dates, and Ellis's statement in the book of 1732 that he had not yet started writing monthly periodicals, has compounded the confusion as to which publications contain the original and which the duplicated text. Fussell writes despairingly of Ellis's literary output that: 'No two bibliographies or catalogues give them alike or use the same titles and dates'. It is hoped these bibliographic notes will not add to the confusion.[3]

## William Ellis, *The Practical Farmer: or the Hertfordshire Husbandman* (London, 1732)

Like many of Ellis's books, this is in two parts but the pagination is continuous. There is an indication that the parts were produced and sold separately because the bookseller has included an unpaginated catalogue at the end of part one and part one only is present in the first edition. Part two is appended to the second and subsequent editions, with the same publication date as part one in each edition.

This is probably Ellis's earliest book but confusingly he refers to farming methods, 'I have already wrote of' (p. 180). The short preface is a humble plea to the public to buy the book and encourage Ellis to further efforts, reinforcing the view that this was his first publication.[4] In pursuance of agricultural improvement, 'I have here humbly thrown my Mite into the Publick Treasury: And, for the sake of my good intentions for the common weal, I hope the Generous will excuse the deficiencies that may have accompany'd my Rustick Pen.'

Much of part one follows what was to become the standard pattern of Ellis's books on husbandry: discussion of soils and their improvement, chapters on wheat, barley, peas and beans, discussion of the new 'grasses' – trefoil, clover, lucerne and so on – and an encouragement to farmers to plant fruit trees on the edges of their fields. He also deals with keeping tame rabbits and pigeons, cows, calves and sheep.

The second part gives more information on many of the topics listed on the frontispiece of part one but includes more information on his own farming,

---

3   Rothamsted Experimental Station, *Library Catalogue* (Harpenden, 1940), p. 53; Fussell, *Old English Farming Books*, pt 2, pp. 7, 11; Donald McDonald, *Agricultural Writers* (New York, 1968), p. 209.

4   Further evidence is his reference in *Chiltern and Vale Farming* (p. 211) to his seed steep, 'mentioned in my first book, Page 25'. There *is* a recipe for a seed steep on p. 25 of *Practical Farmer*.

ending with *General Observations on the Summer*, 1734. The details provided indicate that Ellis was keeping a farm diary. He had, apparently, not started publishing his monthly journals at this time (see above, p. 174). He explains:

> for these seven Years past I have been making Collections and Experiments, and wrote the Success and loss of several Farmers' Proceedings in our Country, as well as my own, which I intend to publish by way of Monthly Books, that consequently must be a great service to the World.[5]

He demonstrates his intention by a final chapter, 'A comparison of different methods of farming in several countries'.

**William Ellis, *Chiltern and Vale Farming Explained, according to the latest improvements*. Printed for the author William Ellis of Little-Gaddesden near Hemstead in Hertfordshire (London, 1733)**

This early work follows the usual pattern of Ellis's books; it is in two parts, although they are not labelled as such in this case. The first half covers soil types and how to cultivate them successfully, and timber and fruit trees, with a chapter on each, beginning with the oak. This part is repeated, word for word, in *The Timber-Tree Improved* of 1738 (see below). There follow chapters on the main grain crops and then other crops, including turnips and 'improvement' fodder crops. There is also a chapter on weeds.

Many examples of good (and bad) local practice are described, as well as some of his own experiences. The book draws on many examples from 1732, and he gives cost and profits per acre for several crops grown in that year. Ellis sometimes gives precise dates for his examples, such as when discussing weeds: 'About the fourth of May, 1730, the Black-bennet [a weed] began to shew itself a Foot long'.

*The London And Country Brewer. Containing The Whole Art of Brewing All Sorts Of Malt-Liquors, By a Person formerly concerned in a Common Brewhouse at LONDON, but for Twenty Years past has resided in the Country* (London, 1734) [and six subsequent editions]

This anonymous work is clearly by Ellis, from the references to him in it and references to this book in others by Ellis. To give just one example: in *The London And Country Brewer*, extolling the excellence of seed steep for barley, he refers readers to his *The Practical Farmer*, p. 25. *The London and Country Brewer* was originally issued in one part; by the fifth edition (1744) it

---

5   Ellis, *Practical Farmer*, p. 128.

consisted of Part I, Part II, Part III and a Supplement. Pagination is continuous. Chapter 1 in most of the sections is devoted to barley and barley malts. Ellis moves on to discuss the other ingredients of beer and ale, water and hops. Ellis clearly knows a lot about brewing, and Kalm says that this book was well received (it went through seven editions). Present-day writers on brewing also look favourably on this work. Ellis's first occupation was that of brewer and he ran a large London brewery left to him by his uncle for some time before starting to farm in Little Gaddesden (see above, pp. 11–13). The book draws on his experiences in the London trade as well as detailing information about brewing, both commercial and private, in other parts of the country. This he picked up on his business tours: he stayed at many inns and talked to many brewers. The overall aim of this book was to improve the quality of beer and other malt liquors in England – Ellis was very critical of many of the beers he came across in his travels, although he occasionally found something he liked, such as the White Ale brewed in Plymouth.

**William Ellis, *The Practice of Farming and Husbandry in All Sorts Of Soils, According to the Latest Improvements, By William Ellis, Author of the Practical Farmer, or the Hertfordshire Husbandman* (Dublin, 1735)**

The earliest edition of this work was first published in Dublin. It may have been an unauthorised edition because Ellis complains about Dublin editions, which pay no royalties (see above, p. 156). Its arrangement is: chapters on soils, subdivided into the nature of, the culture of, and the improvement of, various types of soil; then chapters on forest and fruit trees, beginning as usual, with the oak; followed by similarly arranged chapters on farm crops, starting with wheat, and including 'improvement grasses'. Elimination of weeds has a chapter, and there are chapters on ploughing, sowing and hoeing. But all of the content of this work appears elsewhere in Ellis's publications, in *Chiltern and Vale Farming Explained* (1733) and/or *The Modern Husbandman* (1743-4). Maybe it was thought that the English-reading public of Ireland would not have already acquired these works. We will deal with the salient points of this work when discussing those from which the text originated.

**William Ellis, *The Timber-Tree Improved: Or The Best Practical Methods Of Improving Different Lands With Proper Timber* (London, 1738) [Part 2 first appeared in 1742 and is often bound as part of the 3rd and 4th editions. There were subsequent editions in 1741, 1742 and 1745]**

The book is in two parts and bibliographers list the second part as a separate work, but it appears that all extent copies of part two are found bound with part one. The first part of this book appeared several times in Ellis's other works. It was originally part of *Chiltern and Vale Farming* (1733), and also appears in *The Practice of Farming* (1735) and volume eight of *The Modern Husbandman* (1750). Ellis introduces the book by acknowledging that his subject has been already 'set forth by able hands', but he justifies another book because he lives in a wooded area, comes into contact with skilled woodsmen and, in his extensive travels, he has picked up information from all over the country that he will include in the book.

Part one is arranged in chapters under tree types: the oak comes first as it 'claims the Priority of Regard in this Nation', and is followed by beech, elm and ash, then a number of trees of lesser importance to the English countryman. Each chapter deals with 'The Nature and Improvement' of each tree. As usual, Ellis draws on examples from his own experience and that of his neighbours, but the text is largely free of digressions and anecdotes.

Part two is larger than part one but has a similar arrangement, with separate pagination but no preface. Any gentleman buying part two would find some extra information on the culture of trees drawn from Ellis's experience and some may have been impressed by his knowledge of trees in antiquity. Others would have recognised that much of each chapter is a paraphrase of John Evelyn's *Sylva* of 1664. Ellis draws on other writers – William Lawson, John Houghton, John Worlidge and so on – and also reports conversations with wheelwrights, wood turners (his neighbour was a turner), lath-renders and the like. In the final chapter (on 'furz') he advises caution in using the dried haulm of this plant for fuel – a spark ignited some of it in 1724 and fire partially destroyed his house.

There was a German translation of this book: *Von Erbauung des Zimmerholzes. Oder, die vorzüglichste Art, verschiedene Länderyen mit gutem Zimmerholze zu versehen. Nach der vierten Englischen Ausgabe ins Deutsche übersetzt und hrsg. von H.v.F.P.* [d.i. Peter Graf F. von Hohenthal-Königsbrück 1726–1794], published by Carl Ludwig Jacobi (Leipzig, 1752).

**William Ellis, *The Farmer's Instructor Or, The Husbandman and Gardener's Useful And Necessary Companion, First begun by Samuel Trowell*, Gent. and Now completed [...] By William Ellis, Farmer, [etc.] (London, 1747)**

The chief glory of this book, for many readers, is the sole illustration: a frontispiece showing a small horse pulling a seed drill. The horse is being whipped by a small boy and the machine is guided by a man holding two handles at the rear. The man wears shoes and gaiters, a kerchief at his neck, a loose-fitting coat with capacious pockets and a wide-brimmed hat. He is bending forward in concentration – this could be a portrait of William Ellis, although it is more likely to be of his son, who he trained to work this machine. There is a brief description of the machine (it looks like a more elaborate version of John Worlidge's drill illustrated in 1681). It was invented by William Ellis in 1745, and 'any person may view the same' at his farm, where 'it is now in use'.

This book was originally written by Samuel Trowell and appeared in 1738 and 1739 as *A New Treatise of Husbandry, Gardening, and Other Matters Relating To Rural Affairs.* Trowell, for a long time Steward of the Inner Temple, and a nurseryman specialising in bulbs, died in 1746 and Ellis was invited to augment the text for this 1747 edition.[6] Ellis decided to add supplements to Trowell's original agricultural chapters (which follow the usual pattern of crop by crop chapters beginning with wheat) 'which the Reader will much better understand [...] than [...] if I had blended our Observations and Directions together'. This is debatable; the real reason was probably that it was simpler for Ellis to just add his own text. Ellis did not supplement Trowell's gardening chapters, for 'what he was short in his Accounts of Husbandry, he made up by his writing on Gardening as being a celebrated Artist in that Science'. In any case, Ellis had no interest in garden writing.

The main thrust of Ellis's preface was that his newly invented four-wheeled drill-plough, together with some of his other invented implements, plus a compost invented by him that could be sown by the drill-plough with the seed, would transform agriculture. Much space is devoted to extolling the virtues of Ellis's inventions: 'For this Purpose the following Treatise is chiefly wrote to recommend the Practise of a perfect, new, and more profitable System of Husbandry; than ever was yet invented, and wrote by any Author whatsoever.'

The supplements added by Ellis to each agricultural chapter are mainly composed of the experiences of himself and his neighbours in cultivating various crops. They are also full of references to his mechanical inventions, composts and seed steeps. This edition appeared in the year following Trowell's death. As was usual with Ellis's books, the text must have been written fast – and no doubt at the expense of tending his farm.

**William Ellis, *The Country Housewife's Family Companion, or Profitable Directions for Whatever relates to the Management And Good Oeconomy Of The Domestick Concerns of a Country – Life, According to the Present Practice of the Country Gentleman's, the Yeoman's, the Farmer's, &c. Wives, in the Counties of Hertford, Bucks, and other parts of England: Shewing How great Savings may be made in Housekeeping [etc.]* (London and Salisbury, 1750) [modern edition: Prospect Books 2000, introduction by Malcolm Thick]**

---

6    Blanche Henrey, *British Botanical and Horticultural Literature before 1800* (Oxford, 1975), vol. II, pp. 455–6.

There seems to have been some confusion as to what title this book should have. The title page is headed *The Country Housewife's Family Companion*, and the Introduction is 'To the *Country Housewife*', whereas the Preface is to *The Country Family's Profitable Director*. There is an engraved frontispiece of a farm and farmyard within a picket fence, with poultry and a plough, a cow being milked, and a well. Cattle lie or stand in the foreground.[7] The fence is decrepit and the farm buildings are untidy – not a good advertisement for the book. But Ellis probably had nothing to do with this picture, which has its origins many years before the book appeared. The two most prominent cows in the foreground are exactly the same as those in the etching *Two Cows Seen from Behind*, produced by the Dutch artist Paullus Potter in 1650. Potter specialised in pictures of cows. The background farm may also be by Potter and in any case the buildings do not look English.[8]

This was a late book by Ellis and, to many historians, it is the most interesting of his works. Ellis announced that he planned to write this book on country living by criticising Bradley's *Country Housewife and Lady's Director*:

> I intend to compile a Treatise of their whole oeconomy in the management of a Farm, in opposition to Mr Bradley, who has packed a large parcel of foreign and English receipts together in two books, intitled The Country Housewife, and sold for 2s 6d each, more fit to be perused by Quality or City Cooks, than by a farmer's wife or maid servant.

In another attack he dismisses Bradley's book as 'filled up with little else but cookery – Receipts more fit for a Nobleman's kitchen than a farmer'. Ellis had a point – among Bradley's book were recipes for roast turtle, oysters, turbot, sturgeon and dressed ortolan – hardly English country fare. A number of Bradley's recipes were donated by Londoners, such as cooks at noted taverns, including 'Mr John Hughes, a celebrated London Cook'. Ten of Bradley's recipe informants were residents of France or the Low Countries, one was resident in Germany and one in Barbados. Mr Du Pont of Lyon and 'Mons. la Fontaine, an excellent Cook in Paris', made contributions. Five titled ladies and one noble gentleman gave Bradley recipes and many of his other contributors were designated Mr, Mrs or Esq. Whereas many of Bradley's recipes were sent to him by literate gentry,

---

7   The picture is signed 'I. Ross'. There was an engraver and printer called James Ross in Worcester but he was probably born in 1751 – could he have had a father in the same profession?

8   Paullus Potter, *Two Cows Seen from Behind*, Harvard Museums, Cambridge, MA, Spencer Album 10., S10.92.8. I am grateful to Professor Christiana Payne for her identification of Potter as the origin of this frontispiece.

Ellis went searching out recipes from country housewives, many of them his neighbours, who may well have been illiterate. Ellis tapped into a rich vein of cookery and household management lower down the social scale than Bradley's informants.[9]

Compared with his other books it is a large tome, some 379 pages plus an index, and is in two roughly equal parts. There is no evidence that they were published separately, but the work does not read as if planned as one volume from the start. Some topics – meal, grain and bread making, the dairy, as well as a miscellany of recipes – occur in both parts. Others – poultry; harvest food and pork preservation; bacon and ham; preserving vegetables and fruit; veal production; pig keeping; cures for cows; brewing and malting – occur only once. The medicine and dairy sections are short and sketchy in the first part and much fuller in the second. The first part ends with a piece praising Scroop Egerton, late duke of Bridgewater, and reads like a conclusion. I suspect Ellis was pressed by his publisher for a work on rural household management and he quickly gathered together the information to hand and produced the first part. The publisher (then as now; they were hard taskmasters) probably said the book was too slim and did not cover everything fully. Ellis did more research, pestered his maid, farm servants, neighbours, friends, visitors, correspondents and casual acquaintances for information, lifted more material from books and, pressed for a finished manuscript, simply grafted the new material on to the existing text as a second part. The result, rushed and unpolished, is all the more interesting to the historian of rural life. The charm of *The Country Housewife* is that it has little organisation: Ellis frequently digresses in order to relate a choice anecdote or even, one suspects, just to fill out the work. Although he uses material from published sources, the bulk of his information comes from his own employees, his neighbour's wives and people he meets in his home village and on his extensive travels.

The recipes he puts forward are homely, country ones and often he will give such a recipe, then provide a more luxurious variation, adding cream or extra eggs, for gentry tables. He has much to say on the subject of how to feed temporary harvest workers – treading a fine line between feeding them well and feeding them cheaply. He tackles the problems of storing food, protecting against insects, damp and vermin. Recognising that country wives were usually the first call when someone in the household was ill, he devotes many pages to medical recipes. These are culled from men and women in all walks of life, ranging from gentry wives to beggars – mostly not physicians.

---

9   Bradley, *The Country Housewife*, pt II, pp. 43–7; Ellis, *Modern Husbandman*, December, p. 147.

Farmyard animals were the province of the country housewife and Ellis covers keeping pigs, poultry and cows, making butter and cheese, and home brewing. Throughout the book, there are digressions and tales of remarkable local events, letters to and from Ellis and other pieces of text just apparently included at random – what a later editor called 'all those random and ridiculous details which have so disgraced his page'.[10] But to present-day historians they are of great interest.

Rather than attack Bradley's book, Ellis should probably have criticised the other country-living manuals that were published in his time. Three were dictionaries: Salmon's *Family Dictionary* (1710); Bailey's *Dictionarium Domesticum* (1736); and *Dictionarium Rusticum et Urbanicum* (1704). The other two were manuals: *The Complete Family Piece* (1741) and *The Family Magazine* of 1747. These books all covered cookery, preserving, medicine, dairying, brewing, home-made wine-making and those parts of agriculture traditionally assigned to women, such as poultry and cow-keeping. Like Bradley's book, however, they sought to educate the yeoman's or gentleman's wife rather than the spouse of a husbandman or labourer. A work closer to Ellis's was the *Farmer's Wife*, published anonymously in about 1780. This was clearly aimed at farmers' wives, but was more limited in scope, concentrating mostly on pickling, preserving and country-wine making, although the management of fowls and pigs was also explained.[11]

**William Ellis,** *Agriculture improv'd, or, The practice of husbandry display'd: chiefly shewn by facts, perform'd in all sorts of land, according to the old plain, and the new drill, way of farming: in two volumes: containing, a receipt how to improve an acre of barley for six-pence charge ... with many other curious and serviceable matters, never before published* (London, 1745–6)

This is a two-volume work dating from 1745, originally in monthly parts. Volume one covers May and volume two June. It is likely that this is the surviving part of another failed attempt at a periodical in twelve monthly parts. Ellis opens both volumes with a critique of part of one of John Worlidge's husbandry books. For May he starts by:

*reciting* Mr. Worlidge's *Notes on the Month of* May, *who was certainly a most ingenious, learned Gentleman, which enabled him to touch on many Branches of Husbandry but, for want of being acquainted with the practical Part, was forced to write very, very little on them: And therefore I shall here attempt some*

---

10 Ellis, *Modern Husbandman*, January, pp. 99–100; [Ellis], *Ellis's Husbandry*, Preface by the Editor.
11 *The Farmer's Wife* (London, 1780).

*of their several Explanations, according to the present Practice of Husbandry.—* See his Book, intitled, A Complete Body of Husbandry and Gardening: Or, The Gentleman's Companion in the Business and Pleasures of a Country Lise. *Printed in the Year* 1716. *Price Six Shillings.*[12]

Ellis underestimated Worlidge's practical knowledge.

In the June sections he starts by quoting in full Worlidge's summary for that month, but makes no criticism of it. The book is a composition of Ellis's in his normal style – examples of husbandry practice from his own farming and that of his neighbours or others he has seen on his travels; letters from gentlemen requesting some of the agricultural goods he sells or requesting or giving advice; requests for Ellis to look out for specialist agricultural workers seeking a position (e.g. ploughmen); and oddities such as the experiments one of his workers did, applying soot to slugs to destroy them. There is, as always, much subtle advertising of all the things Ellis traded in. He refers to *The Modern Husbandman* several times in this volume and it is curious that, at the time that periodical was being published, he should embark on another one. *Agriculture improv'd* has chapters in it on topics he does not tackle anywhere else – the natural history of British snakes, a detailed examination of microscopic pond life, essays on pigeons, sparrows and bees. One has the feeling that these two volumes contained the 'overflow' of farming material that was surplus to requirements for the *Modern Husbandman*, bulked out by these essays on natural history together with many letters from gentleman readers and critiques of Worlidge's work. This mixture evidently did not sell well, hence the discontinuance of the parts after two months. The texts of these volumes are the same as that of volumes six and seven of the 1750 edition of *Modern husbandman*.

**William Ellis, The Modern Husbandman: complete in eight volumes. Containing I. The practice of farming, as it is now carried on by the most experienced farmers in the several counties of England, for every month in the year. II. The timber and fruit-tree improved, or the best practical methods of improving different lands with proper timber. III. Agriculture improved, or, the practice of husbandry displayed, shewn by facts performed on all sorts of land, according to the old plain, and the new drill way of ploughing. IV. Chiltern and vale farming explained, according to the latest improvements. Necessary for all landlords and tenants of either ploughed, grass, or wood grounds (London, 1743–50)**

---

12   Ellis was apparently not aware that this book was a posthumous amalgamation of Worlidge's books on agriculture and gardening.

*The Modern Husbandman* was the most ambitious writing project Ellis undertook. The work came out in twelve monthly parts, each part being about 45,000 words long. It was meant to come out in 'real time', each month's instalment appearing in the month it was dealing with, and the farming operations it discussed were to be those that farmers undertook at that time of the year. This schedule was evidently too ambitious, for a correspondent complained about 'your publication of your monthly books, after the month for which it is designed, is past, so that they can be of no use, for at least ten months to come. It is now February, and you have not yet published that for November'. Ellis replied that the printer was to blame for the delay: 'I am forced to stay delivering one copy, till the former is printed off.'[13] The instalment for January was priced at 13d; Ellis said he could write larger instalments, but that would involve a price for each instalment of over two shillings.

It seems that the twelve monthly parts were probably issued from May 1743 to April 1744 (a letter in the part published in January 1744 is dated May 1743, adding weight to this conjecture).[14] A collected edition of the twelve parts was issued in London with the dates of 1743 and 1744 on it – there is no title page and these were probably monthly issues unsold which were simply reissued as four collected volumes. A similar three-volume edition was printed and published in Dublin. A London edition in five volumes was priced at £1 11s 6d in 1745. Another edition in 1750 was of eight volumes, and included not only the original monthly parts but also three previously published works, *The Timber Tree Improved*, *Chiltern and Vale Farming* and *Agriculture Improved*.

This publication is the most informal and intimate of Ellis's works. Letters to him and his replies are scattered throughout the work, giving a feeling that the reader has almost eavesdropped on a conversation between Ellis and another of his readers. This informal style, with advertisements for goods and services cunningly inserted into the text, and letters from satisfied customers, was calculated to encourage readers to buy his offered wares. He was writing, he claimed, particularly for his fellow farmers in the Chiltern and Vale country (especially for the gentry?) so that

> with the help of these my monthly books, they may prevent their being imposed on by the advice of ill neighbours [...] because, by my several years travels on purpose,

---

13 Ellis, *Modern Husbandman*, February, p. 97.

14 An advertisement in the publisher's catalogue at the end of the February instalment of the *Modern Husbandman* seems to confirm this timetable. It can be interpreted as follows: monthly parts for May to November are in print and available; February has just been published, as has January; December has been recently published; March will be speedily published. There is no mention of April, but presumably this monthly part concludes the set.

and holding my own farm, and the glebe lands of the parish that I rent in my own hands, the former for near thirty years together, I am enabled to write such cases and informations as may be serviceable to all those who undertake the farming business both in Chiltern and Vale countries, so as to prevent their suffering in a great measure by the deceitful advice of those that know the management of affairs better than they do.[15]

## William Ellis, *New experiments in husbandry, for the month of April. Containing several processes of plowing various lands. The transcendent uses of the late invented Hertfordshire-double-plough. The improvements of grain, grasses, manures and trees* (London, 1736)

This book contains what had originally been (monthly) productions for April and May. All of this book is reproduced in the 1750 edition of the *Modern Husbandman*. In the preface Ellis advertises various ploughs and other mechanical contrivances he has invented, as well as medicine for sheep. The preface includes a letter from a gentleman ordering goods from Ellis. He hopes Ellis is not discouraged by a general lack of interest in new works on agriculture and comments that there have been many agricultural books published lately that are rehashes of old ideas or contain text copied from other works (ironic in that Ellis was a prime example of recycling, albeit of his own works in the main).

Ellis's seed steep for barley is heavily recommended. He advises that the seed not be sown too close together, because he has known well-spaced seed-barley thus treated to produce very large heads. As usual, he also makes prominent mention of his machines, especially the double plough. Throughout the work it is made explicit or is implicit that many of the experiments and practices Ellis writes about have taken place on his own farm.

It is noteworthy that this book was printed 'for the author' and sold by several book shops. Was the text in this book originally an attempt by Ellis to write and self-publish a farming periodical, as he had said that he took books with him on his travels to try to sell?

## William Ellis, *The Compleat Cyderman; or, The Present Practice Of Raising Plantations Of The Best Cyder Apple and Perry Pear-Trees, With The Improvement Of Their Excellent Juices* (London, 1756)

Ellis is not named as the author of this book but internal evidence clearly shows that it is by him (many mentions of Hertfordshire, examples from Little Gaddesden, a description of Ellis's Parsnip Apple and so on) – or it would be more accurate to say *compiled* by him for, in the preface, he

---

15  Ellis, *Modern Husbandman*, p. 52.

includes: 'EXPERIENC'D HANDS, *living in the Cyder Countries of* Devonshire, Cornwall, Herefordshire, *etc.*' as contributors to the book. He also quotes from published works, most notably Sir Jonas Moore's *England's Interest, or, the Gentleman and Farmer's Friend*, first published in 1676 and reprinted in many editions. He inserts some long letters on cider he has received from those involved in producing it, such as an eight-page letter headed 'An Account of Cyder-making, as sent the 13th Day of *July*, 1753, to this Author, by an eminent Doctor of Physic; shewing different Ways of making and improving Cyder by several Persons in the Country about him', or '*An Account, by another Hand, of the Moss on Fruit-Trees, and their Cure*'.

Ellis begins the preface with reasons for encouraging cider:

> THE many and great Advantages that might be made to accrue to *Great-Britain* and *Ireland* by increasing Plantations with the right Sort of Cyder Apple and Pear-Trees, is of such Importance, that not only Thousands of Acres of barren Lands may-be improved by it in the highest Degree, but a most, rich, vinous Liquor may be enjoyed in the greatest Plenty and Perfection, that is as strong, and as pleasant, and I am sure is much wholesomer, than most Foreign Wines; and by which the Importation of them may be much lessened, our Treasure more kept at Home, the publick Revenue increased, and great Numbers of the Poor imployed.

Such arguments, especially that of import substitution, are standard mercantilist ideas that would not look out of place a hundred years prior to this book.[16]

Ellis is keen to promote cider from the South Hams district of Devon, which he feels has been neglected as a cider-producing district, although he claims many thousands of barrels of cider from there are imported yearly to London, landed at the Southwark wharves of Chamberlain's, Cotton's and Beal's. Ellis had contacts in this part of Devon; in his role as employment agent he had placed a young man in a position there and received regular letters from him. Ellis deals with all aspects of cider making: the trees, gathering the fruit, making cider, keeping it in good heart, and its claimed medicinal virtues.

**William Ellis, *A Compleat System of Experienced Improvements, Made on Sheep, Grass-Lambs, and House-Lambs, etc.* (London, 1749)**
The title page of this book (which first appeared in 1742), advertises that it is 'A Work different from all others yet published, as it is explained and

---

16   For example, Sir Hugh Plat thought in the 1580s that a good perry was the equal of French white wine and advocated this as an import substitute. British Library, SL 2210 f.141; SL 2244 f.19; SL 2245 f.38.

improved by great Numbers of various Cases that have really happened' – Ellis is making a virtue of the many examples of sheep husbandry he cites. The book *was* different from others in being the first English book devoted entirely to sheep husbandry. In the preface Ellis draws attention to the great advances in agriculture over the previous forty years and the important part sheep have played in this – he singles out folding sheep at night on arable land after allowing them to range over commons during the day. Sheep are also an important source of meat and wool – one of the major raw materials for manufacturing. He says the book will address the problem of rot in sheep, advise what to look for in a good shepherd and tell how to break in a new sheep dog.

The work is in three books – books two and three have separate indexes but no title page and were probably published always with the first part. Ellis's name does not appear on the title page but the book starts with a two-paged advertisement for his various wares and services, which states that he is the author. Ellis draws on some quite old sources to a considerable degree. He quotes John Worlidge and also James Lambert, whose much-reprinted work on farm beasts was in its fourth edition in 1710. Two books a century or so old are also much quoted, by Gervase Markham and Ad. Speed.

Ellis goes into considerable detail on breaking in a sheep dog. Some of his methods are cruel by today's standards – a dog apt to bite sheep too hard should have its 'four fangs' broken off. Another operation on a dog was to cut out the 'nerve string under its tongue to prevent it biting if it went mad. This was done with the aid of a penknife and a shoemaker's awl!' His section on sheep dogs eventually degenerates into a series of anecdotes about dogs that had killed animals or attacked humans. Finally, he reprints an anonymous doggerel verse on the virtues of a dog.

He spends time on the qualities to be looked for in a shepherd, using many examples from his own experience and that of his neighbours. The correct feeding of sheep (turnips are said to be particularly useful) and tending to their various diseases, including rot, receive much attention, as does choosing the right breed of sheep (he goes into detail on many breeds). A chapter is devoted to raising house-lambs for the London meat market. As with most of his publications, much of the information in this book comes from Ellis's neighbours. Ellis may have been influenced in his decision to write a book on sheep by a shift in eating habits from beef to mutton at the time he was writing. This was exacerbated by a thirteen-year-long outbreak of foot and mouth disease in cattle from 1745.[17]

---

17 Emily Pawley, 'Feeding Desire: Generative Environment, Meat Markets and the Management of Sheep Intercourse in Great Britain, 1700–1750', OSIRIS, 33/1 (2018),

***Every Man His Own Farrier, or the best methods of preventing and curing the injuries and diseases of that truly serviceable creature, a horse*** (London, 1769)
This was Ellis's last book, published posthumously. The title page informs the reader that the author was *the late farmer* of Little Gaddesden. Ellis wrote the preface and the book seems to have been completed before he died. It is a short work without a great deal of organisation: just a succession of recipes for curing horses of all manner of diseases. Ellis obtained much of the information for this book on his travels – there are numerous recipes obtained from ostlers. Many were also given to Ellis by carters and waggoners; he would have had frequent contact with such men as he dispatched the goods he sold to country customers. He also took some material from published works, such as one of the many editions of Gervase Markham's books on farriery.

The recipes in the book are composed of ingredients a farmer would easily be able to obtain – for instance, there are many cures for gripes in horses, with recipes such as: getting a horse to swallow a piece of soap; a drink of parsley roots boiled in gin with pepper; another of four ounces of treacle in a pint of strong ale; two ounces of pepper, a quart of milk and a pound of fresh butter; a spoonful of gunpowder mixed with vinegar. It is debatable whether any of these recipes worked on a horse's upset stomach, but Ellis insists that all the remedies in the book have been 'sufficiently tried' by him and administering them is, in any case, much cheaper than employing a farrier. He also makes the sensible point that often a speedily given medicine might save an animal, whereas waiting for a farrier might prove fatal.

<https://doi.org/10.1086/699233>, p. 57.

# Bibliography

Bell, Vicars, *Little Gaddesden* (London, 1949).
Bell, Vicars, *To Meet Mr. Ellis* (London, 1956).
Blith, Walter, *The English Improver Improved* (London, 1653).
Boerhaave, H., *Treatise on the Powers of Medicines* (London, 1740).
Bradley, Richard, *The Country Housewife and Lady's Director* [1736], ed. Caroline Davidson (London, 1980).
Bradley, Richard, *Dictionarium Botanicum, or a Botanical Dictionary for the use of the curious in Husbandry and Gardening* (London, 1728).
Bradley, Richard, *A General Treatise of Husbandry and Gardening* (London, 1727).
Britten, James, *Old Country and Farming Words* (London, 1880).
Buttress, F.A. and Dennis, R.W.G., 'The Early History of Cereal Seed Treatment in England', *Agricultural History*, 21/2 (1947), pp. 93–103.
Cobbett, William, *Cottage Economy* (London, 1824).
Collet, John, 'An Account of the Peat-pit near Newbury', *Philosophical Transactions*, 50 (1767–8), pp. 109–15
Collins, Tony, Martin, John and Vamplew, Wray (eds), *Encyclopedia of Traditional British Rural Sports* (London, 2005).
*Columella of Husbandry* (London, 1745).
Croker, Temple H., *The Complete Dictionary of Arts and Sciences* (London, 1765).
*Dictionary of National Biography*, online edition.
Digby, Sir Kenelm, *The Closet of the Eminently Learned Sir Kenelm Digby, Kt, Opened* (London, 1669).
Donaldson, John, *Agricultural Biography* (London, 1854).
Dover, Thomas, *The ancient physician's legacy to his country, being what he has collected in forty-nine years practice* (London, 1733).
Eales, Mary, *The Compleat Confectioner* (London, 1733)
Ellis, William, *Agriculture Improv'd*, 2 vols (London, 1746).
Ellis, William, *Chiltern and Vale Farming Explained* (London, 1745).

Ellis, William, *A compleat system of experienced improvements, made on sheep, grass-lambs, and house-lambs: or, The country gentleman's and the shepherd's sure guide* (London, 1749).
Ellis, William, *The Compleat Cyderman* (London, 1756).
Ellis, William, *The Country Housewife's Family Companion, 1750*, with an introduction by Malcolm Thick (Totnes, 2000).
[Ellis, William] Anon. (ed.), *Ellis's Husbandry, Abridged and Methodized*, 2 vols (London, 1772).
Ellis, William, *Every Farmer his own Farrier* (London, 1769).
Ellis, William, *London and Country Brewer* (London, 1742).
Ellis, William, *The Modern Husbandman* (Dublin, 1743–4).
Ellis, William, *The New Art of Brewing and Improving Malt Liquors* (London, 1761).
Ellis, William, *New Experiments in Husbandry, for the Month of April* (London, 1736).
Ellis, William, *The Practical Farmer: or the Hertfordshire Husbandman* (London, 1732).
Ellis, William, *The Practice of Farming and Husbandry in All Sorts of Soils* (Dublin, 1735).
Ellis, William, *The Timber Tree Improved* (London, 1742).
Ellis, William and Trowell, Samuel, *The Farmer's Instructor or, The Husbandman and Gardener's Useful and Necessary Companion* (London, 1747).
Ernle, Lord, *English Farming Past and Present*, 6th edition (London, 1961).
Farley, John, *The London Art of Cookery* (London, 1793)
Fisher, James, 'The Master Should Know More: Book-Farming and the Conflict over Agricultural Knowledge', *Cultural and Social History*, 15/3 (2018), pp. 315–31.
Fitch, John G. (trans.), *Palladius, The Work of Farming* (Totnes, 2013).
Floud, Roderick, *An Economic History of the English Garden* (London, 2019).
Fussell, George E., *The Farmer's Tools* (London, 1985).
Fussell, George E., 'Farming Writers of Eighteenth-century', *Agricultural History*, 21/1 (1947), pp. 1–8.
Fussell, George E., *Old English Farming Books 1523–1793* (Collieston, 1978).
Gardiner, H.W., *A Survey of the Agriculture of Hertfordshire* (London, 1967).
Gardner, H.W., *A Survey of the Agriculture of Hertfordshire*, Royal Agricultural Society of England (London, 1967).
Glasse, Hannah, *The Art of Cookery made Plain and Easy* (London, 1760)
Hale, Thomas, *A Compleat Body of Husbandry* (London, 1756).

[Hartlib, Samuel], *A Discoverie for Division or Setting Out of Land* (London, 1653).
Harvey, John, *Early Gardening Catalogues* (Chichester, 1972).
Henrey, Blanche, *British Botanical and Horticultural Literature before 1800* (Oxford, 1975).
Hillman, Daniel, *Tusser redivivus: being part of Mr. Thomas Tusser's Five hundred points of husbandry* (London, 1710).
Houghton, John, *Collection of Letters for The Improvement of Husbandry and Trade* (London, 1681–3).
Jenkins, J. Geraint, *The English Farm Wagon* (Newton Abbot, 1972).
Johnson, George W., *Cottage Gardener*, vol. 8 (1852).
Kerridge, Eric, *The Common Fields of England* (Manchester, 1992).
Laurence, John, *A New System of Agriculture* (London, 1727).
Lisle, Edward, *Observations in Husbandry*, 2 vols (London, 1757).
Lucas, Joseph, *Kalm's account of his visit to England* (London, 1892).
McDonald, Alexander, *A Complete Dictionary of Practical Gardening* (London, 1808).
McDonald, Donald, *Agricultural Writers* (New York, 1968).
McKendrick, Neil, Brewer, John and Plumb, J.H., *The Birth of a Consumer Society: Commercialization of Eighteenth Century England* (London, 1984).
Markham, Gervase, *Cheap and Good Husbandry* (London, 1664).
Markham, Gervase, *The English Housewife* (London, 1615).
Mead, W.R., *Pehr Kalm in The Chilterns* (Aston Clinton, 2003).
Miller, Philip, *Gardeners' Dictionary* (London, 1768).
*Monthly Review, or Literary Journal*, 48 (London, 1773).
Moore, Ian (ed.), *Primrose McConnell's The Agricultural Notebook*, 16th edn (London, 1976).
Moore, Sir Jonas, *England's Interest, or the Gentleman and Farmer's Friend* (London, 1703).
Mortimer, John, *Whole Art of Husbandry*, 8 vols (London, 1717).
Muldrew, Craig, *Food, Energy and the Creation of Industriousness* (London, 2011).
Murrell, John, *Murrell's Two Books of Cookerie and Carving* (London, 1638).
Nourse, Timothy, *Campania Foelix* (London, 1700)
Overton, Mark, *Agricultural Revolution in England* (Cambridge, 1996).
Oxford, Arnold Whitaker, *English Cookery Books to the Year 1850* (London, 1913).
Page, William (ed.), *A History of the County of Hertford: Volume II* (London, 1908).

Pelling, Margaret, *The Common Lot* (London, 1998).
Philips, John, *Of Cyder* (London, 1708)
Plat, Sir Hugh, *Diverse new sorts of Soil* (London, 1594).
Plat, Sir Hugh, *Sundrie new & Artificiall Remedies Against Famine* (London, 1596).
Pryor, Alan, 'The Industrialisation of the London Brewing Trade: Part I', *Brewery History*, 161 (2015), pp. 51–90.
Quincey, John, *Pharmacopoeia officinalis & extemporanea: or, a compleat English dispensatory* (London, 1722).
Rabisha, William, *The Whole Body of Cookery Dissected* (London, 1661).
Radzinowicz, Leon, 'The Waltham Black Act: A Study of the Legislative Attitude Towards Crime in the Eighteenth Century', *The Cambridge Law Journal*, 9/1 (1945), pp. 56–81.
Ransom, Harry, 'The Rewards of Authorship in the Eighteenth Century', *Studies in English*, 18 (1938), pp. 47–66.
Richardson, H.D., *Domestic fowl: their natural history, breeding, rearing, and general management* (London, 1847).
Robinson, D.H. (ed.), *Fream's Elements of Agriculture* (London, 1949).
Rothamsted Experimental Station, *Library Catalogue* (Harpenden, 1940).
Rowe, Anne and Williamson, Tom, *Hertfordshire: A Landscape History* (Hatfield, 2013).
Sherman, Sandra, 'Advertisements for Myself: William Ellis and the Reinvention of the Puff', *Prose Studies*, 24/2 (2001), pp. 65–86.
Sherman, Sandra, 'Printed Communities: Domestic Management Texts in the Eighteenth Century', *Journal for Early Modern Cultural Studies*, 3/2 (2003), pp. 36–67.
Smith, E., *The Compleat Housewife* (London, 1753).
Stafford, Hugh, *A Treatise on Cyder-Making* (London, 1753)
Stanbridge, Paul, *William Ellis, The Forgotten Improver*, unpublished typescript, copy held at Museum of English Rural Life, University of Reading ([1984]).
Sumner, James, *Brewing Science, Technology and Print, 1700–1880* (Pittsburgh, PA, 2013).
Switzer, Stephen, *The Nobleman, Gentleman and Gardener's Recreation* (London, 1715).
Tait, W.E., *The Parish Chest* (Stroud, 2012).
Thick, Malcolm, 'Breads of the English Husbandman and Woman, c.1750', *Petite Propos Culinaires*, 104 (2015), pp. 89–105.
Thick, Malcolm, 'Garden Seeds in England before the Late Eighteenth Century – II, The Trade in Seeds to 1760', *Agricultural History Review*, 38/2 (1990), pp. 105–16.

Thick, Malcolm, 'Intensive Rabbit Production in London and Nearby Counties in the Sixteenth, Seventeenth, and Eighteenth Centuries', *Agricultural History Review*, 64/1 (2016), pp. 1–16.

Thick, Malcolm, *The Neat House Gardens: Early Market Gardening around London* (Totnes, 1998).

Thick, Malcolm, 'The Sale of Produce from Non-commercial Gardens in Late Medieval and Early Modern England', *Agricultural History Review*, 66/1 (2018), pp. 1–17.

Thirsk, Joan (ed.), *Agrarian History of England and Wales*, vol. V, pt 1 (Cambridge, 1984); vol. VI (Cambridge, 1989).

Thirsk, Joan, *Food in Early Modern England* (London, 2007).

Walker, R.B., 'Advertising in London Newspapers, 1650–1750', *Business History*, 15 (1973), pp. 112–30.

Weir, Robin and Liddell, Caroline, *Recipes from the Dairy* (London, 1998).

Werner, Sarah, *Studying Early Printed Books* (London, 2019).

Worlidge, John, *Systema Agriculturae* (London, 1681).

Worlidge, John, *Vinetum Britannicum* (London, 1678).

Young, Arthur, *General View of The Agriculture of The County of Hertfordshire* (London, 1804).

# Index

References to illustrations, maps and tables are in *italics*. References to footnotes are suffixed 'n'. Main topic references are shown in **bold** text.

Advertising 43, 73–100, 158
Agricultural Revolution 153
Ale *see* Beer
Alms giving 136, 139n
Animal health 58–62
    country housewife primarily responsible for 58–9
    *see also* Cows, Farriers, Horses, Sheep
Antimony, cure for horses 60–1
Apples 49, 51, 111, 118, 119
    cider, sweet 87n
    orchards 87
    Parsnip 50, 89, 118
    *see also* Cider, Recipes
Ashes 19, 28, 66, 112, 123, 150
Ashridge Park 14, 18, 19, 97, 131
Astley, Thomas, publisher 79, 156
Aylesbury 99
    Vale of 15, 78

Bacon 110, 112, 116, 119
Barbers' Company 129n
Barley 20, 23, 39, 40, 63, 66, 71, 84, 98, 154, 159
    as ingredient 102n, 104, 105, 108
    drilled 43, 45, 95, 96
    in open fields 35
    seed 41–2, 83, 91
    sown after turnip crop 66
    *see also* Rotations
Barley-End 124
Barnstaple 126
Beale, John 49
Beans
    broad 116, 117, 119
    drilled 43, 95, 96
    field 20, 63, 64, 69, 72, 84, 96, 99, 129, 154
    french 111
    in open fields 35
    seed 91, 99
Beaver 118
Bedfordshire 57, 63, 65, 109
Bedlam, Matilda Ellis confined in 7, 20, 21, 129, 134
    Tom o' Bedlams 134
Beef 109, 110, 116, 117, 119, 139
    in cookery books 55
    typical country food 102, 103
Beer 9, 11, 59, 64, 115, 118, 119, 121, 122, 132
    ale 104, 125

brewed at Ellis's London brewery 125
brewing 125–8, *126*
Devonshire White Ale 125
small 115
strong 115, 116
yeast 127
Bell, Vicars 14, 15, 163
Bethlehem Hospital *see* Bedlam
Bielke, Baron Sten Carl 3
Bishop's Stortford 5
Blith, Walter 29–30
Boerhaave, Herman 120
Book agriculture 144–8
Books, agricultural
  about farming outside his neighbourhood 23–4, 62–74
  as vehicles for advertisements 24, 43, 75–100, 158
  cookery 55, 102–3, 107, 111, 142n
  income from 73–4, 155–7
  material reprinted in 140–2
  medicine 120–2, 124
  printing method 157n
  *see also* Book agriculture
Bradley, Richard 2, 42, 49, 128, 145–6, 164
  and house-lambs 58
  Ellis critical of 84–7, 105, 147, 179–80
  rival author 1, 103
  social status 86
Brazier, Mary 137
Bread 11, 105–8, 110, 112, 116, 117, 118, 119, 139
Brewing *see* Beer
Bridgewater, duke of 90, 120, 121, 124, 126, 131, 148, 180
Brining 41–2
Bristol 126

Britten 163
Broadcast, seed sown 37, 43, 45, 63
Brompton Park 64
Broth 103, 139
Buckinghamshire 8, 14, 57, 63, 65, 124, 135
Burgoo 109
Butter 54, 59, 85, 103, 110, 122, 123
  London as a market for 113
  recipe ingredient 55, 102n, 104, 105, 109n, 111, 115, 119
  Welsh, coloured with marigolds 112

Cabbage 111, 116, 117
Cake 116
  seed, Hertfordshire 118
  plum 118
Cake, oil (cattle food) 66
Calves 54–5, 112–13, 149
Cambridgeshire 112
Caraway 36
Carmarthenshire 65
Carrot 20, 66, 111, 116, 117
Chalfont 150
Chalk, solid geology 15
  soil 16–17, 26, 28, 31, 34, 41, 44, 72, 93
Chalking 32–3, *33*
Cheddington 8
Cheese 51, 54, 85, 113, 116, 117, 118, 119
  -making 112, 115
Chelsea 39, 63, 64n, 150
Cheshire 102, 109, 112
Chester 82
Child, Robert 91n
Chilterns 30, 33, 36, 39, 36, 38, 69, 117, 149–50, 154
  and Vale, 24, 28, 35, 39, 63, 146, 163

clover early adopted in 40
geography of 14, 15
Ellis's farming in 24 *et seq*
peas and beans sown in 63, 64
Church Farm 8, 13 *et seq*
Cider 49, 50, 51, 87, 128, 185
   criticism of Sir Jonas Moore's book on 87
Cinnamon 104
Clay
   cultivating in different types of 31
   variety of in Little Gaddesden's fields 15, 17
Clements, farmer 43, 95
Clover 17, 35, 36, 37, 38–9, 44, 57, 71, 73, 153, 158, 161, 174
   Hertfordshire early to adopt 154
   initial resistance to by Vale farmers 40
Clutterbuck, Rev. J. 51
Cobbett, William condemned growing of potatoes 110
Cole-seed 36, 54
Colemore, Rector 16, 124
Collins, Ted 108
Colonies, American 1, 96, 152, 167
Coney-clippings 28
Cookery 85, 102–5, 107, 111, 120, 146, 179–80, 181
   veal 55
   *see also* Bread, Pies, Recipes
Coriander 36
Cows 18, 23, 40, 54–5, 59, 66, 90, 93, 99, 112, 130
   *see also* Dairying
Cucumber 116
Cumberland 83
Cures
   Sloane, Sir Hans, asthma cure of 124

   Southampton innkeeper's cough cure 124

Dagnal 69
Dairying 54, 112–13
Derbyshire 121
Devon 65, 93, 102, 112, 125
   South Hams cider 87 128
Diaries
   farm diary 25, 128
   Pehr Kalm's 3, 4, 47
Digby, Kenelm 103, 146
Dodson, Matilda *see* Ellis, Matilda
Dorking Fowl 88
Dorset 65
Dover 67
Dover, Thomas 120
Drill husbandry 4, 42–9, 69, 72, 81, 92, 94–5, 154, 161, 165
Du Pont, M 179
Dublin 90, 156, 173
Duke's Place, St James' 5
Duncomb, Justice 124
Dunghill fowls 113

Eales, Mary 111
East Anglia 2, 63, 65, 114, 153
Egerton 14, 180
Eggs 53, 56, 88, 99, 113, 149, 154
   as ingredient 102, 105, 109, 110, 123
Ellis, Frances 11–13
   Henry 16, 21n, 129
   Mary 5, 13
   Matilda, nee Dodson 5, 7, 8, 20, 21, 24, 130
   Philip 5, 21
   Richard 8, 11, 12, 13, 125, 130
Ellis, William
   appalled by unfairness to poor by enclosure 140

awareness of economic change 148–55
enforces distribution of alms to poor 137, *138*
fairness towards dayworkers 139
family 1–13, 20–1, 130–1
farm and farmhouse 15–19, 25
favours employing servants 'in house' 19–20
favours extension of 1723 Black Act 133–4
frustration at neighbours' conservatism 25, 45, 130, 153, 166
income 155–60
interviewing technique 130–1
morality 132–6
neglects his own farm 24, 73–4
participates in parish administration 136–9, *138*
puritan ideals 132–3, 135
reputation, posthumous 160–4
scared of vagrants 134–5
self-plagiarism 140–2
social status 140
values knowledge of ordinary workers 131
Ellis, William (Ellis's son) 129n
Ernle, Lord 165
Essex 11, 65, 66, 166
Evelyn, John 2, 50, 141, 146
Excise 8–9, 123, 128
Experiments (agricultural) 32, 69–71

Fallow 29, 30, 35, 36, 38, 39, 56, 57, 69, 150
 plough 29–30
Farley, John 55
Farriers 60, 124, 131, 148, 187
 Ellis wary of 58, 59

Fenugreek, cure for horses, in *Farmer's Weekly* 61
Fertilisers *see* Soil
Fisher, James *see* Book Agriculture
Flair 109n
Flax 36
Flummery 109n
Fowls 1, 41, 53, 56, 77, 79, 88–9, 113, 140, 158
 ornamental 100n
Fruits, dried 104
Fuel 26, 140
Fulham 63, 150–1
 open fields at 36
 seed barley from 39, 91
Fussell, George 29, 75, 108, 162

Gage, Colonel Thomas MP 11
Games, rural 132n
Garden, Ellis's 17, 18–19, 50, 62, 71
Garden, Market 36, 39, 71, 151n, 154
Gardiner, H.W. 15, 28, 162
*General Advertiser* 79
Glamorganshire, Vale of 112
Gloucestershire 112
Godalming 65, 67–8
Godden, James 95
Goodwyn Mr 121
Grass 28, 34, 36–7, 50, 56, 57, 96, 98, 116, 153, 167
 Lady-finger 54, 85, 90
 ley 36–8
 seeds, price of 158
 sown for fodder 17, 69, 57, 85, 90–1, 99–100, 112, 149, 150, 151–2
Grew, Nehemiah 146
Gruel 103, 104, 109

Hales, Dr 146
Hampshire 34, 65, 134
Hanowell, Mr 122
Harrow (implement) 35, 37, 39–41, 47, 48, 63, 94
Harrow (town) 63, 64
Hartlib, Samuel 49, 91n, 166, 172
Harvest 4, 35, 38, 36, 49, 51, 65, 68, 70
　bean 35
　gleaning after 115
　oats 40
　saffron 67
Harvest workers, food for 101, 105, 114–19
Harvey, John 91n
Haslemere 65
Haslet, recipe 103
Hauxton 66
Hayseed, advertised for sale 78
Haystacks, roofed 18
Hedging 25–7
Hemel Hempstead 63, 64, 78, 122
Hemp, growing near Dover 67–8
Hertfordshire 3, 18, 23, 24, 32, 34, 46, 51, 53, 63, 65, 78, 88, 93, 99, 114, 119, 120, 131, 132, 154, 162, 163, 165
　Ellis identifies with 1, 2, 13
　geology of 15
　influenced by London markets 113, 149–50
　ploughs 29–31
　recipes 102, 105, 108–10, 116, 117, 118
　sheep in 56–62
　wheat grown in 38
Higley, Sarah 137
Hockley 63
Hops 36
　Kent 67–8

Horse-hoes, advertising and selling 93–9
Horses, care of 40, 58–61
Hot bed 151
Houghton, John 68, 84, 86, 103, 146, 177
House-lambs 53, 56
　how raised in Hertfordshire 57–8
Housewives, frugal 104–5
Howard, Widow 122, 131
Hughes, John 179

Improvements to vehicles 143–4
Ireland 23, 51, 82–3, 91, 96, 156, 166
Ivinghoe 123

Johnson, George W. 162

Kalm, Pehr 3, 4, 8, 12, 16, 18, 24, 47–9, 44, 45, 64, 73, 78, 85, 95, 97, 129, 130, 131, 139, 159, 163, 164, 165
Kensington 63, 150, 154
Kent, 11, 65, 66, 68
Kerridge, Eric 36
King, Edward 95

La Fontaine, M 179
Lancashire, visitors from 102
　Manchester, potatoes for sale in 110
　letter of criticism from 141
Land reclamation 152
Langford, T. 49, 50n
Lawrence, John 50n, 146
Lawson, William 49, 144, 177
Laybourne 135–6
Leaven, preservation between bakes 107
Leighton 54, 109, 111, 134, 149

Lent harvest 115, 116
Lent seed-plough 30
Lilley 137
Lime 26, 28, 32, 41, 42, 72
Linnaeus, Carl 3
Liquorice 36–7, 67–8, 124
Lisle, Edward 2, 34, 35, 147
Little Gaddesden, Ellis's farm at 16–19
  farming at 24 *et seq*
  geography of 13–15
  Kalm's visit to 3
Livestock 53–62, 77, 79
  *see also* Calves, House-lambs, Sheep, Fowls
Loam, 28, 44, 63, 71, 94, 150, 151
  in Little Gaddesden's fields 32, 17
Loblolly 109n
London 5, 7, 11, 14, 20, 26, 60, 74, 78, 79, 81, 82, 86, 89, 90, 97, 102, 105, 107, 122, 130, 136, 139, 144, 158, 166
  brewing in 8–9, 125, 127
  market gardening near 63, 151, 154
  produce sent to 41, 53, 54, 55, 56, 57, 113–14, 149, 152
  waste from, as fertiliser 32, 34, 149–50
Lucerne 17n
  as a fodder crop 37, 41
  hoes used on 96

Mail order 81–4
  goods Ellis had for sale 99–100
Manure 31, 34, 37, 45, 46, 47n, 48, 65, 66, 69, 72, 73, 85, 86n, 94–5, 150, 151, 161
Markham, Gervase 60, 62, 103, 146, 172, 186, 187
McDonald, Alexander 50n

McDonald, Donald 74n, 173–4
Mercantilist 68n
Middlesex, agricultural techniques in 63–4, 65, 146, 150–1
  farmer-gardeners 154
  sheep 57
  vagrants 134
Milk 58, 112, 115
  as ingredient 104–5, 106, 108, 109, 110, 111, 116, 118, 119
  as medicine 123
  cows' diet affects quality of 54
  for a sick lamb 62
  for suckling calves 54–5
  London demand 113
Miller, Philip 50
Moore, Sir Jonas 87, 185
Morgam 65
Mortimer, John 39, 146, 147, 164
Muldrew, Craig 119
Murray, William, First Earl of Mansfield, dedication to *10*, 81
Murrell, John 103, 146

Newbury, peat deposits in Kennet valley near 66–7
Newcastle 83
Nitrogen 17n, 28, 36, 37n, 40, 73
Norfolk 65, 66, 154
Nottinghamshire 65
Nutmeg 104

Oats 20, 35, 37, 38, 39, 40, 43, 65, 91, 96, 98, 99
  black 38
  oatcake 109
  oatmeal 109–11
  seed 91
Onions 115
  Welch (Welsh) 18
Open fields 35–6, 38, 39, 63

# INDEX

Overton, Mark 162
Oxford A.W. 163
Oxfordshire 56, 57, 88, 89

Palladius 2, 62
Pancakes 105
Paris 179
Parsley 115
Peas 19, 117, 119
   as food 103, 105, 151
   drilling 45, 94–5
   seed 91
   sown with beans 63
   varieties sown by Ellis 40
Pelling, Margaret 121
Philadelphia, 127
Philips, John 50
Pie 51, 102, 103, 104, 111, 117, 118, 119
   Tring 55
Plashing 26, 27, 27
Plat, Sir Hugh 18, 42, 88n, 173n, 185n, 189n
Ploughing 25, 28, 29, 32, 40, 146, 150
Ploughman 19, 20, 28, 30, 74
Ploughs 20, 38, 78, 79, 92, 140, 144, 146
   advertised for sale 93–100
   demonstrated to Kalm 47–8
   Hertfordshire 28–31
   income from sales of 158–9
   *see also* Drill husbandry
Plums 109, 113
Plymouth 125, 176
Poems
   *Cyder* 50, 87
   praising apple pies 104
Pontefract 67
Pork 116
   dishes made with 103, 110, 117

pickled 11, 19, 102, 112, 116, 119
pork products 102n, 103–4
Porridge 103, 104, 105, 109
Posset 103, 104, 115, 116, 118
Postage 83, 91
Potatoes 109–11, 117
Potter, Paullus 18
Preserving 110, 111–12, 113, 117
Puddings
   apple 104
   baked 19
   Hog's 102
   importance to English diet 103
   oatmeal 109
   plain 104, 116
   potato 111
   Sussex pond 102

Quincey, John 120

Rabbits 55–6, 150, 100n, 154
Rags, as soil improver 28, 150
Reading, Museum of Rural Life 163
Recipes
   apples, 104–5, 115, 116
   beer 126–8
   brawn 103
   bread 108
   collecting, 101–5, 121, 130–2
   culinary 118–19, 142n, 179–80
   haslet 103
   medicinal 121–4
   oatmeal 109
   potato 109–11
   veterinary 130–1
Rochester 11
Romney Marsh, sheep 57, 66
Ross, J. 179n
Rotations, crop 35–9
Rothamsted 173–4
Ruislip 63

Russell, John 159
Rutland 65
Ryegrass 17n, 57

Saffron 36, 67–8
Saffron Walden 67
Sailcloth 66, 68
Sainfoin (animal fodder) 41
    as fertiliser 17n
    Bradley's error re 84
    in rotation 37
Salmon, William 181
Salt 54, 111, 113
    as ingredient 102n, 104, 109n, 110
    see also Preserving
Salts (chemical) 19, 41, 46
Sand 28, 31, 32, 63, 66
    dunging 15
    liquorice and 67
    ploughing 28, 44, 93
Savery, Captain 8
Scientific method 70–2
Scot, Reginald 172
Scotland 51
Scythe, Kentish husbandmen use for harvesting 65
Seabright, Sir Thomas 127
Seed steeps 41–2
Seeds 1, 34, 35, 38, 39, 40, 47, 48, 63, 66, 67, 71
    caraway 118
    fenugreek 61
    for swards 54, 78, 85, 90–1
    preference for heavy 42, 91n
    trading in 2, 41, 76–9, 89–91, 99–100, 149, 158
    turnip 66
    see also Grass, Drill husbandry
Sheep 17, 56, 73, 135, 161
    best pasture for 85
    can supply 99
    characteristics of breeds 56–7, 66
    effects of growth of mutton consumption 16
    Ellis's book on sheep 1, 17, 56, 79, 92, 162
    fodder for 40, 41, 57, 66
    folding 34–5, 36, 40, 53, 56
    medicines for diseases of 59, 61–2
    useful products from 56
    wether 25
    see also House-lambs
Shelburne, Richard 21
Sherman, Sandra, Ellis's methods of advertising analysed by 75–7, 76n, 83–4
Shropshire
    brewing 126
    cheese-making 112
Sibley, Mrs of Water-End, herbal tonic 123
Sieve
    for drying fruit 111
    for yeast 107
    hand sieve for sale 99n
    to isolate heaviest grain for seed 42
Smith, Eliza 55, 111n
Smut 35, 72
    experiments to eradicate 69, 72
    seed steeps to prevent 41–2
Smyrna
    wheat 70
    raisins 118
Soil, management of 27–41
Soil fertility, ways to improve or maintain 19, 28–41, 46, 62, 72, 66, 150–1, 154
    experiments with 32
    mixing to improve fertility 28, 31–2

*see also* Chalking, Loam, London waste, Sand, Sheep folding
Somerset 65
   dairying 112
   grey and blue poll wheat 66
Soot
   for slugs 182
   for soil fertility 28, 150
   in tonic for cows 59
South Carolina 127
Speed, Adolphus 146, 166, 186
Spices
   as ingredients 55, 103, 104, 111
   spice-loaf 118
St Clements Danes 5
St James's, Duke's Place 5
St James' Westminster 9, 11, 125
Stafford, Hugh 87
Stanbridge, Paul 16n, 21n, 140n, 163
Suffolk 65, 66
Sugar
   as ingredient 55, 102, 104, 105, 109, 111, 116, 118–19
   as medicine 123, 124
   bottling without 112
   sugar beet 32
   sugar syrup 87
Sumner, James 127, 143n
Surrey, Ellis's travels in 65
Sussex 65
Switzer, Stephen 1, 65n, 173

Textbooks, agricultural 144–7, 172–3
Thatch *see* Vetch
Thirsk, Joan 163
Thunen, von, theory applied to London and hinterland 154
Tillage 28, 73, 161
Trading in goods and services 73–100

Travels, on horseback 63–5
Trees, fruit 26, 49–53, 79
   London fruiterers buying fruit crop on the tree 51n
   nursery of 51, 53, 81, 89, 100, 118
   orchards 51
   *see also* Apples
Trees, timber 26, 53, 89, 99
Trefoil 17, 37, 44, 57, 158
Tring, livestock market at 57
Trowell, Samuel 178
Tull, Jethro 75, 94
   drill plough 44–5, 84, 86, 95
   theory of soil fertility 45–6, 75
Turnips 35, 78, 150, 152
   cultivated on sandy soils in Norfolk and Suffolk 66
   Ellis's enthusiasm for 41, 153, 154
   sheep and cattle fodder 34, 37, 66
   sold in London streets 149
Tusser, Thomas 114, 166

Upnor 11

Veal, London demand for 54, 55, 154
Vetch 34, 40, 54, 57
Vinegar 55, 102, 115, 123
Virgil 2, 42

Wales 63, 65, 102
Weeds 35, 85, 86–7
   kept down by hoeing 43, 45, 46, 65, 69, 96
Westbeck, Zacharias, Swedish inventor of a seed drill 47
Westminster 9, 11, 125
Wheat 20, 30, 37
   bread made from 105–8
   drilled 43–5, 46, 98
   experiments with 70–1

French, as green manure 66
foreign, sown experimentally 70
given prominence by Ellis 23, 38, 66
secret method of sowing 71
seed 38, 91
soil preparation for 28–9, 38–9, 40
varieties of, sown in England 66
*see also* Brining, Seed steeps, Smut

Wills
  Ellis's 17, 21, 130
  Ellis's uncle Richard's 8, 11–13
Wiltshire 65
Wine 50, 89, 128
Woad 36, 44
Woburn 63
Woodhouse, Dr 121
Worlidge, John 43, 50, 84, 86, 87

Xenophon 2, 86

Yeast, bread 107–8
  brewers 127
  ingredient 118–19
Yorkshire 65, 67
Young, Arthur 2, 27, 32, 34, 38, 47, 57, 150, 166